LANTERNE ROUGE

MAX LEONARD

LANTERNE ROUGE

The Last Man in the Tour de France

PEGASUS BOOKS
NEW YORK LONDON

LANTERNE ROUGE

Pegasus Books LLC
80 Broad Street, 5th Floor
New York, NY 10004

ISBN: 978-1-60598-786-6

10 9 8 7 8 6 5 4 3 2 1

Printed in the United States of America
Distributed by W. W. Norton & Company, Inc.

So the last shall be first, and the first last.

Matthew, 20:16

CONTENTS

Prologue

ISSOIRE

...success, especially your own, is not a good subject; failure is.

Tim Krabbé

17 July 2011: the Auvergne, central France.
My day begins in a hotel car park at 4.45 a.m., applying wet weather lube to my bicycle chain as warm, fat raindrops fall slowly all around. It is my first real moment of consciousness on the journey from the short hours of sleep to the start line. I'm one of the 4,500 amateurs riding the Étape du Tour, the closed-road event that gives cycling fans the chance to emulate their heroes and ride one stage of the Tour de France. This stage, 208 kilometres through the mountains of the Massif Central from Issoire to Saint-Flour, is one of the toughest in the 2011 race.

We had known the storm was coming, had watched the black clouds gather for days over the extinct volcanoes surrounding the start town but had hoped in vain that ignoring them would forestall the inevitable. But by the time we are in the start pen waiting for the 7 a.m. gun, those clouds have been making good on their promise. It has been raining for hours. The mayor of Issoire counts us down, and then we're off, over the start line early and riding easily with a fast group, the bike sliding smoothly through the wet.

For a year as a student I lived in Clermont-Ferrand, the regional capital just 20 kilometres from here, and a French friend from that time, David, who still lives in the area and teaches in a primary school, has promised to be out on the road clapping us through. It is miserably early on a Sunday morning and, with the road spray and the rain jackets, the cagouls and the umbrellas, I am not sure either of us will recognise the other, but the idea that he is there gives me comfort. That there are any spectators at all for this amateur jolly through an unseasonal storm is astounding.

Forty kilometres in, the first climb, the Côte de Massiac, splinters the bunch. The gradient takes its toll and each man settles into his solitary rhythm. At the top is a featureless plateau and a long drag up to the 1,200-metre Col du Baladour.

Up above 1,000 metres the wind rises, the temperature drops and the remaining groups split. No hiding in the bunch from the gusts. Rain stings the eyes, then hail, yet for 20 kilometres or more it feels OK. Hands? Not too cold. Feet? Not too cold. Head down, watch the wheel in front, take a turn and drop back off. The mist closes in, the world shrinks. A small square of black tarmac ahead of the front wheel, the sound of the wind, raindrops pelting my rain jacket. I begin to see riders on this closed road heading the other way, turning back for the start. Then a descent. Five kilometres? Three? Long enough to numb the feet and strip feeling from the hands, making it near impossible to work the brakes. Glasses discarded, head bowed to stop hail hitting eyeballs, arms and shoulders chilled rigid, suppressing shivers with every breath. Wobbling along, buffeted from side to side, gripping the bars. At the bottom in Allanche, the first feed station, my faster companions are waiting for me, blue-lipped and unable to speak. We watch as riders young and old travel erratically down the slope. Looking shell-shocked, they dismount and dump their expensive bicycles on the ground before sitting down next to them or running for warmth in the village hall, which has been opened because of the weather. Two degrees at the top of the next col, someone says.

So we do something professional riders very rarely do, and especially rarely in the Tour. We give up. DNF – did not finish. Thousands of others that day did the same.

In normal circumstances I do not quit. I hate failing. Coming into the feed stop I remember thinking – somewhat confusedly – that I should keep rolling through, because if I climb off the bike I will not get back on it. But the sight of my friends, better riders than me, already resigned to abandoning alleviates any residual guilt or self-recrimination. I feel curiously blank about giving up. The coaches that will take us to Saint-Flour are next to the long racks of abandoned bikes, which will be trucked to meet us there. We climb on board and wait, and as we warm up we steam. The windows cloud with condensation that obscures the scene outside, making the extreme, miserable cold seem far away, and we begin to laugh about how awful it had been. My friend Joe, a late addition to the coach party, is asked to get off just as the bus is preparing to leave as he does not have a seat to himself. I feel sorry for him, back out in the chill.

It's only when I see him at the hotel that evening, wandering around glassy-eyed, full of beer and calorie debt, that I realise that instead of waiting for another coach he'd retrieved his bike and cycled to the end. I feel obscurely jealous of his feat of suffering, and my pride begins to dent. That was where the itch kicked in. Nobody I was with blamed us for abandoning: in the circumstances it was the right thing to do. I had not asked for sponsorship, since my friends knew I cycled events like this for fun, had not sacrificed my social life for months of training (the Saturday and Sunday before, I'd ridden 380 kilometres, Brighton to Paris and back, so hadn't felt the need to get fit specifically); I knew I had enough free time and was enthusiastic enough to go and ride on beautiful mountain roads again pretty soon. In short, it didn't matter to anyone else that I'd failed. Only to me. Those feelings of stubborn pride and thwarted tenacity, it would turn out, took a long time to shake off. The challenge would not be as easy to relinquish as simply getting on a bus.

A week before, albeit in better weather, the pros' experience of the Tour stage on those same roads had been no less dramatic: on a fast, narrow descent, a horrific crash broke collarbones and wrists and forced six riders to abandon their journey to Paris. Alexander Vinokourov, leader of Team Astana, was lifted out of a tree by his teammates, a broken elbow and femur ending his valedictory Tour; other big names including Dave Zabriskie and Jurgen Van den Broeck fared barely any better. Later, Team Sky's Juan Antonio Flecha was sideswiped by a France Télévisions car that, against race authorities' orders, was passing a breakaway group on a narrow road. He hit the floor in front of Johnny Hoogerland, catapulting the Dutchman into a barbed-wire fence. Despite deep lacerations to his thigh, which would require 33 stitches, Hoogerland got back on his bike and finished the stage, 17 minutes behind the day's winner.

Even before my inglorious dismount I'd been in awe of the demands of professional racing. Trying – and failing – to ride just one stage in the wake of the pros really puts you in your place. Their fitness levels and the lengths to which they push themselves are almost unimaginable. For those shooting for a place in history, the pain and the sacrifices might – just – be worth it (Hoogerland went on to take the King of the Mountains jersey for several stages). But professional cycling is not a zero-sum game. Behind every winner there are a hundred other riders, indistinguishable in the swarm of the peloton as they go about the dangerous business of racing. Guys who, for little reward or recognition, ride hard, crash, get back on and keep on going. Then get up the next day and do it all again, one more time, with feeling. Repeat to fade. In modern Tours there are the prologue and stage wins, four jerseys, the combativity prize and the team prize; barring the odd team time trial, that's a maximum of 35 'winners' each year. And the corollary: 163 guys – if miraculously nobody drops out – who wake upon plump duck-feather pillows and Egyptian cotton bedlinen at the Hotel Concorde La Fayette the day after the Champs-Élysées party, officially unrecognised and unrewarded, with only sore legs, deep tanlines, a raging metabolism and some flaking scabs to take home with them. And don't forget the hangover.

One of them each year is the *lanterne rouge*, to give the last man in the general classification his popular title. It is probably cycling's most notorious prize and it exerts a peculiar pull on many fans. Some see the *lanterne rouge* as a joke, simply a booby prize for an untalented rider; others as a survivor's badge of honour awarded to a man nobly struggling on against the odds. At once emblematic of failure and yet imbued with the most sought-after qualities, the *lanterne rouge* is a paradox – both celebrated as a symbol and yet, for the most part, forgotten as an individual. What is for sure is that, for better or worse, the *lanterne rouge* does not quit. Each year, by the time he lays his head on that Parisian pillow, he will have outlasted approximately 20 per cent of the starting field – his competitors mainly dropping out because of injury or illness.

Fresh from my fiasco, with the experience of abandoning a Tour stage still raw, I wanted to find out more about the man behind the *lanterne rouge*. With the spectator's feeling for the underdog, I had rooted for a few *lanternes* through various Tours. One stuck out: Kenny van Hummel, a Dutch sprinter. In 2009 he had occupied last place for much of the race, often finishing half an hour or more behind the stage winner. Though manifestly not greatly suited to the task put in front of him, he had won himself a legion of new fans around the world with a gutsy ride in which he refused, through high mountains, heatwaves and tumbles, to bow to the inevitable and leave the race (until he crashed badly in the Pyrenees and had to withdraw).

Every year when the Tour comes around a story or two surfaces about the *lanterne*, either from that edition or from a journalist digging deep into the barrel of the race's rich history and coming out with an inspirational, sad or funny tale. Kenny's was that year's, and he attracted more attention than most. But aside from a few media opportunities each year, the back of the race is relatively unexamined.

So I began thinking: if you turned the Tour upside down and gave it a shake, what would fall out?

Really, I knew very little about the *lanterne rouge* or why I was interested, except for a few vague and interconnected notions.

First: I am not that keen on winning as a concept. Competition, yes; racing, yes; shooting for a goal and trying to be the best you can, definitely. And beating a rival can be an incomparable feeling, for both good and bad reasons. On the flipside, I am definitely not a fan of winning's opposite, losing . . . and that's OK, because this most certainly is not a book about losers. However, once the race is run, the whistle blown or the results in, I lose interest in the idea of the winner, it feels somehow shallow. We're often told that it's not the winning but the taking part that counts. It is said consolingly to a bereft child at a school sports day, to someone who's just missed out on a job opportunity and to a thunderous-looking bloke whose team has just been thumped in the derby on home turf. But, if there is more to life than winning, what, exactly, is there?

Second: I was bored of listening to most winners. Their point of view, it seems to me, is potentially one of the least interesting on any contest, yet they hog the limelight. Listen to certain great champions from any sport and you'll hear platitudes about focus, toughness and achieving one's dream, but precious little insight into what actually went on. Dig down into the peloton, on the other hand, and there are as many stories as there are men and stages. Riders who experience lots of different facets of the race, who, after spending hours and hours in the saddle, watch for the umpteenth time the backsides of the fast guys disappear up a hill – they must have had some time to reflect on winning and losing and why they do what they do. For those of us outside sport, who probably never actually come first (or last) in anything in life, that might be useful.

A third and final thought: if there is more to life than winning, it must be contained somewhere in the Tour de France. Because the Tour is more than a race: it is a bastion of France and French culture, a three-week lesson in that country's geography and history; it is a drama of ethics and emotions; a tragicomedy in which 200 people want the same thing yet only one will get it, and many aren't even capable; a melodrama of (false) hope and (doomed) endeavour, desperation and despair, optimism and disillusion; a human zoo and life in microcosm.

Not to mention that it's a three-week test of the commentators' ability to fill dead time with chat about châteaux and cheese.

Tony Hoar, the first British *lanterne rouge*, wrote an article for *Cycling* magazine in 1955, giving his impressions of the first British sortie on to Continental cycling's biggest stage. 'The Top Tour Rider needs the Qualities of Zátopek, Marciano, Harris, Tenzing and Coppi', ran the overly long headline. Respectively, the era's greatest long-distance runner, world heavyweight champion boxer, record-breaking trackman, Everest-conquering mountaineer and the *campionissimo* – cycling's champion of champions.

Could this ever be one rider? I wanted to go in search of men who had once aspired to these qualities and definitively fallen short – who indeed could not have fallen any shorter. To find out more about these riders who were unable to win and yet unwilling to fail, and to talk candidly with them about the race in a situation in which they did not have to explain why they didn't get the yellow jersey.

To ask them: what keeps you – keeps us all – going? Why not simply get off and do something easier and less painful instead?

Chapter 1

THE FIRST LAST MAN

Now all the truth is out,
Be secret and take defeat
From any brazen throat,
For how can you compete,
Being honour bred, with one
Who, were it proved he lies,
Were shamed neither in his own
Nor in his neighbours' eyes?
Bred to a harder thing
Than Triumph, turn away . . .

'To a Friend Whose Work Has Come to Nothing',

W.B. Yeats

I'd been searching for signs of life – signs of *a* life – for so long
it came as a relief when I finally saw his face.

For days I'd been scanning the pages of the defunct sports
newspaper *L'Auto*, picking out his name in 110-year-old race
reports. Days among snoozing old men and equally somnolent
students in the basement of the Bibliothèque Nationale de
France, the French national library, on the windblown Left Bank

of the Seine, scrolling through rolls of scratchy microfilm, chasing ghosts on bicycles on their maiden journey around France.

I was looking for Arsène Millochau, who I'd plucked out of obscurity because, I'd reasoned, the story of the last man in the Tour de France has to start with the first to have that dubious honour. But I was beginning to regret setting myself the task. It hadn't proved easy to unearth any facts about him, and what I'd intended to be just a simple historical sketch was turning into a manhunt, a cross between an archaeological dig and a missing person's investigation. The only thing I could be sure of, it seemed, was that he'd been last, first. In 1903 he'd crossed the finish line a whopping 64 hours, 57 minutes, eight-and-two-fifths seconds after the winner, Maurice Garin, 21st of 21 finishers.

Millochau raced the first Tour – and raced pretty badly you might say – then never attempted it again.

Some things about the first Tour are pretty well established. That it was, for example, the last throw of the dice to save L'Auto, a French sports newspaper, from failure in a bitter circulation battle, and that its editor, Henri Desgrange, was a fierce, athletic ascetic who seized upon the idea of sending riders on a wild six-stage tour of France when it was suggested by his junior reporter Géo Lefèvre over a glass or two of Chablis and a lobster thermidor, as they tried to dream up publicity wheezes to save the crisis-struck paper.[1] Ever since the world's first road race, Paris–Rouen in 1869, and especially after the success of the first Bordeaux–Paris in 1891 for the weekly Véloce-Sport, French newspapers had organised promotional

---

1 Less well known was that Desgrange, a former publicity agent and lawyer, was also a velodrome owner, entrepreneur and recordman over several distances (his 100-kilometre tricycle record still stands). The younger of twins, he wrote novels and published a theatre and arts revue, while living in sin with an avant-garde artist called Jane Deley.

races. Paris–Brest–Paris (1891) and Paris–Roubaix (1895) are two of the best known that still survive in some form today, but this was even more ambitious. A tour of France. It is a crazy plan, but it might just work.

Aside from these known knowns – to paraphrase Donald Rumsfeld – there are a lot of known unknowns, too, but also a lot of half truths, maybes and facts bordering on myth. After all, what do most of us know about Maurice Garin aside from he had a period-correct set of moustaches, a nice line in chunky knitwear and was partial to a gasper every now and then? That he won the first Tour de France, yes, and that he was disqualified from the second Tour for taking the train. Or maybe that was Pottier. Or was that 1906? And the Tourmalet was the first mountain they climbed? In the Tour, more than in many other historical events, it's a case of you tell me your truth, I'll tell you mine.

Until the bibliothèque in Paris all I'd had to go on was a very brief Wikipedia entry and some tantalising references on distant strands of *le web*. I was pretty sure Millochau had been born in Champseru, near Chartres in north-western France, in 1867, but couldn't quite be sure of his name: many sources had it as 'Millocheau' with an 'e'. Old Arsène was a shadowy figure, almost coquettish in his reluctance to let himself be known, and I had been drawn into the chase. I'd been sending out fruitless enquiries on Internet forums, and missives via obscure genealogy sites, but the bibliothèque was where I hoped a few scrappy facts might be saved from the waste-paper basket of history. As the old *L'Autos* unspooled in front of me so did the first Tour, as if happening for the first time. And Arsène's role gradually came into focus. Unfortunately for him, right from the off that role predominantly involved bringing up the rear.

In January 1903 Desgrange officially launched the Tour de

France, 'The greatest cycling test in the world'. Europe's cyclists, however, were not as gung-ho as he was; initially scheduled for June, the start was pushed back to July because of the lacklustre response. From May onwards the race, the regulations Desgrange was dreaming up and in particular the prizes were regular 'news' in *L'Auto*. It cost 10 francs (around €100 in today's money) to enter and a list of new *engagés* was published daily but, despite Desgrange's efforts, sign-up was slow. The 15 June deadline loomed and the front-page exhortations to riders, by turns cajoling and pleading, became more frequent and urgent.

1 June: 'Almost all the "cracks" of the road have already entered,' *L'Auto* says, as if this might encourage lesser riders to part with their money and throw their names in the hat. Millochau, probably not being regarded as a 'crack', is not one of them. 7 June: Lucien Pothier, who will finish second, becomes only the 37th name on the list; Arsène's still not there. 11 June: Desgrange resorts to publicly naming and shaming such stars as Lucien Petit-Breton (a future winner) who have signed up but have yet to pay their fees. Come and have a go if you think you're hard enough; Millochau is still conspicuously absent.

Finally, on Tuesday 16 June, the first edition after the Monday evening deadline: 'A. Millochau (Chartres)', 67th out of an eventual 80 conscripts – the paper magnanimously promises to honour entries posted by 5 p.m. the day before. Even though his participation had never seriously been in doubt, it still sent a thrill down my spine to see the name in print for the first time.

What was Millochau thinking at that point? Riding 2,428 kilometres around France as fast as you can is a big commitment, and 10 francs would have been a lot of money to waste if you didn't have serious designs on the race, even with the allowances paid to each rider to defray the cost of participation. On the other hand, anyone who's ever signed up late for a race or a sportive knows that getting your entry form in at the last minute is hardly a sign of overweening confidence. Arsène was a bicycle mechanic after his racing career, and probably during it too, so riding the Tour would conceivably have lost him money but also been potentially good for business. He may have fancied his chances, or have been lured as a bear to honey by the rather generous allowances, but he must have balanced the pain, hardships and loss of earnings against the gleaming possibility of glory, fame and fortune.

On the start line at the Au Reveil Matin café in Montgeron, just south of Paris, there are only 60 men. Present are the favourites, among them Maurice Garin and Hippolyte Aucouturier, but Millochau is there too, meaning he has already outlasted one quarter of the original field. They are about to embark on a super-sized 467-kilometre first stage to Lyon in central France.

'My sportsman's heart delighted in the spectacle of these courageous men, silhouetted in golden dust by the sun, before whom the road stretched into infinity,' writes Géo Lefèvre, gearing up for the reams of lofty copy he will be expected to file over the next three weeks. But for all the highfalutin words, genuine doubts remain. Can it even be done, this Tour de France? In many remote parts of the country the bicycle is an unknown machine, and the sight of charging riders frightening for the locals; even in large towns there is outright disbelief that a man might pedal to the next town. At the inaugural Bordeaux–Paris race, villages along the way prepared banquets and beds, believing the riders would take several days to cover the 560 kilometres whereas, fuelled by a combination of raw meat and an unidentified special 'tonic', the fastest rider took only 26 hours. Ditto, Paris–Brest–Paris (1,200 kilometres) seemed unimaginably far until a bloke called Charles Terront made it look easy, conquering it with barely any sleep in 71 hours and 22 minutes. Dirt roads and primitive technology – heavy, unreliable bicycles, rickety wheels, no gears – were but two of the major impediments: everywhere in early racing there is a sense of pushing the boundaries of human endeavour, of finding out through trial and, if necessary, error what the limits of the possible are.

Desgrange is very keen on pushing limits but he also feels these doubts. He is there to wave the riders off, but, betraying his fear of failure, he will not follow the Tour. That job, which comprises timekeeping, marshalling and reporting, he leaves to little Géo Lefèvre, who must chase the race in a madcap succession of train journeys. In a further sign Desgrange is hedging his bets, the front page the day before the Tour starts is consecrated to the marvellously named Gordon Bennett Cup, an annual motor-racing challenge between moustachioed gentlemen amateurs from England and the United States.

The *Grand Départ* is scheduled for around 3 p.m. in the hope that the riders will arrive in Lyon on the morrow in time for the results to be telegraphed to Paris before the next day's paper goes to print that evening. At 3.16 precisely they're off, and Desgrange retires to his newsroom. Lefèvre follows the first 60 kilometres in a car – long enough to see Arsène dropped from the main group. In the first four hours, 20 men join those 20 who didn't start, and get off their bikes. Millochau rides through the crowds thronging the route and passes the first checkpoint, at Cosne after 174 kilometres, in just over six hours – 19 minutes after Garin. According to the account that appears the next day, the roadside support does not let up all night. Édouard Wattelier, one of the favourites, abandons at some point in those dark hours but Garin is in Lyon at 9:01 a.m., having covered the rough roads at an incredible 26 kilometres per hour. Millochau comes in almost 10 hours later, just before 7 p.m., 33rd out of 38 finishers.

What happens during those extra hours of brittle, sleep-deprived cycling through the blinding daylight? Perhaps there are mechanical problems – this is, after all, an era when riders are responsible for all their own repairs, and where several hours can easily be lost mending a wheel or taking a pair of forks to the blacksmith. Perhaps Millochau finds a quiet corner and has a nap under a tree, his bicycle stashed behind a hedge for safekeeping. What is easier to know – yet far less revealing – are the implacable, inescapable numbers. By the end of the second stage, in Marseille, Millochau is almost 25 hours behind Garin and has slipped into last. After a terrible third stage to Toulouse, Millochau has been riding for 84 hours, 48 minutes and 55 seconds, almost a day and a half longer than Garin. Steadily, many of those above him drop out, but Arsène keeps going. He is now last, and will be last for the rest of the race. Toulouse to Bordeaux, Bordeaux to Nantes and, completing the circuit, Nantes to Paris.

Once or twice he disappears from the official classifications only to be magically reinstated the next day – a result of carelessness, or an understandable lack of interest in the tail-end Charlie, I conjecture. Save for the official inscription of his name at the checkpoints he passes, he appears only once more in *L'Auto* during the whole Tour: at Orléans, 155 kilometres from Paris: 'At 9.50 a.m., Millochau, very fresh. He lunches.'

He gets dropped, and he lunches. Is that it? I think. Any old fool can do that, but this man, in between those two mentions, cycles 2,200 kilometres – on his way to becoming one of only 21 men ever to loop around France – and all they can say is he lunches?

That was where I left Arsène one evening: him eating, me turfed out of the library at closing, frustrated at bumping up against what was both a practical and philosophical problem: how to tell the story of the back of the race. Races, if you'll forgive the basic point, are really one-directional. They're teleological, goal-oriented: everyone's trying to get to the top of the pile. The attention of the riders, organisers, fans and media is focused at the front and there's very little interest in what goes on at the other end, so what happens there is likely to get lost. Throw the historical distance into the equation and it becomes doubly tough: go all the way back to 1903 and the swirling mists of time and bad historians have almost carried the winner off into obscurity, let alone that pariah figure, the last-placed man.

I repaired to a canalside Parisian bar where a beer or two did much to quell such pseudo-profound angst. Then I *vélib*-ed back to where I was staying. At a red light in the Rue de Charonne, I checked my inbox on my phone for the 473rd time that day. And there they were. Two emails: one from Millochau's great-grand-nephew, and one from a Tour historian containing a scan of a *Miroir Sprint* article from 1947. Accompanying the article there are two photos of Arsène Florentin Millochau, fit and healthy at a grand old age and still mending bikes on – I'm not making this up – the Rue de Charonne. In the first, he's wearing a workingman's jacket and a peaked hat like a bus conductor's, and is cycling along the street on a town bike with flat handlebars. 'Still alert and smiling' deadpans *Miroir Sprint*, '«Papa» Millochau prefers his bike to *Le Métro*' – managing to make this historic Tour finisher sound like your average fluoro-clad commuter on a Halfords-bought hybrid. In the second picture Arsène, a small, elven man, is in his kitchen, which also doubles as his workshop. The walls are festooned with old bike parts, yellowing photographs, advertisements and race numbers, including his one from the 1903 Tour, and the crankset he used in the first ever

Bordeaux–Paris. He is inspecting a chainring over a vice and looks like a follower of the bash-it-with-a-hammer-and-hope philosophy of bicycle repair. And why not: it's not one that ever goes out of style, and is probably just the job when you're faced with riding a heavy bike with no gears over dirt roads for more than 20 hours at a time. It's those kind of hardships that leads him to scoff: *'Le Tour d'aujourd'hui? Une simple randonnée.'* Today's Tour? A walk in the park.

As for his other achievements, Emile Toulouse, the *Miroir Sprint* reporter, is all ears. 'Just think: my bike weighed 33 kilos[2],' Millochau says, of the first Bordeaux–Paris, in which he claimed to have come 28th (held back, perhaps, by his hugely heavy bike). 'I had provided for all eventualities and had armed myself with several spare parts.' After that, Arsène says, he was on the start line of the first Paris–Brest–Paris, and later at the first Paris–Roubaix in 1895. Add those three – still undisputedly the classics, the most prestigious races of their kind – to the first Tour de France, and suddenly Arsène, far from an unworthy straggler, becomes a kind of proto-racer, a pioneer present at all the most significant occasions marking the birth of road cycling.

As for Millochau the man, I'd found Thierry, Millochau's great-grand-nephew, through a French genealogical website. Like Arsène, Thierry was happy to share his stories. In his email, he wrote:

Uncle Arsène was a family character. What I know of him was told to me by close relatives who knew him directly. My grandmother in particular has tender memories of him. She talks about him as a handsome athletic man,

---

2 By way of comparison a modern Tour de France bike weighs 6.8 kilos.

a seducer who was appreciated by women long
after the end of his sporting career.

[...]

Arsène came from a family of 11 children,
all of whom we know about. One of his brothers,
Louis, is my direct ancestor. Arsène was twice
married. As the family legend has it, in his
youth he would leave for long periods of
solo training on the road. He also invented
mechanical parts adapted for the bicycle racing
of the day (I don't know anything more).

His participation in the Tour remains, at
least in the family's mind, an exploit that
was very far from being a failure. He was
himself very proud of it, and not at all
cynical as today's sportsmen are. At the end
of his sporting career, he maintained his
passion by opening a bike shop in Paris.

I remember when I was a child a newspaper
cutting that showed his premises. The memories
of him that remain portray a kind, independent
hard-working man.

I send Thierry the cutting from *Miroir Sprint*, to rekindle
that childhood memory.

The next morning I return to the library buoyed by the
emails, ready to follow Arsène into Paris and triumphantly
over the finishing line. In *L'Auto* of the morning of the final
stage, Desgrange, mirroring my mood, is in superlative mode.
His riders have overcome . . .

. . . the steepest mountains, the coldest, blackest nights,

the most violent, most atrocious winds, the most unjust and numerous misfortunes, the longest roads, never-ending hills . . . nothing got the better of these men's dogged will. Is that to say that every man finished who started? No. But it seems at this time fair to applaud the victor and the vanquished, and to spare a thought for those who could not finish.[3]

At the final control in Ville d'Avray, just a few kilometres from the ceremonial end in the Parc des Princes velodrome, Garin arrived first, sealing his win. There, each rider was given a board with his finishing time painted on it, which they then took on, in their own time, to the velodrome. In the early days it was common for road races to end on the track – witness Bordeaux–Paris at the Porte Maillot, or Paris–Roubaix, which has made a legend of the Roubaix velodrome – at least in part because the huge crowds they'd attract would provide bumper ticket revenues for the track owner.[4] On 19 July, 1903 there was a programme of events including a paced 100-kilometre race and the French Speed Championships, to whip up the spectators before the Tour riders arrived. They would be introduced, all freshened up, on to the track in order, displaying their finishing time at Avray, for a celebratory few laps.

And Arsène wasn't there.

He was not given a finishing time in L'Auto that day. He was not, in fact, even recorded at Rambouillet (48 kilometres from the finish) or Versailles (13 kilometres away). At Ville d'Avray, he didn't get a board, and he didn't get to ride his laps of honour

---

3 Desgrange was often very dismissive of what he called 'Barnum', after the circus ringmaster, preferring the hard, honest truths of bicycle racing to showbiz flummery. But he was never shy of blowing his own trumpet.

4 Which in the Tour de France's case was Desgrange himself – he'd established the Parc des Princes in 1897. Handy.

in front of a roaring, delirious crowd.

Did he simply pack up and go home, I wondered, or perhaps, judging victory laps pointless, head straight for the Au Reveil Matin in Montgeron, his departure point three weeks previously, for a slap-up meal and a vat of red wine? He was, after all, a man barely noted in contemporary accounts for his capacity to race, but very keen on lunch.

After I got over the temptation simply to wind the microfilm back up and tell nobody – least of all Thierry – about the terrible secret I had found, I sat there for a minute or two, pondering this turn of events and my pursuit of Arsène in general. On the whole, it didn't surprise me that the identity of the first last man might have been misattributed or forgotten somewhere along the long road to the present day. One of the difficulties with the history of the early Tour is that in 1940 the Tour organisation, fearing the Nazis, packed up its archives and sent them by train to the south of France for safekeeping – where, ironically, they were completely destroyed in a fire. Hundreds must have consulted these public microfilms to study the Tour, but how many were really concentrating on the bottom of the GC? It appeared, having gone back to the source, that Arsène was not the first *lanterne rouge*.[5]

It brought me down with a bang. My *grand projet*, which is in some senses about failure, was starting with a big fat failure of its own. What was I doing resurrecting the career of this nobody, instead of poor Émile Moulin, the last man to have a recorded finishing time in that Tour-finishing edition of *L'Auto*? I felt like a mad pirate trying to nail mist to the mizzenmast. Would I have to start again with Émile instead?

---

5 In fact, he is definitely not the first *lanterne rouge*, since the term had not yet been coined – of which more in the next chapter.

Perhaps I should not have been trying to elevate one man at the expense of another, possibly equally deserving one. Perhaps they should all simply be left in obscurity and a tomb of the unknown cyclist erected in their honour.

One by one, I checked the rest of Arsène's 'known' achievements, as listed by the man himself in *Miroir Sprint*, against outside sources, and he quickly proved to be not only a Houdini in print but also an unreliable witness to his own life. Twenty-eighth in the first Bordeaux–Paris was the wonderfully named Pierre Tardy, not Millochau. Nor was he on the start list for the first Paris–Brest–Paris or the first Paris–Roubaix. He might have beaten the Paris–Amsterdam record in the 1890s (also mentioned in *Miroir Sprint*), but I couldn't back that up. None of Arsène's many claims, in fact, seemed at all grounded in reality, and it wasn't looking at all good until I skipped forward to the second PBP, in 1901, just to check. There, his name *was* on the start list; more heartening still it was on the finishers' list too – a very respectable 47th.

And that was where my research time in Paris ran out. I'd come hoping to firm up my story but departed knowing less than before: yes, I'd succeeded in putting flesh on the bones, but I was now less certain that they were the bones I wanted. Arsène was AWOL on the Tour and, aside from one other confirmed sighting, the histories I had were wrong, the journalism shoddy and the star, if not a charlatan or fantasist, then perhaps at best a teller of tales.

Back in the UK, I resorted to trawling the Internet once more – forums, history websites, all the usual suspects – but it felt futile. If you've been back to the primary texts and found them wanting, how could these secondary sources help out? I needed a specialist to help me make sense of what was going on all those years ago. To my rescue came a Frenchman called

Pierrot Picq, a Tour historian who has given the first Tour close study. Arsène, he told me, had not failed to finish, only failed to cross the finish line before the evening's print deadline.

In a flash, those gaps that I had seen in Arsène's attendance at certain stage finishes became entirely comprehensible: with everybody's attention on the front-runners, and an imperative to publish a daily newspaper, the presses simply could not wait for slow cyclists. Had I been able to check the next day's paper, Arsène's final stage time would have been there in black and white (for the record: he wasn't last), and his final place in the GC confirmed.

Millochau had reclaimed the throne of first last man. For my part I was relieved that all my work had not been wasted. It had felt cruel taking away a man's only extant achievement, and I also felt, somewhat bizarrely, proud of him.

Picq also helped me to fill in the details of Arsène's racing life and *palmarès*. He called Arsène 'one of the pioneers of racing, on the road and track', and gave me some of his race results:

1895	Bordeaux–Paris: 9th
1896	Bordeaux–Paris: 13th
1897	Paris–Roubaix: 24th
	Bordeaux–Paris: 5th
	Bol d'Or (a prestigious 24-hour paced track event): 4th
1902	Marseille–Paris: 13th

Much later on, in 1921, he came 34th in Paris–Brest–Paris and the following year started Bordeaux–Paris, but abandoned. He was 55 years old.

All in all, not bad for a loser and, given that Millochau was talking to *Miroir Sprint* at half a century's remove from the events in question, it's understandable he might have got a

few dates wrong. But it is impossible to ignore how far behind
the winner he was: Arsène's 1903 Tour was the best part of
65 hours longer than Garin's. It's not quite the record: Antoine
de Flotrière, *lanterne rouge* in 1904, took an astounding 100
hours and 28 minutes (and 52 seconds) more than that year's
fastest man, on exactly the same course as Millochau. Four
other *lanternes* in the 1910s and '20s finished 65 hours or more
behind, too.[6] Sixty-five hours is a very long time: a modern pro
could ride most of a whole Tour de France in the extra time
Millochau spent on the road over Maurice Garin. Speed-wise,
Garin did not let up (his winning margin over second place,
at almost three hours, was the largest there's ever been) and
he was so fast he almost outran Géo Lefèvre, *L'Auto's* roving
correspondent. Lefèvre, commissaire and timekeeper, failed
in his roles at the first hurdle: when his train got to Lyon for
the end of the first stage, Garin was already tucking in to
breakfast. Millochau's average speed, by contrast, was around
11 kilometres an hour slower than Garin's.[7]

Survey the whole history of the Tour and the average speeds
are interesting. Technology, road surfaces, training, nutrition and
on-the-road support have all contributed to their steady rise,
though today's Tours are slightly slower than those during the
EPO years in the late 1990s and early 2000s. As for the gap
between front and back, in the early days, when riders were

6 *Lanterne rouge* Daniel Masson also took 65 hours longer than 1922's winner, Firmin
Lambot, but that year distances were so vast that was only some 29 per cent longer
whereas Millochau's time was 70 per cent greater than Garin's.

7 The slowest Tour was in 1924 – the winner rolled at 23.97 km/h – but that
route was almost twice as long as in 1903. The issue of Tour stats is vexed – even
contemporary official Tour publications and the *Guide Historique* give varying times,
speeds and stage lengths, with a startling amount of divergence, so I have gone with
what seems the consensus. However, the average speeds given for the *lanterne rouge*
and the percentage gaps to the leader were worked out by Feargal McKay in a great
article on the PodiumCafé website.

racing solo on dirt roads and were forced to do their own repairs, it fluctuated wildly. After the Second World War, however, once the Tour became definitively a team endeavour, mechanical help was allowed and the road surfaces became decent, the gap between leader and lantern stabilised and shrank. Post-war, all that separates first and last over thousands of kilometres and 60 or more years is an average speed of between one and two kilometres per hour. Take the recent example of Adriano Malori, a former under-23 Italian national time-trial champion and 2010's *lanterne rouge*, who completed the 3,642 kilometres at an average speed of 37.7 km/h – only 1.9 km/h less than the winner, Alberto Contador (who in any case was subsequently stripped of his title). Or José Berrendero, who rode for Spain in the 1960 Tour: 35.63 km/h, as compared with yellow jersey Gastone Nencini's 37.21 km/h. There are many, many more: the rule really does hold, despite the increases in the averages overall.

One or two kilometres per hour, over three or four thousand kilometres. Such is the margin between success and defeat.

Compare the slowest professional to the fastest amateur and the sliver becomes much wider. The winner of the hail-blighted amateur Issoire-to-Saint-Flour Étape I briefly took part in was a full hour slower than the slowest pro over the same *parcours* in that year's Tour. There are many mitigating factors to explain that chasm – better weather, the aerodynamics of the peloton and closed roads all being significantly in the professionals' favour – but the pros had already raced for eight days and the fact remains that very few of us could stick with any of them, even the *lanterne rouge*, for more than a kilometre or two.

Remember that when you scoff at Arsène's performance. His 65-hour delay may seem laughable but it does, at least, seem honest. Maurice Garin won himself eternal fame by winning the first Tour, and forever inscribed his name in the history books, yet he barely blotted his copybook with cycling fans by cheating the next year. It's worth repeating what happened in 1904: in the middle of a cycle race, the defending champion got off his bike and took the train. Garin is only the first of many Tour winners to have cheated; is it right that we forgive – and even fete – some cheaters and excoriate others?

As for Arsène, he is only barely remembered. There were no teams in the first Tour de France, no outside help allowed whatsoever; he was on his own and we shall never know his full story. 'There's not a competitor lining up without the hope of placing honourably,' Desgrange said of his magnificent men in 1903. And, while it seems obvious, he's right: I bet Arsène had high hopes of his endeavour. Pretty much nobody enters a race with the idea that they're going to come last, and by such a long way. Let alone an accomplished bike racer, possessed of the talent, courage and tactics to place honourably. My guess is that somewhere on that long road back to Paris his luck and his equipment failed him, perhaps multiple times, dumping him into a time deficit that he could not climb out of and making simply finishing the only realistic goal.

Henri Desgrange and many others of his time were fond of talking about *la vélocipédie* – Cycling, with a big 'C' – as a movement, an industry, a calling. Arsène was a fanatic, a true part of the bicycle boom of the 1890s. A poor mechanic (still working at 81, remember), he was bred to a harder thing than triumph, relying on his legs for a few top-10 placings to make a little extra money.

'His whole life is a bicycle race,' *Miroir Sprint* said in 1947, and Arsène was competitive to the last. The paper continued: 'Just a few months ago, M. Millochau's desire was to live to an older age than Gaston Rivierre, his glorious adversary from that

heroic era, who died four years ago aged 80 and four months.'
Millochau died on 4 May 1948, less than a year after the
article, at the age of 81. He had won his final race.

1903
60 starters
Winner: Maurice Garin, 25.68 km/h
Lanterne rouge: Arsène Millochau, 15.24 km/h @ 64h57'08"
21 finishers

Chapter 2
THE SURVIVOR

The ideal Tour would be one in which a single rider succeeded in completing the challenge.

Henri Desgrange

Back in the bowels of the bibliothèque, trying not to join the napping ranks, and a curious thing pops up. I'm buried in microfilm reading about the 13th Tour in 1919 and suddenly there are the words: *'lanterne rouge'*.

'Devilly did not depart in our Tour de France,' writes Henri Desgrange a day or two after the race starts, 'because he could not find tyres in sufficient quantities. A shame: the ex-*lanterne rouge* might have given lessons in courage to many a rider.'

Georges Devilly was *lanterne rouge* in 1909 when he had been riding as an *isolé* – a rider unsupported by one of the bicycle manufacturers such as Clément, Peugeot or Alcyon. They were the principal sponsors of professional riders at the time and advertised on the back of their victories, consequently acquiring a level of power and influence over the sport. But the line between pro and amateur back then was incredibly porous, and not being sponsored did not make you a bad rider: the first *isolé* in 1909

placed sixth, winning a substantial cash prize.[8] Georges had
ridden previously for Alcyon and Le Globe but perhaps owing
to poor form (he came third bottom in Paris–Brussels just the
week before) he was participating in the Tour as an *isolé* and
completed the race in 55th and last place.[9] *Isolés* were responsible
for all their own travel expenses over the 14 stages. That's a lot
of money out of his own pocket for the privilege of coming last.

I'd been wondering about the origin of the phrase *lanterne
rouge*. French dictionaries of cycling slang date the expression
to 1924, when it was used by the journalist Albert Londres
in his famous article 'Les Forçats de la Route'. But clearly it
went back a lot further than that. I made the inference that it
was born in the first decade of the Tour – based on a couple
of assumptions. Number one: if Desgrange was calling Devilly

---

8 Albeit with a little help. His name was Ernest Paul and he was the half brother
of François Faber, a Luxembourgeois rider for Alcyon-Dunlop who won five of the
first six stages and whom the organisers asked to slow down lest he completely run
away with the race. Faber backed off and then helped Paul to victory in stage 7
before taking the overall win.

9 The 1909 race was decided on a complicated points system, with the winner of
each stage receiving one point and everyone below him a point corresponding to his
finishing position (2, 3, 4 etc), plus a point for every five minutes or portion thereof
that separated him from the man before him, up to a maximum of 10 extra points.
The rule was instituted in 1905 (along with much shorter and more numerous stages
that removed the need for night riding) in an attempt to stamp out the egregious
cheating in 1904 that eventually saw six riders including Maurice Garin, the winner,
disqualified. Over the 14 stages Georges accrued a total of 713 points, 43 more than
Alfred Guidez in 54th and a monstrous 676 more than François Faber.

So if accumulating points is your thing, the *lanternes rouges* between 1905 and
1912 – Clovis Lacroix, Georges Bronchard, Albert Chartier, Henri Anthoine, Devilly,
Constant Collet, Lucien Roquebert and Maurice Lartigue, Frenchmen all – are the
men for you. It's an alternative points race, if you like.

What's more, it's theoretically possible (if very unlikely) that these *lanternes rouges*,
bottom on points, were not the slowest men in their respective races since the points
system created very flat racing. If Devilly, for example, beat Guidez by four minutes
on one stage he'd receive one point fewer than his rival. But then if they came in
the next day within 30 seconds of each other, but 10 places apart, Guidez would
be eight points to the good but still three-and-a-half minutes down on time overall.

There may therefore be an anomalous *lanterne rouge* or two from those years who
was not actually the slowest man in the race.

lanterne rouge in 1919, it must mean the epithet was in use before the First World War. The 1919 race was the first since 1914, and for the epithet to survive the four-year hiatus it must have been firmly established in the everyday cycling lexicon. It was not necessarily current by 1909, however, since Georges might have received his epithet only retrospectively. Number two: I'm going to stick my neck out and say that the nickname came into being in the Tour and not before. Partly because of the language clue but mainly because it seems a good bet that the cult of the *lanterne* did not originate in a one-day race. I'll explain: in a common or garden, unhandicapped one-day race, everyone lines up at the start unranked in any official hierarchy. The race unspools, everyone hurtles towards the end and tries to get into first place; many different people occupy last position on the road until the classification is set in stone on the finish line.

First place wins; last place finishes last. Race over. If the last-placed man races again the next day the slate is wiped clean and he is theoretically once more equal to all his rivals.

Perhaps, in those interminably long races such as Paris–Brest–Paris, the last man in the peloton might have been referred to as the *lanterne rouge*. But only in a stage race, with the invention of the general classification, does a rider occupy last place for days on end. He goes to bed last and wakes up again last; gets back on his bike and races still in last place . . . potentially for almost a month. I'm not sure if the Tour invented the GC, but it was the world's first stage race of any note and generated significant discussions in the local, national and international press. Only in these circumstances, it seems to me, might a folklore grow up around the man who occupies last place.

After spotting the *lanterne* reference to Georges Devilly, I hunted through many of the pre-war editions of *L'Auto*, but didn't spot the magic words again. It may not be the first ever

printed use, but I'm happy with 1919: it seems poetic justice
that the red lantern first appears in the same year the yellow
jersey (according to official records) made its debut.

So that was the when, more or less, pinned down. The why
was more interesting. The prevailing wisdom has it that the idea
of the *lanterne rouge* was borrowed from the railways, and was
inspired by the red lantern that used to hang on a train's final
carriage. Its presence indicated to guards and signalmen that no
carriages had decoupled along the way and the line behind was
clear – that the brake van with its red light swinging behind
was truly the last carriage of the train. Railway and automotive
historians on both sides of the Atlantic have confirmed this was
the case: it seems to have been an international standard practice
that set the colour coding for all transport to come. It might seem
more natural that the bicycle borrowed its customs from the
car, but trains were the first mode of transport where distances
and speeds were such, and the possibilities of hitting things real
enough (no swerving!), that widely followed conventions were
needed. Moreover, lights were not obligatory on cars until well
after the First World War. The Ford Model T, first made in 1908,
had oil lamps on its rear end but these were not introduced until
around 1915. And though red was the long-standing convention
for tail lights on cars – thanks to the railways – this was not
codified until the Vienna Convention on Road Traffic of 1949.

Red: stop, don't hit this. It's an example of 'aposematism'
– using colour to signal a warning, effectively the opposite
of camouflage. Red has the longest wavelength in the visible
light spectrum, which means it's less likely to be scattered by
particles in the air and red lights can be more easily seen at
distance in fog. Going back to first principles, it has always
been used to signify danger. The red-winged blackbird that
flashes its plumage to deter attackers, the coral snake and the

poison tree frog. *Dictionnaire Le Robert*, the Gallic equivalent
of the Oxford English, states the *lanterne rouge* is the lamp on
the last vehicle in a convoy. It does not mention the railway
specifically, but wagon trains seem more an American than
a French idea – the *fin de siècle* Frenchman being more
interested in absinthe, cabaret and madeleines, if popular
culture is anything to go by. The Robert also references the red
lanterns of *maison closes* – brothels – hence 'red-light district'.
But let's not get distracted by red herrings. Racing cyclists in
the good old days really did carry lamps. Graeme Fife, author
of books such as *Tour de France: the History, the Legend, the
Riders*, told me of a drawing from a late 19th-century edition
of the *Illustrated London News*, depicting clubmen on a motley
assembly of bicycles leaving a meeting in a procession of
Chinese paper lanterns, spherical and cylindrical, attached
to rods on their bikes.

Professionals, too, relied on lamps, mostly oil lamps, since
many races in the early days would continue through the hours
of darkness as riders toiled on bad roads to accomplish the
distances required of them. Even if the symbolism was current,
it's unlikely the last rider ever carried a red lantern during the
Tour, for logistical reasons as much as anything, but throughout
its history, as the Tour reaches its end, the last rider has often
been presented with a ceremonial lantern, usually on the final
stage when there was no room left to wriggle up the standings.
Fife also showed me a photo from the '20s in which two Tour
cyclists ride side by side. One of them is holding a stick, to the
top of which is tied a tin-can lantern. They are both grinning
broadly and somewhat mischievously, 'like a couple of kids on
the way home from a tadpoling expedition', as he describes it. It
certainly looks like a ceremonial lantern, and that would support
the idea that the *lanterne rouge* has, since the earliest days of

the Tour, been an award with a certain amount of self-aware and self-deprecating humour. The last man in the Tour still often receives a ceremonial lantern before the Champs-Élysées, either awarded by the press photographers, or by the rider's own fan club. Every year a few staged publicity photos emerge of the rider with the *lanterne*, sometimes riding off the back of the peloton, turning to smile at the camera; sometimes being presented it by other riders; sometimes standing with a fan on the side of the Champs-Élysées or by the team buses. They are characterised by stilted poses and something indefinable in the rider's eyes as he stares into the lens. Not shame, exactly, but everything on a continuum from amused to bashful to awkward to defiant, a discomfort at being captured on film celebrating last place. *I did not get into bike racing for this.*

But they still finish. Georges Devilly did, and did it alone, without a team or even the broom wagon for company (that wasn't introduced until 1910), perhaps weighing up in his mind the relative cost of continuing versus abandoning and slogging to the finish to collect his things and, defeated, make his way home. And, if it weren't for a shortage of rubber, he would have come back for more in 1919.

Devilly and Desgrange had sent me on a long detour, on a railway ride to the Ford factory in Michigan via Paris's seedy nightlife and the Natural History Museum. But I'd been researching 1919 for an extraordinary story of endurance, in which one unlikely winner helped the French nation feel like it had survived the Great War intact. So there I returned, to a year when half of Europe was counting the cost of war in devastated towns and cities, destroyed fields, roads and railways. The mood in France was painful and muted. Almost 2.5 million Frenchmen had either died or returned from war as invalids. Among them, former

Tour winners Octave Lapize and Lucien Petit-Breton both dead. François Faber, the Luxembourgeois who had steamrollered all opposition in 1909, was also killed in action. The rest of the peloton was depleted, dispersed and lacking race fitness, and even getting them to the start line proved difficult.

There was, however, great public demand for the Tour, a national emblem, as entertainment and spiritual succour. 'The Tour is reborn from the ashes,' Henri Desgrange wrote early in 1919. Its delivery would not prove easy and it was not the only race that year to run into trouble. In January, less than three months after Armistice, *Le Petit Journal* newspaper tried to steal a march on *L'Auto* with a new race, *Le Circuit des Champs de Bataille* (the Battlefield Circuit), to be run that April. Tracing a route between Strasbourg, Luxembourg, Brussels, Amiens, Bar-le-Duc and Belfort, the organisers ignored warnings from the local papers that there, in the heart of the devastation on the borders with Belgium and Germany, the roads would be unusable. In fact, they argued, it was precisely the terrible state of the region that made it worth visiting: such a race would be a symbol of solidarity, regeneration and hope, and would welcome some former German provinces back into France. The week before the *Circuit*, Paris–Roubaix was held in conditions so bad that only five of the 40 following cars made it through the no-man's-land to Roubaix, and the *Circuit des Champs de Bataille* also had a terrible attrition rate. Snow, sleet and hail added to the poor road conditions, and eventually only 13 'heroic survivors' (as one paper called them) made it to the finish.

Sweeping all these difficulties aside, Desgrange had planned an ambitious 5,560-kilometre route that would take the race through Switzerland and into the neutral zone, then through the newly captured Alsace-Lorraine region and the battlegrounds of the Somme to Dunkirk. It was to be the longest Tour to date, covering the ground in 14 stages, and it would prove to the world – and to France herself – that the country was getting back on her feet.

He hit immediate logistical challenges. Aside from the terrible roads, there were checkpoints and military bureaucracy to hinder the race's passage, and the riders were under strict instructions to remember their passports. And the challenges were not confined to the *parcours*: the lack of tyres faced by Georges Devilly [10] was only one of a multitude of shortages making Desgrange's job difficult, shortages Desgrange took personally – as if, rather than a complex geopolitical event and massive global tragedy, the war were a vendetta against him and his race. Writing in *L'Auto*, he is uncharacteristically browbeaten by his responsibilities:

> Not since our newspaper began organising the Tour de France has the long challenge appeared to me as difficult, nay, fearsome, as this year. Before the war, the start of each of our «Tours» seemed like the dawn of a beautiful month of magnificent exertions and splendid courage. I have the impression this year of a very valuable canvas smeared by muck-throwing scoundrels. Some details will make my point clearer: for each stage we planned to supply fresh tyres, but, having knocked on every door, have found none. The cost of living, another gift of the war, has provoked strikes in the factories. How will our riders fare? We resolved to feed them twice each stage but we lack sugar – the war again – and the useful amount we ordered in Antwerp was, yesterday (despite no restrictions on imports), stuck at the border.

---

10 Although Devilly didn't make it to the start line, Bronchard, Chartier, Anthoine and Roquebert (*lanternes* in 1906, 7, 8 and 11) did, and they were joined by Henri Alavoine (1913). None of them would finish. And this would not be the last time tyres would seal the fate of a *lanterne rouge*, as Tony Hoar (1955) will testify.

The litany of disasters continues, with hotels full or out of action and the Tour's motorcycle outriders in doubt: 'Our motorcycle guard has caused us unheard-of difficulties. War – again! – has requisitioned all the motorbikes.'

The bicycle manufacturers were also in dire straits. Many of France's factories had been converted to the war effort, had been destroyed by fighting or were short of precious raw materials. The bike industry had been hit so hard they could not afford to field separate teams. Instead, they joined forces to sponsor just one team, La Sportive, which, though under-resourced, effectively resurrected the idea of professional cycling and helped make the 1919 Tour viable. Desgrange knew he needed the manufacturers' help; he had a keen eye for a show and knew the money and publicity they brought to the race was vital. But he hated the control they exerted over their riders, and the way these riders in their hands became stars – both of which factors diminished his own dictatorial grip on the race. Under the cover of expediency and post-war austerity, he saw an opportunity to grab back some power. Once La Sportive had committed to the race, he announced that *L'Auto* would not be giving any publicity to the manufacturers behind the team, nor to the team at all while the race was going on: 'The 1919 Tour de France will be the rider on his own,' he said. It was, all in all, a bad deal for La Sportive, which could only help its riders at the beginning or end of stages, and could not even deck them in brightly coloured clothes since there wasn't much dye to spare. Drab grey was all they got.

Desgrange's second objection to the manufacturers' presence was the team element they introduced. In his eyes it diluted the pure element of competition. The manufacturers had quickly worked out that many cyclists in their pay could usefully work together for the greater glory of one of their own. It was

Desgrange who, in 1911, coined the cycling term *domestique* –
literally 'servant', or for women 'maid'– for cyclists who worked
for others, and he meant it as an insult. Now, the manufacturers'
weakness and lack of resources meant he could sideline these
team tactics. He saw the race in 1919 as moving away from
'. . . the distressing injustice in the past that allowed some
to ride the Tour as big stars and obliged others to ride it as
beggars', he wrote. 'Theoretically, the least significant, most
deprived racer, the most *isolé*, if he has quality, has the same
chance as the great lords of the pedal, the stars of the road.'

It was democratising in an autocratic way, as was Desgrange's
wont – he was on the side of the little man, so long as he could
make that man's life as difficult as possible. Among the many,
many regulations, it stated that no rider was allowed to give
another food or drink, a spare tyre or a jersey or a tow in the
wind. Official *ravitaillements* were open to everyone, there were
no *musettes* – too expensive – and outside the feeds no man was
allowed any drink or food he did not buy personally, save for the
water from horse-troughs, fountains and public taps. And what
tyres there were could only be distributed by officials during
the race. Really, Desgrange just wanted things to be hard and
for men to be alone, gloriously alone, in their suffering. Just a
man and a bike on a road, hopefully in the rain. Going uphill.
With a broken spoke and possibly some chafing. A bracing, not
to say Nietzchean, conception: *The ideal Tour would be one in
which a single rider succeeded in completing the challenge.*

The 1919 Tour was to be a harsh survival of the fittest.

Having waged war against the war, against the manufacturers
and against kindness and fellow feeling, Desgrange (who
was himself freshly demobbed, having voluntarily enlisted in
1917 at the age of 52) was ready to start the race. Lining up

against La Sportive 'A's were the unsponsored riders, the not-so-meritocratically named 'B's, effectively no different from the *isolés* of the pre-war years. There were official prizes available only to Bs to encourage participation, and they were paid 20 francs a day indemnities, twice that of the As.

At first the enlisted riders were mainly Bs, perhaps because of the disarray in the sponsorship arrangements for the As. However, all cycling's remaining big guns and rising stars eventually signed up: Odiel Defraye; Eugène Christophe; Firmin Lambot; Francis and Henri Pélissier, the brothers who would later walk out on the 1924 Tour in protest at Desgrange's despotism. Less heralded, and in by last post, was a certain Jules Nempon, from Calais. He'd placed pretty well in minor races before the war, including top 10s in Paris–Le Mans and Paris–Beaugency, and by the end of his career would notch up 10 Tour de France starts. Nevertheless, he was placed in the B category, which was not unusual despite his pedigree: owing to the war, everyone had a fractured racing record.

The day before the race starts, *L'Auto's* front page features a photo line-up of Tour hopefuls. Bang in the middle is Jules, a Dickensian figure. His face is slight and dominated by a large flat cap, he has a small moustache over a lopsided smile and a slightly rodent cast to his jaw. His eyes tend towards melancholy. He is 29, weighs 61 kilos and he will be riding a development of 5m 50cm.[11]

---

11 That's how the French measure a gear – how far the bike travels in one complete revolution of the pedals. 5m 50cm is equivalent more or less to a 52-tooth chainring and 18-tooth sprocket on a bike today. The riders in 1919 would have had one other cog on the other side of the rear wheel, a bigger one for climbing. They would change gear by undoing the axle nuts and flipping the wheel over. This presented a great opportunity for bluffing, by turning your wheel all the way round and powering up the slope in your big gear while your adversary was stuck spinning up in his little gear, literally powerless.

Freewheels were grudgingly allowed in the 1919 Tour, as long as riders promised not to make use of the greater safety this afforded groups riding together and spend too much time conserving energy in pelotons. I'm not joking.

In total 130 riders registered, but only 69 made it to the start line, mostly because of the lack of tyres. And of those only 68 made it from the ceremonial start at the Place de la Concorde to the *départ réel* in Argenteuil in one piece, after Francis Pélissier crashed in the neutralised roll-out and spent two hours mending his bike. His hopes dashed even before one kilometre of racing, he, surely, was a prime candidate to receive the 15-franc *prime* offered to the unluckiest rider that first day by ex-soldiers in Sainte-Adresse, just outside the stage finish in Le Havre. There was particular sympathy for the riders' hardships from soldiers, probably because the majority of riders had fought alongside them. Those who had fought had had no time to get into shape after five years with no cycling, and no new generation of young riders had come through to supplant the older men, all of which contributed to the attrition rate.

Twenty-six riders drop out before Le Havre – 18 of them Bs, and in total more than a third of the combined field. Among those who abandon in the first stage is Philippe Thys, a two-time Tour winner. He gives up just before Le Havre through illness. Jean Rossius, a fellow Belgian, had taken pity on him and given him food, an act for which Rossius was penalised 30 minutes, forfeiting the race lead. Jules, meanwhile, starts as he means to go on, coming in 20th, towards the back of the pack. He is, however, first of the Bs.

For three days along the northern coast, from Paris to Le Havre to Cherbourg to Brest, a headwind beats the riders back and in Brest in the driving rain the celebrated Pélissier brothers, believing the whole world to be against them, abandon. That stage, the holder of the *lanterne rouge*, one Henri Leclerc, finishes at midnight and spends the whole of his rest day in bed. The following stage Nempon stays easily in the lead group for more than 200 of the 412 kilometres, prompting the correspondent to declare him a safe bet for the B category and to exclaim: 'By faith, I found him in fine condition.' Nempon eventually trails in last by a good long way, but he holds a lead over his nearest B rival, Alois Verstraeten, of over three hours.

By the foot of the Pyrenees, which the riders reach in two gigantic strides along the length of the Atlantic coast, the terrible weather and the shocking roads have reduced the field to only 25 men, one third of those who left Paris; Géo Lefèvre declares it: 'The most beautiful Tour de France I have ever seen.' His reporting is salacious and sadistic, deliberately exaggerating the drama of the road. Many of the classic images of suffering, endurance and determination that dominate the way we think about the Tour were pioneered in the early coverage – the hollow cheeks, the sweat-stained brows, straining muscles and shell-shocked expressions – all to make the feats of the 'Giants of the Road' seem more heroic. Sadistic, but not without a certain admiration and even compassion. There was, to use a phrase coined by Christopher S. Thompson, author of a book called *The Tour de France: a Cultural History*, a 'cult of survival' around these terribly tough races. If, like Nempon, you showed you had a certain self-sufficiency and ability to suffer, you'd be celebrated no matter what place you occupied in the standings, cheered on for your attitude, dignity and determination in the face of terrible challenges.

Over the next couple of stages, Nempon flags and Verstraeten rallies, and Jules is in real danger of being overtaken. Before the Tour, *L'Auto* had hyped the prospect of a ding-dong battle between the French and the Belgian heavyweights – Eugène Christophe, Jean Alavoine and the Pélissiers lining up against Firmin Lambot, Émile Masson and the Buysse brothers – and now, at the back, it is being fought in miniature. There are only 17 riders left. 'The small rider from Calais seems too weary to confront the numerous difficulties still to surmount,' Lefèvre writes.

It is in the Pyrenees that Nempon begins his fight back. First, a stage from Bayonne to Luchon, taking on some of the Tour's most celebrated climbs: the Aubisque, Tourmalet, Aspin and Peyresourde; in 1919 they are barely goat tracks in their upper reaches. 'Our men, having uttered their cry of "convicts" up the interminable climbs, pulling on their handlebars and pressing down on the pedals, appeared as silhouettes, their bodies bent over, on the blue horizon at the top of the col,' wrote Desgrange, 'and then they dived, so it seemed, into nothingness. In the time it took us to get to the summit, they were already no more than tiny dots, rolling down the white road in the gulf beneath us.' Nempon flies over the cols, crossing the Portet d'Aspet and the Col de Port in the first group of three. Despite getting dropped, falling and having numerous punctures, he is gaining confidence. Verstraeten, on the other hand, crashes in the dark after a 2 a.m. start. Battered and bloody, he limps on.

After the Pyrenees, Verstraeten's world falls in when an allegation surfaces that he took the train in Normandy. A day passes, nothing more emerges, and then Verstraeten is gone, chucked off the Tour after being seen hanging on to the shoulder of a motorbike rider near Montpellier. Desgrange investigates and finds no substance in the train accusation, but the motorbike seems irrefutable, even though there are dark mumblings about dissent in the Belgian camp: 'They had wanted to exclude him from the B category because he was riding too well,' says the Belgian manager Karel Steyaert.

With Verstraeten's departure, Jules is the only unsupported

rider left – the 'last of the Romans' – and the coverage about him becomes more extensive and more affectionate by the day, even as the list of abrasions, haemorrhoids, rashes and swellings suffered by the riders grows. The organisers, realising the publicity value of the sole survivor, begin to take special care of him. Ahead of the Alps, Jules is 12th out of 13 riders, one place ahead of *lanterne rouge* Paul Duboc, an apple merchant from Normandy, who but for a time penalty for swiping an illicit drink would be almost half an hour ahead of Nempon. They survive the Alps and the now tiny peloton hits the *pavés* of northern France, the neutral zone and the battlegrounds. Jules holds on until all that remains for the *rescapés* – the term is much used in the era and translates as 'survivors' – is a 340-kilometre slog from Dunkirk back to Paris, a stage that passes through Nempon's home town of Calais. He receives a huge reception on the roads around Calais and is escorted through the stage by Henri Desgrange himself, who historians say applauded from the official race director's car for much of the way from Dunkirk to the Parc des Princes.[12] It is, in many ways, a triumph.

Nempon finishes the race both last and first: last place in the GC, over 21 hours behind Firmin Lambot; first of the Bs to Paris. The only B, in fact. The winner, the loser, the survivor.

Little matter that he had been aided and abetted by the canny, publicity-seeking organisers. That he had reportedly been fed and groomed, and also had cleaned up on prize money.[13]

---

12 Nempon punctured once during the stage, at a place called Nempont-Saint-Firmin – which is an uncanny amalgam of his name and that of the winner, Firmin Lambot.

13 Nempon had led the B category since the start and his prize pot rose after each stage, but, given there were so few other competitors, he also picked up sundry other primes – for the first French B, for instance, and after the Aubisque stage, 20 francs for being the last finisher. It meant that for much of the race his total winnings rivalled those of the yellow jersey.

He was an underdog, continuing in the face of terrible odds, like the Tour and like France itself. His last-placed triumph had helped to give the French public something to cheer about, some sense that normality was returning after the war. The 1919 Tour had united the nation and there is no doubt Jules played his part. *L'Auto* reports the 'touching reception afforded the courageous little Nempon, sole survivor of the B category', as he entered the velodrome packed with 30,000 spectators.

His picture appeared one more time, on the front page of *L'Auto*, on the final day alongside all the Tour finishers. This time he is in a shirt collar, no hat, a shock of black hair sticking up. He looks both half asleep and slightly startled, as if just woken from a daydream in which he has just completed the 13th Tour de France. And also ever so slightly fleshy, as if the meals and other *soins* laid on by the organisers for their prize B had actually caused him to gain weight over the four-week ordeal. Some six weeks after the race, Paul Duboc was disqualified. An inquiry had determined that in one of the closing stages Duboc had hitched a lift in a car to find somewhere to repair a broken pedal. Consequently, Nempon found himself promoted from 11th to 10th place. He would survive several more Tours, but would never improve upon this top-10 placing.

In further proof that neither the organisers nor the crowds were fixated on winning, there was also wild adulation for Eugène Christophe from his home in the Parisian suburb of Malakoff all the way to the end. By common reckoning the unluckiest Tour rider ever, Christophe, who had led for most of the race, broke his forks on the penultimate stage and lost his yellow jersey to Firmin Lambot. In the final stage, Christophe had a record number of punctures and lost his second place to Jean Alavoine. Wrote Desgrange: 'The sky is gloomy and washed out. Huge, grubby clouds extend to the horizon. It is as if nature itself were grieving. In the outskirts of Valenciennes, Eugene Christophe stands on the pavement. He pushes in front of him, the saddle towards the earth, his bicycle: the fork is broken. It seems to me a mighty lyre whose broken strings sing his final misery.' The authorities, recognising perhaps that there is more to winning than coming over the line in the shortest time, awarded him the same prize money as Lambot, and after public donations he took home much more than the Belgian.

In the 1919 Tour Desgrange got a race that had exacted a harsher toll than even he might have hoped for – though his willingness to bend the rules showed a sense of compassion and moral justice that his public pronouncements and persona tried to keep under wraps. And, in Nempon, Desgrange got what he wanted too, his victor in glorious isolation. A lone wolf battling against the odds.

1909
150 starters
Winner: François Faber, 28.64 km/h, 37 points
Lanterne rouge: Georges Devilly, 713 points, no time recorded
55 finishers

1919
69 starters
Winner: Firmin Lambot, 24.06 km/h
Lanterne rouge: Jules Nempon, 22.02 km/h @ 21h44'12"
10 finishers

Chapter 3
THE YELLOW JERSEY

The Tour de France is made great as much by what it eliminates
as by what nourishes it. Its refuse is sublime.

Antoine Blondin

Follow the Seine's sinuous course west out of Paris towards
Ville-d'Avray, the location of the final control in the first Tour
de France, and just beyond the clotted *Périphérique* ring road
you get to Issy-les-Moulineaux. Its leafy urban sprawl is a
little anonymous, with a tramway and busy roads processing
people from one place to another. The sort of town with plenty
of modern corporate headquarters but no traditional cafés in
which to grab an *expresso*, that curiously French perversion of
the espresso where the 'ex' signifies 'used to be coffee'. It is
also chock-a-block with street furniture of the sort that would
make Jean-François Pescheux mad.

As the Tour's technical director between 2005 and 2013,
Pescheux was responsible for making sure that each day, each
week, each year, unfurled seamlessly. That each story and drama
was allowed to play itself out, without unwanted interference
from hazards such as race vehicles, media, spectators, gravel,

dizzying drops and the speed-humps, chicanes and other traffic-calming measures that have accreted in depressing abundance in and around French towns like potentially deflating road crud on a wet bicycle tyre. He joined the Société du Tour in 1982, working his way up under race directors Jacques Goddet and Félix Lévitan, Jean-Marie Leblanc and Christian Prudhomme. Before that he sprinted, riding three Tours de France and twice achieving a podium place in the individual sprint at the French national track championships.

When the Tour began it was organised from the offices of *L'Auto* in the Rue du Faubourg-Montmartre in central Paris. Now *L'Équipe*, the newspaper's successor, and ASO, which organises the race, have been spun out to the south-western suburbs. The ASO offices are next to those of Sodexo, one of France's largest multinationals, and inside is Monsieur Pescheux, who is waiting to chat about the *lanterne rouge*. Before I meet him I want to look over my notes, possibly over an *expresso*, but I can't find anywhere to do so. It's going to be an interesting interview.

First, because he has a reputation as a straight-talking, practical man: look up the word 'pugnacious' in the dictionary and you might well find his picture. Now 61, he doesn't look like he gets out on a bike much but he retains something of that elbows-at-70-kilometres-an-hour presence that some sprinters have. An air that promises that if you got in his way after the *flamme rouge* or threatened the smooth running of his race he could swat you aside as easy as look at you. And as a race director he worked for Jacques Goddet, son of one of the founders of the Tour, who in turn first worked on the race with Henri Desgrange in the '20s and '30s. That's an unbroken line back to the birth of cycling: fixed-wheel bikes and 460-kilometre stages, woolly jerseys and flat caps, brandy and cocaine at only two removes.

Second, because, well, what does the *lanterne rouge* mean to ASO? The venerable organisation puts on a race each year, the main idea of which is to get to the end in the shortest time possible. Yes, there are other prizes too, but they're invariably for superlative achievements – such as climbing really quickly, charging towards the finish line in the sprint – and critics would say that the honorific of *lanterne rouge* is at best frivolous; at worst, it is antithetical to the point of the race. Doesn't it take attention away from the real business of trying to win? Isn't it celebrating failure? And what if, in some sort of conquest of the useless, people actually raced to be last? (Which indeed they did, as we shall see.)

You don't have to dig too far to find negative feelings towards the *lanterne rouge*. 'It adds nothing,' Jean-Marie Leblanc, Tour director from 1989 to 2005, said to journalist James Raia. 'Today it is part of the lore of the Tour de France, but it no longer exists officially or unofficially.' That's a bit hostile. And also a bit futile – it is, after all, something that lives with the fans and is therefore out of his hands. Roger Legeay, once a rider, renowned DS – *directeur sportif* – and now chairman of the Movement for Credible Cycling, was more moderate in a *Procycling* magazine piece by journalist Sadhbh O'Shea: 'It is not the philosophy of the sport. The principle of the sport is to do your best and not to be the last one,' he said. 'It was never an objective for me, I wanted to do my best.'

Directeurs sportifs, though they sometimes appreciate the publicity the *lanterne rouge* brings, can often also be hostile towards it. Marc Madiot, DS of La Française des Jeux, is one who definitely is not in favour. Wim Vansevenant (*lanterne rouge* 2006–2008) told me he'd heard Madiot berating a rider for his last place in the GC, while Graeme Fife also reports Madiot giving a rider a real dressing down: 'Last in the Tour de

France? It's shameful. A disgrace. I do not like *lanternes rouges*.' Riders, although they usually bear the title with dignity and grace while they're holding it, seem to try to avoid the subject as long as is humanly possible: 'I don't care to think about that,' the decent, if not stellar, stage racer Gianluca Bortolami has said. 'There are always plenty of guys behind me.'

Other races are more accepting of the tradition of celebrating last place. In the second edition of the Vuelta a España the last-placed man wore a red jersey: 'To hold the last place in a race such as this is no cause for shame,' the race jury explained. Red, if you didn't know, is the colour of the modern leader's jersey in the Spanish Tour (in the second edition, in 1936, the leader wore orange) and the original red jersey seems only to have been awarded for one year. In 1937 the Spanish Civil War enforced a four-year break in racing and there is no sign that it survived the gap, so the sole Vuelta rider ever to wear the red (loser's) jersey was Ramón Ruiz. In Italy, on the other hand, the jersey for the Giro's last-placed rider stuck around for a few years. Between 1946 and 1951 *la maglia nera*, the black jersey, was given every day to the race's last man. Imagine how *that* must have weighed on your shoulders. Since there was, according to *Gazzetta dello Sport*, a substantial cash prize due to the wearer of the *maglia nera* at the race's end, it was hard fought over and, while in 1946 and '47 Gino Bartali and Fausto Coppi made do with sharing the *maglia rosa*, Luigi Malabrocca had the black jersey all to himself, reportedly hiding in barns and cellars, and puncturing his own tyres to do so. In 1949 Malabrocca was so confident of success that, thinking he'd won before the last stage, he took his eye off his main challenger Sante Carollo on the run in to the finish in Monza. He believed that in the rush to crown Coppi three-times king of the Giro the timekeepers would not be concerned about the *grupetto* (the

Italian name for the riders who bunch together at the back of the race) and they would all be given the same finishing time. He was wrong: Carollo managed to sit up and lose time, and was correctly awarded the black jersey, depriving Malabrocca of a historic third win. The *maglia nera*'s most famous winner, however, was also its last. The final recipient before the custom was abolished was a certain Giovanni Pinarello. He had been riding for Bottechia, but the team wanted to make room for an up-and-coming star, Pasqualino Fornara, and so in 1952 offered Pinarello 100,000 lire – around six months' salary – to give up his place in that year's Giro. He invested this money in his fledgling shop and bike-building business in Treviso, perhaps throwing in his last-place prize money for good measure. One suspects his abilities as a bicycle racer were inferior to his skills as a businessman: 60 years later, his bikes have been ridden to numerous Grand Tour victories and the Pinarello brand is one of the most respected and influential in cycling.

Back at the Tour, there have often been unofficial prizes awarded by sponsors to the last-placed rider. From one *lanterne rouge* I heard talk of the year a car manufacturer presented its latest model, although I couldn't verify this. There have also been scores of *primes* donated by individuals for the last man to pass through a town, or to the 'most unlucky' rider, but the *lanterne rouge* has never been officially recognised and an official prize has never been awarded. Indeed, the French Cycling Federation, the FFC, forbids any *primes* for last-placed riders.[14] It sits, therefore, alongside other prizes like the *Prix de l'Humour*, awarded to the funniest rider that year, and the *Prix Orange* and *Citron*, awarded by the press corps to the most

---

14 Over and above those connected with his place in the GC – i.e., if 50th place is due to receive 100 francs and 50th is also last, he still receives 100 francs.

friendly and uncooperative riders respectively, as a well-known but entirely unsanctioned honour.

I wonder if Pescheux shares this ambivalence towards the *lanterne rouge*. On the one hand he might have inherited the early veneration of the 'cult of the survivor' from Goddet, but he also had a ringside seat at an almighty ding-dong between Tour director Félix Lévitan and one particular *lanterne rouge* in the late '70s. There's only one way to find out.

Pescheux turns out to be a kind, gentle and very helpful man, with refined diction and an elegant turn of phrase. Straight away he confirms the thinking behind the FFC rule: if there were prizes for last, 'then the battle happens at the back, whereas normally it should happen at the front,' he says, spelling out the uncomplicated truth in that direct way that racers, used to always focusing forward, sometimes can. And it turns out that J.F. Pescheux isn't hostile towards the *lanterne rouge*; he just thinks that since the early '80s it has diminished in stature. That it has become insignificant in the modern era.

'In those days there used to be a red lantern given to the last in the Tour, that he hung on his bike on the last stage. It was symbolic and he was treated like a star. But all that disappeared,' he says. 'Now . . .' he pauses to interrogate his memory, 'I can't even name the last man in the Tour this year.' Pescheux admits that some of the things in the Tour that fall out of fashion are worth bemoaning – he is sorry that the Team Classification, which used to be second in importance to the yellow jersey, is no longer celebrated by the public. But the *lanterne rouge* is not one of them. He continues: 'Today it's almost more of a dishonour than an honour. We've passed from the phase of it being an honour to be *lanterne rouge* to just being last in the Tour. [And riders now, they say] "I'm not the last in the Tour, I'm 135th . . ."'

He sees many reasons for this shift, one of which is simply that there are many more riders in the race now – 198 took to the start line in 2013, compared with 120 or 130 in the '60s and '70s. Another is the rise in salaries in professional cycling, which has made the post-Tour criterium races less important. The post-Tour crits take place in the weeks following the Tour, originally organised by businesses in towns that weren't visited by that year's Tour in France, and also across Belgium and Holland, in order to bring the action to their own doorstep. Promoters would sign up the Tour's stars for large appearance fees and fill the start sheet with lesser Tour riders and local makeweights. Then, as dusk fell, the riders would put on a carefully orchestrated show on a tight city-centre course, giving people a taste of the excitement of the Tour and letting them see in their own high street the stars they'd followed in the papers or on TV for those three weeks in July. Unsurprisingly, the yellow jersey would always win, often snatching the victory by a wheel from his bitterest rival. At their height there were as many as 50 criteriums in northern Europe in the few weeks in August before serious racing re-established itself, with many riders racing twice a day and catching specially chartered flights between races. And the *lanterne rouge*, the fans' favourite and an entrenched part of the pageant of the Tour, was much in demand. For a journeyman pro on a low wage and with uncertain job prospects, the idea of a well-paid invitation to a two-week party was very alluring.

So much so that many Tour riders, once they found themselves near the bottom of the GC, would deliberately lose time by fair means or foul in order to 'win' the *lanterne rouge*. Abdel-Kader Zaaf, an agitator and a schemer, was *lanterne rouge* in 1951: 'I thought hard about my situation and I didn't find it too bad at all,' he said. 'The last man is more noticed in the classification than one who is in the middle, lost in the masses, but the last man

in the peloton isn't marked. He is allowed to act as he pleases.'
Zaaf claimed to have made 35,000 francs at the criteriums (his
daily wage had been something like 7–10 francs).

Later, Don Allan, an Australian, was initially enthusiastic
about racing for last: 'You have to have a first and last rider.
I'll never be the first, so I might as well be the last.' In 1974
Allan was headed for the *lanterne rouge* but missed out when
Italian Lorenzo Alaimo stopped and hid by the road to lose
time and take the lucrative criterium cash. In 1975 he was
again scraping along near the bottom before missing out. When
looking back, Allan admitted losing his enthusiasm for being
last: 'Everyone said: "It's great, you'll get a lot of publicity for
it,"' he was reported as saying. 'The team said: "It's great, you'll
get money." But I hated it. I didn't enter races to finish last.'

Today, the post-Tour crits still take place, and even a popular
jobbing rider can make his salary over again in the two weeks
following the Tour, but they number no more than 12 or 15 and
they are less important to a cyclist's livelihood. Jimmy Casper
was *lanterne rouge* in 2001 and 2004, when the criteriums had
definitively waned: 'Being last or second last doesn't change
much,' he said. 'It's just a bit more in the media spotlight.' He
did used to get invited to the criteriums that remained, he says,
but more for his abilities as a sprinter than for his lantern.

One last factor Pescheux mentions is that the shape of the race
has evolved. In the '60s and '70s the high mountains were usually
over and done with around the start of the second week, leaving
at least a couple of flat stages on which the riders could mess
around and lose time. These days, and especially since Christian
Prudhomme took over as race director, the conventions are less
strict. Sometimes there is only a time trial separating the final
high mountain stage from Paris – more exciting for spectators
but more difficult for the riders. 'The race design has changed

attitudes,' he says. 'The topography of today's Tour means you can't just do what you like. You don't take risks in the mountains.'

For 30 years Pescheux has been working on these evolutions from the inside. One of his last acts was overhauling the time-cut rules, which set a limit each day on how far behind the winner a rider can be. It's calculated as a percentage of the winning time that day, with extra allowances for mountainous terrain and if the race is fast, so that sprinters are not unfairly penalised when gravity makes their lives difficult. Miss the time cut and you are eliminated from the race. It is not, however, intended to be punitive: 'The goal of the time cut is to eliminate riders who ride with their hands on top of the bars, taking it easy, and then on the next day's flat stage attack from the gun. They lose an hour on one stage and attack the next day,' he repeats contemptuously. 'Voilà. It's a question of fairness.'

That's probably not quite how he viewed it when he was still in the *autobus*, the group of sprinters and slower riders who band together in the mountains for solidarity and self-help, assuring mutual survival when the road goes up and the time cut threatens. Because riders – especially the heavier ones, or any who are weak, ill or injured – often view it as harsh and unforgiving, and for the last-placed man in a stage it is a guillotine that hangs above him, threatening his existence as a Tour rider.

Yet it is also flexible and prone to being bent. As anyone who has ever done intervals on a turbo trainer will understand, time is a wonderfully, torturously elastic thing. The one minute of recovery, arms bent, head bowed, legs turning slow shaky circles, passes in a flash, while the 30 seconds of effort extend into a continuous sludge of eternity, the liquid crystals on the stopwatch mired in thick time and barely advancing. Just so the time cut, which can be extended or even dispensed with altogether according to the whim of the commissaires.

The history of the Tour is full of examples of *repêchage*, men being let back in after missing the cut, due to their courageous attitude in the face of injury or other similar reasons. *Repêchage* is a great word that suggests the hand of some more-or-less beneficent higher power casting around in the pit of despair, fishing riders out and putting them back on their bike.

Before Pescheux's modifications, if something like 20 per cent of the peloton came in outside the time gap they would all have been let báck in. In 2013 the cut off became absolute, but the way it was calculated became more specific, prescribing more leeway for short, mountainous stages than long ones, for example, to take account of the increased pace set by the climbers and GC stars in such stages. As an example, on 2013's 125-kilometre Annecy–La Semnoz stage everyone got in fine, more than 10 minutes before the cut-off. However, there has not as yet been a mass elimination scenario to test how hard the organisers' hearts really are.

If tinkering with the back of the race was one of Pescheux's last acts, it was one of the first things Jacques Goddet did when he inherited the position of race director in 1936. Both he and Desgrange, who, after abandoning the race at Charleville still followed the race from his desk, were preoccupied with the question of how to keep the racers actually racing. They bemoaned the lazy riders who would take flat stages easy and then ride hard in the mountains, hide in pelotons to reduce the individual graft or 'only' race the final 200 kilometres of a 350-kilometre stage. 'Goddet would have put a sprint bonus every five kilometres, to liven up the race,' Pescheux says about his old boss. 'He always had extraordinary ideas. He didn't like it when people spun along at 20 kilometres an hour and nothing happened. There always had to be action.'

For 1939 Goddet shook up the race. He increased the number of stages from 15 to 24 and made them all much shorter, as well as introducing a number of measures designed to provoke faster and more spectacular racing. Of these the easiest to understand were the 'Departs Séparés', or what we'd now call time trials, including the Tour's first mountain TT up and over the highest pass in the Alps, the 2,770-metre Col de l'Iseran. In 1939 there were a lot of them. Next, there were a lot more time bonuses, including mountain bonuses, and a complex system of sharing the prize money at the stage end. If a rider won by more than 20 minutes, he'd pocket half of everyone else's prize money for the stage. With up to seven arriving together the judges would try their best to classify them to receive the prize money they were due, but if up to 12 arrived together the group would share the pot equally. Finish in a group of 13 or more and the shared pot would be reduced. Moreover, any large group faced being summoned for an eliminatory 1,000-metre sprint on a velodrome the next day.

Think you've got all that? There's one more: 'After each of the first 14 stages, the first excepted, the last rider in the general classification will be eliminated.'

This rule, Article 41, introduced something like a road-going version of the popular track event known as the 'Devil' (after 'Devil takes the Hindmost', and in the modern Omnium event known as the elimination race). In 1938 a previous draft of the rule had allowed for a mass cull at several points in the race, of riders falling either an hour, two or three behind the leader – in other words those who were within the time cut but hadn't been able to hold any kind of contact with the front. This improved version, it was hoped, would be less barbarous, and though it would daily remove the last man from the race, it was not designed specifically to target the *lanterne rouge*.

Rather, it was intended to encourage team spirit and to remove the 'unfair' advantage conferred by having *domestiques*: team leaders would have to 'change martyr' – that is, not rely always on the same man to help them through. Climbers, too, would have to work harder to stay in the race during the first week; they could not save their forces for their preferred terrain. 'Every man will have to pitch in kneading the dough,' Desgrange wrote.

And so the 1939 Tour started. After the first stage, won in a sprint by Amédée Fournier of the north-east regional French team,[15] the Belgians dominated at the front and, sure enough, with each subsequent stage one man was eliminated – first Leisen then Dubois then Bouffier then Bidinger – with little fanfare or fuss. Little fanfare, that is, until the sixth stage from La Rochelle to Royan when Jean Majerus of the Luxembourg team was caught in last place and summarily shown the door. The 'big, handsome' Majerus was something of a star. A master tactician on the flat stages, he had worn the yellow jersey for five days in the 1938 Tour. 'I waited for Pierre Clemens today when he punctured. After that I was dropped, adding to my deficit,' Majerus said, explaining why he'd found himself losing so much time. 'But I believed I'd make it through since Maestranzi, who was the last, was lagging behind.' Reassured by Maestranzi's presence as backstop, he faced up to the long, lonely road to the finish line. 'Only [Maestranzi] was so far back,' he continued, 'that he didn't arrive in Royan within the time limit, being thus eliminated and leaving me as *lanterne rouge*.'

With Maestranzi shown the door because of the time cut, it was Majerus who found his head on the block. He wasn't

---

15 Regional teams were another innovation, bolstering the numbers since the political situation in Europe meant that Italian and German teams had not been invited. The 'Black Squadron', the Belgian team, also had back-up – though the Belgian Bs wore green.

used to being at the back, and he blamed his bad form in this, the fastest Tour to date, on racing too much beforehand and on a particularly tiring Bordeaux–Paris. He had battled fatigue, lumpy terrain and a vicious headwind but it had been a long, slow ride to elimination.

The next day, a rest day, saw a big outcry against the injustice of Majerus's departure. It was judged catastrophic by Mathias Clemens, the leader of the combined Swiss/Luxembourgeois team which, having lost three of its personnel to the new rule, was now reduced to four men. Majerus was a pillar of the team and the one responsible for keeping team spirits high, according to Clemens: 'Without Majerus I think I've now lost this Tour,' he lamented.

Majerus himself wrote a letter, published in *L'Auto*, to Henri Desgrange, expressing his disappointment, but the authorities held firm and the elimination stood.[16]

The 1939 Tour had from the outset been short of stars, in part because of the absence of the Germans and Italians. With Majerus gone, they were yet fewer and further between. It would soon get worse. Amédée Fournier had been a late entrant into one of the regional teams, but had made his mark by taking the yellow jersey in a first-stage sprint, and a second win at the velodrome finish in Nantes in stage five. From the off the organisers had been keen to promote the regional stars as a disruptive threat to the dominance of the big guns of Belgium and France, and Fournier, along with the gifted climber René Vietto, was delivering. The papers had been touting Fournier as

---

16 Curiously, there was far less outcry in *L'Auto's* rival, *Le Petit Parisien*, which was not dedicated to sports. Yes, there was less Tour coverage – the *Petit Parisien* mistakenly attributing front-page space to insignificant things like the annexation of Poland and the Tripartite Pact – but is there a sniff here of Henri Desgrange being a backseat driver and briefing against his successor while Goddet, who is out on the road, can do little about it?

a potential *recordman* for stage victories that year but, though talented, he was inexperienced. Stage eight was a split stage, with a short road stage in the morning and a time trial in the afternoon.[17] By the time trial, Fournier was so exhausted he struggled to cut up a hard-boiled egg in the feed station. We can assume that the TT did not go well because, at the end of the day, he had tumbled into last place. Yet in the stage results in the next day's paper there was no *'eliminé'* by his name. The day after that he was still there – and there was a note explaining that due to the excessive difficulties of the Tour this year, he was being allowed to stay.

A week later another note appeared stating the automatic elimination regulation was being suspended until further notice. No further notice would come.

Were the commissaires acting out of expediency? Fournier was leading the sprint classification at that point, and to knock out another high performer risked alienating fans and causing even more of a stir than they had with Majerus. If pleasing the public and selling papers was the basis for the decision it paid off, as Fournier was from that point on good value and gave the reporters plenty to write about. Early in the race, he'd admitted he had never climbed a proper mountain. 'The mountains? They're a completely different kettle of fish,' he'd said, employing a more-than-averaged sized portion of understatement and stoicism. 'I've only ever climbed the small ridges of Wolber, but in theory climbing is a bit of a grind and I don't like it much.'

---

17 The split stage was a format beloved of the Tour organisers for many years; the riders were less enamoured. 1934 was the Tour's first split stage, with the first-ever individual time trial in the afternoon. According to Feargal McKay of the PodiumCafé website, the *lanterne rouge*, Antonio Folco, had only 10 minutes' rest between one and the next, since he was trailing the field in the morning and, as is tradition, was first off in the TT.

The difference between riding up a hill and a mountain is pretty substantial; that between riding up a mountain and racing up one even more so. Amédée's dislike and apprehension proved well founded. Stage nine took the riders into the Pyrenees, and over the Cols de Porte, Aubisque, Soulor, Tourmalet and Aspin. Fournier suffered and suffered and suffered some more, clinging on desperately over the 2,115-metre Tourmalet, the highest pass in the Pyrenees. He became one of those tortured survivors whose praises journalists love to sing: he does not have mere bad luck, but a 'rosary of misfortunes'; he doesn't relax in his hotel, but 'slumps in his cell', 'features drawn, cheeks hollow, hair in disorder, desperately unhappy lying on his bed.'

Out of the mountains and in the flat wine-growing south, Fournier ate too many grapes and was violently sick. Further on, he removed a wheel and gave it to Archambaud, when his leader needed a spare, but the replacement he was eventually handed rubbed on his frame's seat stays. He lost even more time finding a spectator who could give him washers from their own bike to make the wheel fit properly, before riding 60 kilometres to the finish on his own.

'He rides, rides, rides some more. He rides and rides to the finish line where he learns he is last in the general classification. And tomorrow he will get back on his bike,' writes L'Auto's correspondent Perrier, who devotes almost a page to Fournier headlined 'The Martyr of the Tour'. Which is wrong because he was absolutely not martyred – he was saved from elimination, spared martyrdom – as Perrier should know. Perrier continues: 'How right you were, Messieurs les commissaires, to suspend this rule that ordered the elimination of the last man in the general classification. You wouldn't have had the heart to eliminate pour little Médoche.'

Eventually Fournier, or Médoche as he has become known,

claws some time back, rises in the ranks and Armand Le
Moal of the Breton regional team sinks into last place. Also
a debutant in the mountains, Le Moal had been blasé, even
cocky, and had professed himself to be unconcerned by these
little lumps he had never seen ('The Alps and the Pyrenees, I
can easily imagine them'). However, he proved to be terrible
at both climbing and descending – 49th best out of 50 riders
at going up, and bottom of the table going down – and was
1939's definitive *lanterne rouge*.

It may come as a surprise to hear of yellow jerseys toiling along
at the back and fighting not to be eliminated, but Fournier and
Majerus are not the only two *lanternes rouges* to have worn
yellow. 'It was my dream as a kid. You always look wide-eyed
at the *maillot jaune* and frankly I never thought I'd wear it
one day,' Jacky Durand (*lanterne rouge* 1999) said to me about
wearing the leader's jersey, which he took in the prologue and
then wore for two long stages in 1995. 'It's a different kind of
feeling to a victory. A victory is that intense moment crossing
the line. I savoured [wearing yellow]. It's not the same emotion
as lifting your arms in the air. It's less intense, more long term.'

Joseph Groussard (*lanterne rouge* 1965) and Jean-Pierre
Genet (1967) have also worn yellow for a stage or two, and there
are multiple Tour stage winners among the *lanternes* including
Gilbert Glaus (1984), who beat Sean Kelly on the Champs-
Élysées in 1983, depriving the great Irishman of any stage
wins to go with his green jersey that year. The *lanterne* corps
is also rather winning outside the Tour de France. Groussard
took Milan–San Remo and Edwig Van Hooydonck (1993) was
a two-time Ronde van Vlaanderen – Tour of Flanders – winner.
There is also a winner of the Dwars door Vlaanderen (Rob
Talen, 1994), Bordeaux–Paris (Glaus again), a French national

champion (Anatole Novak, 1964), a national TT champion (the Canadian Svein Tuft, 2013's last man), a Deutschland Tour winner (Guido de Santi, 1949) and at least two medalled Olympians (Claude Rouer, 1953, and Philippe Gaumont, 1997, who both won bronze in the men's team time trial, though obviously at different Olympics).

Open it up from what you might call 'proper' *lanternes rouges* – those who finished last in Paris – to men last on the GC for simply a stage or two and you find the trophy cabinet completely flooded. There are world champions (Mark Cavendish, Thor Hushovd), *maglie rosa* (Cavendish again and Danilo Di Luca), Paris–Roubaix winners (Magnus Bäckstedt) and many more. The paper lantern might not look good in the trophy cabinet, but it's often not the only prize in there.

Back at the ASO headquarters in Issy-les-Moulineaux, Pescheux is getting carried away in a discussion about *la notion du vrai grimpeur*, the idea of the true climber. That's how it goes in France – begin a conversation about cycling and sooner or later it ends in philosophy.

'Bahamontes was the best climber, but he never wore the polka-dot jersey[18] – people knew it because he was the first man over the cols,' Pescheux says. 'These days, the King of the Mountains tries to take points on the hills. It's a bit out of kilter. That's why we put more points on the big cols and double on the summit finishes.' He pauses before carrying on.

'Today, the King of the Mountains classification . . . OK, this year it was good, but it doesn't always correspond to the best climber. When you're the best climber, you command the

18 Federico Bahamontes, 'the Eagle of Toledo', won the mountains classification six times in the '50s and '60s; the polka-dot jersey was not introduced until 1975.

mountain stages, you're in front. The best climbers in the 2013 Tour were Quintana, Contador, Froome.' That seems clear, so he looks to another race to make his point: 'I've nothing against Nicolas Edet, who won the King of the Mountains classification in the Vuelta a España, but that just didn't fit reality. You never saw him fighting it out on the big cols.'

You can see his point. The race organisation should create the best conditions for a good race, one that lives up to the Tour's spirit and heroic image, a race in which the riders are fit to bear the historic weight of the jerseys they are awarded. If the rules produce results that don't live up to this ideal, then that's simply not right. It's a question of fairness. *Voilà.*

Eliminating the last rider in 1939 was unfair, unfair to those who were playing the game by the rules, those who had crashed or were unwell or who had given their all for their team and found themselves at the back. All the tinkering around the edges, forcing the riders to jump through hoops, just wasn't in the spirit: 'The Tour is the best rider, the one who goes the fastest and finishes in the shortest time possible. If we start to put artificial things in, it's not good,' Pescheux says.

Much later on, Goddet acknowledged it too, in his autobiography. Teams used the rule to eliminate their rivals, he said. A rider in last position knew he would be disqualified at the end of the stage, so he had nothing to lose: if he dropped out before or during the stage, or contrived to miss the time cut, another competitor would be last and would leave the race as well. Suddenly, poor old Majerus's elimination, indeed that of almost half of his team, takes on a more sinister air, and Clemens's lament that he'd been robbed looks more credible.

The French don't have a word for 'fair play'. Well, they do, but it's ours: *le fair-play.* Desgrange in his worst moments may have overdone the sadism, toying with his riders like a little boy tearing the legs off a spider, but there was a savage, even cruel, fairness to his diktats; Goddet, on the other hand, was in danger of micromanaging the race to its detriment. There is a fine line between creating the structures that give the race room to breathe and suffocating the competition. A good Tour is Darwinian enough.

Pescheux is still with ASO, until at least 2015, and he will no doubt be stealing a ride or two in a car to watch the race. It'll be a shame for him, though, if he can't squeeze into his old car, which he shared with a driver, Sébastian Piquet (the voice of Radio Tour) and the head of the race jury. Its regular position was squarely behind the peloton at the back of the race. Clearly, he loved that car: 'When there's a big crash, you see immediately if the leader's in there . . . when there's a break you see immediately who's there, who's lost the Tour. You see the race, you see the dramas, everything that happens . . . If you love cycling, being behind is the best place to be. The best place.'

1939
79 starters
Winner: Sylvère Maes, 31.99 km/h
Lanterne rouge: Armand Le Moal, 30.95 km/h @ 4h26'39"
49 finishers

Chapter 4

THE REBEL

What is History, but a fable agreed upon?

Napoleon Bonaparte

I'm not sure Jean-François Pescheux would have got on very well with Abdel-Kader Zaaf, a man whose name is infamous, and not because he was *lanterne rouge* in 1951. An incident the previous year involving a daring breakaway, some wine and a tree has passed into Tour myth. But myths are just that. They are stories we tell ourselves about heroes living in a time more authentic and burnished than our own, stories that may or may not be true.

The post-war period is known by some as the 'Golden Age' of cycling. As before the war, this was the era when men were still men and the Tour still a dusty, dangerously heroic thing to do, but the riders' stories and images were enjoyed by more people than ever before through print, radio and finally TV. It was a time of the Hollywood smile of Louison Bobet, the comb and the slicked-back hair of Hugo Koblet, the effortless cool of Fausto Coppi or the harrowed, debonair chic of Jacques Anquetil – each combining the allure of James Dean, Cary

Grant and Elvis Presley in their own unique way. In such company Abdel-Kader Zaaf stuck out like a sore thumb, not least because he was a Muslim from Algeria and *lanterne rouge* instead of *maillot jaune*. Yet his force of personality, his rapport with the public and the myth he created meant he stood up there with the rest of them. However, the myth of Abdel-Kader Zaaf is perhaps the least interesting thing about the man.

It was on the road from Restinclières to Sommières that the event did or did not happen. Today, it's a dusty highway between the busy southern cities of Montpellier, Alès and Nîmes, where the Languedoc gives way to Provence. On the rise behind Sommières you can see the imposing forested hills of the Cévennes, but the lowlands are dominated by olive groves, swathes of Mediterranean pine forest and bamboo, scrub, smallholdings and horses. And wine: neat rows of vines march away in lines directly from the side of the road. There are expensive *grands vins* too, sheltered by crumbling stone walls, a distant line of trees marking the hidden presence of a château. Either side of the road are the remnants of the twin ranks of plane trees that used to shelter it from the blast of the southern sun. Head from west to east as Zaaf did and you might feel the wrath of the Mistral, the wind that comes off the Alps and funnels down the Rhône valley. When I rode the road on a beautiful September morning, it was just beginning to blow. Locals say that once it starts it lasts for three days, and if it doesn't stop then it will carry on for another three, and so on. In winter the Mistral is cold and savage, terrorising the citizens of Marseille and retired Britons in Provence alike. In the summer it is like a hairdryer, hot and remorseless and no comfort to a pair of Algerians toiling up a false flat on a long, lonely breakaway in the 40°C heat.

It is 1950 and it is the first time there has been a North

African team at the Tour. Only six men strong, it is manifestly underpowered for the task of taking on the European stars riding with 10-man squads, both in terms of numbers and sheer depth of talent. Even most of the French regional squads have a full complement of riders . . . but then in French eyes Afrique du Nord is a regional squad and nothing more. Though its influence in the Maghreb is waning, France still runs Tunisia and Morocco as protectorates and Algeria comprises three *départements* – administratively no different from any chunk of mainland France. That said, the arrival of a fully fledged North African team brings a novelty and a certain exoticism to the 1950 Tour. Comprising four Algerians and two Moroccans, the team is a mix of Arabs, Berbers (the largest group of Berber origin in Algeria are the Kabyles) and what the French call *pieds-noirs*, people of European origin born or living in North Africa. They are all strong riders but the team is chaotic. As with many of the regional teams, there is no year-round structure overseeing cycling – and this region is actually composed of three countries covering a vast area of desert. It has pulled together at the last minute a culturally diverse selection of riders. One shoo-in, however, is Zaaf, the Digger of Chebli, AKA the Old Lion (because every rider in the heroic age of cycling had an epithet or two to garnish his name). At 33, Zaaf is the oldest and no stranger to European racing, having competed in the Tour de Suisse that year. Previously, he'd lived and raced in Belgium, retaining an affection for the country if not for its cobbles, and in 1948 he'd been a last-minute stand-in at the Tour de France, riding for the French south-east regional squad after Ahmed Kebaïli, a gifted climber, had ceded his spot.[19]

Zaaf claimed to have ridden 20,000 kilometres before

---

19 It was an inauspicious debut: he abandoned during stage one.

the 1950 Tour, and he had a reputation as a peerless *rouleur*: aggressive, strong and a specialist in solo breaks. His detractors questioned whether he'd hack the pace in France, given the lower standard of racing in Algeria, but if he'd heard them, he surely wouldn't have cared. He was impulsive, direct and confrontational; a chunky, balding man with huge arms like a boxer's, a ready laugh and an ever-present urge to attack.

He started the race with a saddle sore and suffered on the *pavés*, but had made it through the Pyrenees intact. Although near the bottom of the standings, he was attacking regularly and the press and public, if they hadn't known him before, were much taken with the Zaaf show. 'With Zaaf there's no middle ground,' one of the papers said. 'Either he takes the *prime* for the unluckiest man on the stage (it's already happened twice); or he tries to escape, in a disorderly fashion perhaps, but always full of heart.'

If the Pyrenees had knocked him sideways a bit, by the time the race got to the Midi and the sun had come out Zaaf had rediscovered his punch. He attacked on the 12th stage to Perpignan, near the Spanish border, and was eventually dropped by his breakaway companions. But his tail was up and he warned of more to come in the newspaper: 'I'll give it another go in a stage before the Alps,' he said. 'After that, it'll be too late – but this time I'll go solo!'

The article continued: 'Gifted with fine natural strength, Zaaf recovers rapidly. "When I drink a good wine, I uncork" he said, with a roguish wink.'

The following day the cork popped.

'We had nothing left to lose,' Zaaf said of the attack that he launched with Marcel Molinès, his young *pied-noir* teammate. On the road from Perpignan to Nîmes it was 40°C and the peloton was shuffling along in a stupor, not liking the suffocating heat one bit.[20] Zaaf and Molinès, perhaps better acclimatised than most, took advantage and attacked after only 15 kilometres. Nobody showed any inclination to chase the two Algerians and they built a lead of almost 20 minutes. However, even they were not immune to the sun and the effects of dehydration; in that era drinking too much water was thought bad for performance, drinks were rationed and riders could be punished for taking illegal drinks from team cars. Riders welcomed the bottles held out by spectators on the roadside and Zaaf no doubt did take some drinks. It is here, around 30 kilometres from the stage end, as Zaaf begins to slow, bow his head and wobble on his bike, that we enter the realm of myth.

Zaaf, dehydrated and affected by the sun, zig-zags across the road. He takes a bottle from a spectator and downs it in one. Actually, let's make that two bottles (some accounts do). One or two, it matters little, since the bottles were filled not with water as he expected, but with Corbières, some of the local cheap plonk. For a dehydrated man in a heatwave this would be bad enough, but for a conscientious Muslim, unused to even a drop, it is catastrophic. Disoriented, he falls, remounts, falls again, and is laid down by spectators under a tree to rest. Two hours later, he wakes, gets back on his bike and rides off in pursuit of the peloton. Unfortunately the race is long gone, there is nobody around and, still dazed, he has pointed his bike in the wrong direction and headed back towards the stage start. He doesn't get far and is taken to hospital to recover. Although he implores the Tour commissaires to let him complete the

---

20 Two days later many riders stopped at Sainte-Maxime, near Saint-Tropez, for a swim, some of them cycling straight into the Mediterranean to cool off. Jacques Goddet wished to fine them for it but, finding he didn't have a regulation that covered it, was reduced to metaphorically shaking his fist at them as they played in the waves.

25 kilometres in the morning and then to take his place for the *départ* to Toulon they decline him that courtesy, and Zaaf the drunken Muslim is eliminated.

Or perhaps it didn't happen like that at all.

Three decades later, from his hospital bed, Zaaf recalled the stage to *Vélo* magazine. Twenty kilometres or so out, a spectator gave him something to drink. 'I accepted, because it was as hot as the desert. I'm not a camel, you know,' he explained.

It is too little too late and Zaaf, dehydrated and affected by the sun, zig-zags across the road. He falls, gets up, takes up his bike again. Cycles a little way more before falling again. Third time down, he is KO'd in a ditch; later he gets up and cycles off in the wrong direction. 'Oh! Not far, a few metres. That didn't stop people from claiming I was drunk,' he said. 'Obviously I smelt of plonk, but that's because they splashed my face with a bottle. Do you think I would have done 200 kilometres at 42 kilometres an hour if I'd been drunk? I ask you.' Nobody has suggested that he rode the whole stage drunk, but it is nevertheless a reasonable question.

Let's rewind one more time.

Zaaf, 'the hard worker, the proud Arab, full of dignity and reason', taps out the rhythm of the break for his frailer younger compatriot Molinès, both of them drinking, drinking and drinking some more because they know what the pitiless 40°C heat can do to a man. They pass the cathedral of Béziers atop its hill, together under the crushing sun, and are hosed down by the crowds as they do. Without warning Zaaf attacks his teammate at 60 kilometres out. 'I was suffering at that moment, and I couldn't stop myself crying in impotent rage when I saw him distance me,' Molinès says. He does not see Zaaf again until Zaaf, who has over-reached himself, is laid out cold. Just outside Sommières, 28 kilometres from the end, Zaaf passes between vineyards under rows of plane trees where, dehydrated and affected by the sun, he zig-zags across the road. It is no longer wide enough for him; he heads towards a tree but hits the wall instead, gets up, takes up his bike again. People rush to help him. He is pushed on his way by a man from the crowd of 40 or 50 that have gathered around him. One of the white army-style commissaires' jeeps has also stopped. Zaaf's knee is dripping with blood. Again he falls; this time he refuses all help, apparently shouting and swearing on the Koran that he is not cooked, that he knows what he's doing, that they will not catch him before Nîmes, before remounting his bike. This time he heads the wrong way, back towards Perpignan, and quickly, in a matter of metres, he is stopped by his *directeur sportif*. He turns around. Pedals on. Then, drunk with sunstroke and fatigue, he falls in the dirt. Onlookers lay him out under a plane tree. His bike is in the ditch, its back wheel spinning in the air. Two girls fan him with their handkerchiefs. He does not regain consciousness before he is lifted by four men and put into an ambulance to Nîmes. The doctor at the hospital reassures reporters that Zaaf isn't in any danger. The injury to his knee is superficial. In the morning he will be right as rain. He is seen at 6 a.m. – nobody knows how he escaped the hospital – wandering the streets of Nîmes in his team kit. The Tour's general manager is summoned. He explains to the Algerian that since he travelled the last 29 kilometres of the stage in an ambulance he cannot take his place on the start line later that day. With some reluctance Zaaf takes this in; back in the team hotel, he tells his room-mate Ahmed Kebaïli that he will ask Jacques Goddet if he can go back to where he fell, and ride those final kilometres, to carry on in the Tour. It is not to be.

His passing is mourned practically as a death and marked by fulsome, melodramatic eulogies: 'The unlucky hero' had a 'desire to shine in the twilight hours of an African career', writes one journalist. 'He has been battered, but not beaten. Zaaf will go back to Algiers with tears in his eyes and a full heart, but I am certain that his city will welcome him like a great champion. He who has been so unlucky, eliminated by this curse that has followed him his whole career.'

Abdel-Kader Zaaf promises to come back and complete the 1951 Tour.

Three stories: one myth; one told by an old man 30 years distant; one reconstructed as far as is possible from the TV footage and accounts directly from the time. Pick one.

Even at the time, however, rumours and misinformation had started to circulate. *Miroir Sprint* suggests his *cuite* is down to a lack of experience but that seems fatuous or disingenuous, given his years racing in Belgium, his long Tours of Algeria and other African races, his good showing in the Tour de Suisse. Many of the other factoids that attach themselves to the story have little or no logic to them either. Why is the wine Corbières? This is rural France in the 1950s, in the heart of the wine-producing south; you cannot walk a metre without tripping over people making vino. The Corbières appellation, which is maybe 120 kilometres away, may as well be the Napa Valley for all the likelihood that someone standing in Sommières would have had a flask of it to drink. Some of the stories would prefer the peasants to drizzle him with white wine, or rosé, but this is red wine country – where would they get *that* from? (Then again, pouring it over a dying man might have been the only thing they'd consider doing with a white *vin de pays* . . .) Much later, when he was an old man, Ahmed Kebaïli professed he thought Zaaf to have been an

THE REBEL 71

observant Muslim, so it is probably true that he was sprayed with – rather than drank any – wine.[21]

Kebaïli put Zaaf's collapse down to amphetamine abuse.

So where does the wine-drinking myth come from? It probably originated in an article in one of the illustrated Tour round-up magazines that year, which imagined a scene in which Zaaf's DS jokily reproaches him for taking a bottle of lethal Narbonne rosé from a spectator.[22] And as the myth grew, so did his fame. His attacking mentality and particular brand of beautiful madness were attractive to the cycling public and this haphazard, jokey catastrophe endeared him to them further. Poor Marcel Molinès won the stage yet was overshadowed by the story and disappeared into obscurity, something which maddened him even into his old age; Zaaf's teammate Custodio Dos Reis won the next day's stage, also in the stifling heat, yet the Portuguese-French-Algerian is forgotten. Zaaf, meanwhile, became famous and, for a short while at least, wealthy. He was invited to the criteriums across France and the great Louison Bobet himself, almost more a matinée idol than a cyclist, drove Zaaf from one to another in his car.

Nevertheless, it must have been galling to be known for physically collapsing rather than fighting to victory (and very possibly for something that offended your religion). Walk into a village bar in the environs of Nîmes that summer and order *un Zaaf* and you'd have been served a small glass of red.

---

21 The predominant strain of Islam in Algeria at the time was not particularly strict, so it might have been possible that Abdel-Kader took an occasional drink. By contrast his son Tahar, also a bike racer, was known to like a drink or two, and the drink flowed in Marcel Molinès's home *quartier* of Belfort in Algiers the night he won his stage – though Belfort was a white working-class area.

22 And what to make of the 'uncork' remark in the paper the previous day? It seems sewn in to the narrative as a kind of portent. It could not be more significant if deliberately plotted.

Abdel-Kader himself at least seemed to take it all in – ahem – good spirits. He even appeared in ads for St Raphaël, the fortified tonic wine that would later sponsor one of the most famous cycling teams of the '60s. 'Everybody wants to drink a glass with me,' smiled the Algerian in the newspaper spots. Yet in the photo his grin is tending towards the rictus, and his knuckles look white from gripping the glass rather more tightly than necessary.

Somewhere between the 1950 and 1951 races the joke wore thin, and Zaaf came to the '51 Tour in an even more renegade mood.

This time the Afrique du Nord team was eight strong, but still lightweight in a race of 12-man teams. They rode to the start in Metz from Paris, a two-day journey about which they boasted to all and sundry (they were, however, spotted by a rival team manager somewhere out on the road hanging on to their DS's car). As the race headed into Belgium Zaaf began to plot. He wanted to make a good fist of it there, since he was, he jested, at least partly native; more importantly, perhaps, he'd heard that some of the largest *primes* in the race were being offered on the stage from Ghent back into France. For the first *prime* Zaaf did not make his move: it wasn't that big and he did not want to arouse suspicion. Before the second he moved up the pack but did not attack. Only before the third did he jump, excavating enough of a gap that he could stop at his old friend André Rosseel's house on the way past. He'd stayed with Rosseel when he was racing in Belgium and knew Rosseel's wife well – 'I slowed to shake Mme Rosseel's hand. She is pregnant and I had to be careful not to jostle her' – and then headed off again until, having a gap of four minutes and 40 seconds and being interested only in the *primes* rather than the stage, he stopped to wait for the peloton. Presently two Belgians – Rosseel himself and a chap called Derycke – appeared and Zaaf, reasoning they wouldn't be racing ahead if there weren't more *primes* to be won, promptly remounted and gave chase. Neither was in a good state and Derycke was quickly dropped.

'I could also have dropped Rosseel, but he was my friend and it would have been lousy of me to leave him,' Zaaf said. 'Luckily, he was thirsty. "Why not stop for a beer?" I said to him, since Belgians love beer . . . He stopped, and since I wasn't thirsty I carried on alone.'

A little further and Zaaf was tiring, but when a race official told him there was another *prime* in 20 kilometres, he decided that 1,000 francs per kilometre of effort was a good wage and put in one last dig. At the next feed station he stopped, sat down and ate, and watched the peloton rush by.

Depending on whom you believe, Zaaf won between 80,000 and 100,000 francs that day, but by then he had already lost time on the peloton and was heading for last place. For that, and for the stage win, it seems, he didn't care a jot.

Nor was his attitude towards his 'friends' that caring. His conduct towards Rosseel was of the kind to make a rider glad he doesn't have serious enemies. Unfortunately for Zaaf he was losing teammates and friends all over the peloton. The seventh stage was a massive 85-kilometre flat individual time trial, which Zaaf suspected would be used by Tour favourite Hugo Koblet to kill off some of his GC rivals' hopes. As an elder statesman, he recommended his teammates use a 52×14 top gear and to give it some welly; unfortunately they did not listen, or did not have the legs, and four of the remaining six North Africans were eliminated on time. At Clermont-Ferrand two days later Zaaf was in last place and seven seconds away from being eliminated himself.

It seems by this point, too, his relationship with the French had definitively soured. No more lifts in Bobet's car, only angry, taunting exchanges when they spoke. 'They were making my life hell,' Zaaf said of the French team. 'If I wanted to go, they set the dogs on my tail, dangerous dogs that watched me as if I was a robber.' He was in last place and wasn't a threat – and in any case, the French hadn't once had the yellow jersey to defend. He felt victimised and resolved to get one over on them.

' "Zaaf," I said to myself, "you're going to use the opportunity to attack, and get your name in the papers." ' Rather worryingly as he continues he slips into referring to himself in the Messianic third person: 'They [journalists] can't write anything if everyone buries themselves in the peloton and never comes out again. So Zaaf will entertain them. It's my right to go on solo attacks. I'm only doing my job.'

Perhaps, he reasoned, he could do this and make himself some valuable allies into the bargain, and the Italians that year needed every bit of help offered their way. The great champion Fausto Coppi was in very bad shape. Less than a week before the Tour his brother Serse had fallen on tramlines during the Giro del Piemonte and, though he was able to finish and ride to his hotel, was taken to hospital with concussion. He died in Fausto's arms before an operation could be performed. Fausto was distraught and thought about renouncing cycling for good, but commercial pressures and the shortness of time forced him to line up for the Tour. He wore a leather helmet that year. According to Zaaf, Fausto was a friend who had visited him at home in Algeria; so he went to Coppi's lieutenants to propose a pact. At a certain agreed point he would attack and a couple of Italians were to make a show of chasing, while the rest of the *Azzurri* sat on the front of the pack and put on the brakes. Then he and his breakaway companions could fight the stage out – as long as Zaaf won. Above all, Zaaf wanted help shafting the French and to make a bit of money: 'I'll work for you but let me win a stage. I have a lot of mouths to feed at home,' he said.

Coppi gave his assent and it was set. On the stage between Carcassonne and Montpellier the peloton was again having a siesta under the stultifying southern sun, only rousing itself for drinks raids on roadside bars (*chasser la canette*, chasing cans, as it was known). Around 150 kilometres from the line Zaaf went to the Italians to light the fuse, only to be told it was too early. But for him later just wouldn't do: going early would give him a buffer over the peloton in case the favourites attacked and caused the speed to rise; and if he attacked closer to home even as *lanterne rouge* he would not be allowed to get away alone and would be beaten by a wheelsucker in the sprint. And besides: 'A Zaaf breakaway with 40 kilometres to go is not a Zaaf breakaway,' he harrumphed to the Italians. 'If you don't respect our agreement, I'll go on my own and blow the doors off.' *Si vous ne respectez pas notre accord, je pars seul et je casse la baraque.* No dice.

Considering the pact not only null and void but violated, moreover, by the Italians, he waited for the peloton to take a comfort break – such class! – and launched off regardless. Without Italian aid, however, his attack had no chance of success. He was overhauled by his former friend Louison Bobet (with whom he exchanged some choice words) and the French team, together with Firenzo Magni and Hugo Koblet, on a minor col. And then Zaaf was dropped.

His act may have been dishonourable in the eyes of the peloton, but there is no honour among thieves when one of them looks to steal a race. As Zaaf drifted backwards he realised that something big must have happened behind him to cause all the

favourites to surge forward. Indeed, something had: the great
Fausto Coppi had cracked. Dropped once, and then again, Coppi
was scraping along in front of the broom wagon with almost
the whole Italian team looking after him, while the other GC
favourites were pushing the pace to bury his Tour hopes once
and for all. So successful were they, Coppi and his entourage
missed the time cut and only some judicious arguing with the
commissaires over the rules achieved their reinstatement.

Coppi went to see Zaaf that night, to complain about the
attack, but the Algerian was unrepentant for destroying Coppi's
hopes. 'Fausto,' he said, 'the real culprits are your teammates
who didn't keep their word. I didn't take the Italians for traitors,
but you didn't take me seriously.'

Life is hard in the peloton for a *casseur de baraque*, the
nickname by which he would now forever be known. It
translates literally as 'shed breaker', but in the context of a
breakaway merchant has reckless connotations – 'explosives
expert', 'bull in a china shop', maybe even 'saboteur'. Abdel-
Kader was isolated and in last place; he had only one teammate
left and was hated as much by the Italians as by the French.
Without building some bridges he would struggle to survive. He
also later claimed that he felt sorry for his friend Coppi. Again,
he put himself at the *campionissimo*'s service. The first Alpine
stage was to take the peloton north over the 2,360-metre Col
d'Izoard, a mountain Coppi had won on before. Zaaf approached
Fausto in the bunch and offered to make a suicidal attack on
the flat between the Col de Vars and the start of the Izoard.
He judged the peloton would be nervy and scared of attacking
Coppi before the climb proper, so if he could distract them
by scooting up the right-hand side of the road it would leave
Fausto free to sail off unnoticed on the left. Coppi nodded,
and also agreed not to tell his team (whose distrust Zaaf was

probably right to fear). After the Vars and through Guillestre, between sheer rock faces on the ledge beside the Guil river, Zaaf attacked, sprinting up the road as fast as he could. According to plan, everyone else followed; he put the brakes on and by the time they'd lifted their noses from their handlebars, Coppi was but a dot on the horizon, a heron flying off towards his playground in the mountains. Only a Frenchman who had overheard the conversation, Roger Buchonnet, had stuck to the right wheel, and at the finish even he was almost four minutes behind Coppi. Koblet was four minutes and nine seconds back and the rest of those confounded French were over nine minutes adrift. It was a consolatory victory for Coppi, and a Parthian shot by Zaaf.[23] By helping Coppi he had put himself in danger of elimination (Coppi was back in his hotel by the time Zaaf crossed the line) but stuck two fingers up at his enemies.

Enemies may not be too strong a word. Relations between the French colonisers and the Kabyles and Arabs had been increasingly tense since the Second World War. On VE Day itself a victory parade degenerated into a bloodbath in the market town of Sétif as the police traded shots with demonstrators against colonial rule. The official French report estimated 1,000 deaths at Sétif and in its aftermath, while others in Algeria and across the Maghreb put the number in the tens of thousands. It was a pivotal moment that convinced many future leaders of the Algerian Front de Libération Nationale (FLN) that Algeria should be freed from French rule. Between then and 1954, when a full-scale revolutionary war of independence would rip the country apart, anti-colonialist groups became more

---

23 The Parthians, a people living in ancient Persia, perfected the military tactic of retreating on horseback while turning round and loosing arrows at the enemy who, presuming victory, were advancing behind them.

organised, the acts of uprising and rebellion more numerous, and the consequent repression from the French more brutal and draconian. The issue of the relationship to France was an increasingly volatile part of everyday life in Algeria and it would be naive to think that sport, that arena of controlled or symbolic rivalry and conflict, was immune. A key revolutionary meeting, for instance, took place in Bern in 1954 under the cover of the German-Hungarian football World Cup. And in April 1958 'French' World Cup prospects Rachid Mekhloufi and Mustapha Zitouni, who both played league football in France, were found to have left Europe via Switzerland for Tunisia, along with seven compatriots, where they set up the FLN FC. Despite FIFA's opposition, the team managed to play 91 international fixtures (mainly against Soviet Bloc countries, all preceded by the Algerian national anthem) before independence in 1962 and the establishment of an officially recognised team.

Viewed from a certain angle, then, it was perhaps a brave and inclusive act to invite a North African squad to France's national pageant in the early '50s. Whatever the motivation, it was short-lived: after 1953, the team was no more.

This is not to suggest that Zaaf was a covert revolutionary, or that his attempts to *casse* the *baraque* were anything other than sporting sabotage or personal grudges. There is no indication in the French newspapers of his being overtly political, and he seems to have held good relations with the French establishment – the French cycling establishment, at least – into his old age. But the political situation was inescapable. Ahmed Kebaïli, for one, was good friends with significant revolutionary figures and once was delivered from a potentially tricky encounter at a military checkpoint because the soldiers there recognised him as a famous cyclist. Life for the Algerian cyclists, national figureheads voyaging to the heart of what many of their compatriots saw as an unjust occupying foreign power, must have been difficult.

In his first Tour appearance Zaaf had been drafted in to the south-east squad (him hailing from, presumably, the extreme south-western edge of south-eastern France) and whether for economic or other reasons on the North African side or neglect from the organisers, the North African squad always appeared a marginal affair. *L'Équipe* takes every opportunity it can to mention how well the Algerians are being treated – Zaaf is quoted saying as much on several occasions in '50 and '51 – but that's exactly what the official Tour rag would say. And in the meantime, whether materially looked after or not, the riders were subject to a constant stream of patronising news coverage. Only a few years later, in 1955, the first British team came to the Tour, and the caricatures were duly rolled out. But they soon stopped, and the British were allowed to get on with their job. With the North Africans the power relations were very different, and it's easy to detect a condescending tone in the newspaper quotes I've already pulled out. Yes, Zaaf is praised, as are Molinès and Dos Reis for their stage wins, but it's as if they're being given a gold star for trying – precisely because their achievements do not threaten the normal scheme of things. They are feted for their brave efforts to join the European peloton, filling spare column inches in the inside pages while the European stars continue to fight for the big prizes in the front-page headlines and the photo pages of the magazines. In the reports the North Africans are always *braves garçons* or *gars gentils* – brave boys, good lads – and sometimes Zaaf is a *garçon amusant*. All of which may be just the matiness that pervades all-male sports environments (think of how the not-very-chummy Chris Froome becomes Froomey when his teammates talk about him, or a football manager talks of his lads Lamps, Becks, Wazza and so on). It was by no means solely the North Africans who were called these things in the papers, and if it's OK to call a 34-year-old man a *garçon*, this one was more *amusant* than most: larger than life, an undoubted one-off, an animator of the race. But there's a thin line between diminutive and derogatory. Given the context it's tempting to see it as paternalism of the worst sort, a way of keeping the North African riders in their place.

There are also examples of outright racism and racist stereotyping. During the Belgian stages in 1951 – the very place he wanted to shine – the crowds shouted 'Joe Louis' at the passing Zaaf, in reference to the US boxer of African American and Native American descent, and Zaaf's own dark skin tone. *Le Monde*, France's greatest paper, meanwhile, resorted to calling him a *marchand de tapis*, a carpet-seller, on at least two occasions, and mocked the way he spoke French. Jean Castera, its correspondent on the Tour for several years, detailed Zaaf's physical features using the crudest racial stereotypes and suggested before the 1951 event that thanks to his celebrity and success in Europe Zaaf, 'back in Algeria, could take three more wives and offer his friends great feasts of couscous'.

In this light the invented story of Zaaf forgetting his religion and drinking wine is another way of subtly mocking and putting down – albeit gently and with some affection – this awkward and opinionated figure.

How to explain his erratic behaviour? I like to think he'd had enough of fitting in to other people's narratives. He'd played along with the drinking joke, made some money and gained some friends out of it; played a part in his small Tour team and watched his unprepared colleagues get knocked down like the 10 little Indians of the colonial-era rhyme. Even the idea that he is impulsive and wildly irrational is another narrative imposed upon him. Are his actions really without reason? Another way of looking at Zaaf would be as a sharp operator, ballsy enough while *lanterne rouge* to make the moves to influence the top of the GC and savvy enough to do the deals that needed doing to keep himself in the race, all the while working the system to attract fame – or notoriety – and make the money that came with it. He would ride in only one more Tour after '51 (and abandon very early), but he was a *domestique* on trade teams with Charly Gaul in 1953 and then Federico Bahamontes a year later, so he must have had his merits. There are two sides to every story and perhaps Zaaf had lost his grip on his own, become trapped inside other people's. He was a self-publicist who encouraged and bought into the tales people told about him until the meltdown in the '51 Tour, after which the stories seemed to run out. Patronised at best, racially abused at worst. Pressure to perform, pressure to conform, enough of being Caliban. *You taught me language and my profit on't / Is, I know how to curse.*

But all this is just a story too.

I'd come to Abdel-Kader Zaaf sceptical about the wine incident and hoping to dig into the political situation, to write about discrimination against the backdrop of the impending anti-colonial war, the brutality of which would ravage Algeria and bring France almost to her knees. And, while that's all true, it's impossible to keep this jack in that box. Zaaf was a complex figure, both popular and likeable and mercenary and untrustworthy, and far cleverer than the usual tales give him credit for. The French have a lovely expression for an unruly bunch of riders: *un panier de crabes* – a basket of crabs – which seems to me to perfectly describe the volatility, bad temper and self-interest of a 10-man breakaway, say, 10 kilometres from the finish, in which everyone is fighting their own battle to win and be damned with the rest. Zaaf was a basket of crabs, all by himself.

Critics of TV drama sometimes talk about a 'clockwork universe'. They're usually talking about those big budget, glossy American series with multiple characters spanning multiple seasons, with long arching plotlines and slow-build tension, that have you looking forward to Sunday nights with a takeaway in front of the telly. A clockwork universe, in those terms, is not good. It's where the writers have created a world that seems mechanistic, where the two-dimensional characters are only there to serve the plot and have no personality or agency outside it. Sometimes the Tour is like that. The race starts, a well-organised and well-trained team rides so hard it is difficult to attack. Its leader assumes the yellow jersey at the end of the first week; the team works its socks off to defend the jersey, spends as long as it can on the front to keep attackers anaerobic and deploys a super *domestique* to mop up any last mountain-top surprises. It's all fair and square, very impressive and bloody hard to do, but it's winning by suffocation, as clockwork as it comes.

Take a free radical like Zaaf, on the other hand, who seems to simply float around and make trouble, and you have a different race altogether. He's a cannon loosing off shots in all directions, confounding the certain certainties and daring to disrupt, holding friends and enemies alike to ransom. In Hollywood terms he's the negotiator in the hostage situation who shoots the hostage first and lifts an eyebrow at the baddies. Well then, whaddaya gonna do now?

In that sense, he's a threat: a man of some talent allied to a complete disregard for the normal concepts of winning, losing, success and failure. Only, maybe, the Tour de France, an event that each year encircles a country and holds within itself a hundred men's stories of joy and sorrow, gain and loss, can contain Zaaf and sustain these Golden Age myths – stories we love to tell regardless of how true they are. Just as there is nowhere other than sport in modern life where you can be transported from despair to transcendence in a second, or change from villain into hero in the blink of an eye. I attack without remorse when my grieving friend Coppi is pedalling squares. I help my friend Coppi escape before the Izoard. I am about to win a stage of the Tour. I am unconscious under a tree. No other sport, perhaps, could be as tolerant of a character like Zaaf. He's just one player in a huge ensemble cast − a cast, moreover, in which many of the other actors' roles do not demand of them that they try to win either.

Unfortunately, life is rarely kind to men such as him and the continuation of his story is a sad one. He abandoned his final Tour in 1952 and rode with European teams until 1955, then returned to his homeland, which had plunged into war. There he disappeared, only resurfacing when he was spotted at Paris's Gare de Montparnasse in 1982. The intervening three decades had been cruel: one night, he'd been woken by soldiers demanding he come with them to show his papers. When he resisted he was shot in the leg and thrown in prison, where his wound festered. Owing to untreated diabetes, he also began to lose his eyesight. Upon his release years later, he recovered a small stash of money he'd put away before his arrest and travelled to France for an eye operation. When the French public heard his plight, he was showered with cards, presents and money from cycling fans who remembered his panache on the bike.

At least that's the story told by one historian. Or try this one, told by Zaaf himself, from that hospital bed. He is in Paris, it is 1982, he is wearing a casual blue shirt. His features are slightly thickened by the years, and his male-pattern baldness has not miraculously reversed its progress, but generally he's wearing his age well. Still disgruntled-looking, he is a grumpy old man. In this version there's no mention of the war, but yes he'd had diabetes, and yes he'd neglected it for 14 years. 'Big mistake,' he says. 'So much so my sight dimmed. Very gently. And now it's as if I live in a fog. That's why I'm getting laser treatment.' In this version Zaaf still comes regularly to France for exhibition events. (I imagine it would be like watching McEnroe at a pro-am charity tennis tournament. Yup, the smash might be softer, but that famous temper . . . You cannot be serious. The racket on the ground. The palms and gaze to the sky.) And his passage to one of the best hospitals in France is organised by Henri Anglade, a famous former racer, his friend. He is still hustling, still taking contracts. Fans are ringing the hospital, Belgian TV wants to interview him, but he only wants to talk to his younger son, Ahmed, a racer like his older brother, Tahar. Ahmed is currently on strike, in a dispute with Algerian race organisers over safety. Now that's the kind of scuffle that really lit Zaaf's gas. I can imagine his newly fixed eyes gleaming as he plots how to get stuck in.

In neither story can Zaaf escape meeting his maker in 1986. Two roads, they lead to the same place in the end. Pick one.

1951

123 starters

Winner: Hugo Koblet, 32.95 km/h

Lanterne rouge: Abdel-Kader Zaaf, 31.84 km/h @ 4h58'18"

66 finishers

Chapter 5
THE DEBUTANT

Richer in Courage than in Experience
L'Équipe headline about the British team, 6 July, 1955

'Well, it was very nice but I had just finished a 1,300-mile stage race. I didn't feel I needed to train very hard.'

Tony Hoar is almost certainly the oldest surviving *lanterne rouge*, and perhaps the most laid-back, happy-go-lucky bike-riding character I've ever spoken to. I've just suggested to him that a training camp in Les Issambres on the Côte d'Azur in February 1955, where with his teammates he worked towards the goal of joining the first proper British Tour de France squad, must have been glamorous and exciting, and jolly hard work. His voice, its Portsmouth-bred tones given a Pacific Coast twist from many years living in western Canada, gently puts me straight down the crackly line: he'd just been racing the Tour of Egypt and he'd taken the training camp – as it seems from our conversations he has everything in his long and winding life – completely in his stride. His story is one of inauspicious beginnings, haphazard planning, bad luck and not a little bit of the old stiff upper lip. His words hark back to the days when the continent was a long way away and time trialling, performed in cloak-and-dagger secrecy in dark woollens at the crack of dawn on codenamed routes, was British cycling's version of racing; when the sort of mainstream adulation enjoyed by Mark Cavendish and Bradley Wiggins, Chris Hoy and Victoria Pendleton was unthinkable. They say first is for ever; Brian Robinson, Tony's teammate and friend, was Britain's first major road-racing star – our first Tour finisher (1955), first Tour stage winner (1958) and also winner of the Dauphiné (1961); but Tony was the second British Tour finisher: in 1955 he was the last man across the line.

I'd imagined the scenery and the sheer number of professional cyclists on the Côte d'Azur would have been a shock to Tony, arriving there from the post-war austerity that still gripped the UK. For anyone used to enduring dark northern European winters, the light on the French Riviera in February is dazzling. The air is crisp but the sun falls in arrows from big cloudless skies, warms the pines and rebounds in sheets off the blue waters of the Mediterranean that give the coast its name. Not more than a few kilometres away are the mountains, the Alpes Maritimes, where the snow reflects even more light back on to the towns, villages and wooded hills below. Light is everywhere. The Côte d'Azur was, and remains, one of the heartlands of professional cycling. And the enclave where Tony's team ended up on their pioneering continental training camp was in part popularised by Apo Lazaridès, the legendary *domestique*.[24] Lazaridès was approaching the end of his career and had opened a hotel and mini-golf course in the sleepy resort before he hit

---

24 Apo reputedly cut off his own toe – the better to understand the pain and sacrifice necessary to win the Tour – at the behest of his team leader René Vietto, who had lost his own to sepsis . . . or so the story goes. Since René famously never won the Tour (until he was overtaken by Fabian Cancellara in 2012 he was the rider who had spent the most days in the yellow jersey without taking it home from Paris) this story seems more than usually doubtful.

upon the idea of inviting teams down to benefit from the balmy weather and empty roads in the winter season. In 1955 Raphaël Géminiani was there, as was Louison Bobet. Jean, Louison's anglophile, anglophone brother, was staying next door to the Brits. The region's roads were full of French teams, spinning away companionably and preparing for the early season races. The Brits made an impression: 'There were a dozen of them, true pioneers of British professional cycling, making up a solid and ambitious team that bore the lofty name of Hercules,' Jean Bobet wrote in his memoir *Tomorrow, We Ride*. 'We met them from time to time on the tortuous roads that cross the hinterland of the Var. Poking out of the back pocket of their jerseys was the Michelin map that was both their passport and letter of introduction in this strange and unknown land. My colleagues subjected them to a more or less friendly teasing, but I made sure not to display the least arrogance.'

Hercules was a British bike manufacturer that in the early 1950s sponsored the biggest professional team in the UK. They were cleaning up on the domestic scene and Tony had impressed with a good performance in Egypt where he was racing for Great Britain. 'It was a propaganda race,' he says. 'The Suez crisis was under way, so we actually had bodyguards following us through the bazaars. It was poorly run, I won a stage or two I think.' Though the Armed Services were in his words a 'hotbed of racing', the split life was becoming increasingly untenable. A few years previously he'd had to fight with his superiors to be allowed to take a track bike into barracks when he reported for duty. With a good chance of making the Helsinki Olympics track pursuit team – his favoured event – he'd been reduced to doing laps of the Nissen huts on a brakeless track bike, spoiling his best tyres, just to try to keep in shape. In 1954 he had quickly exceeded the statutory holiday limit. Enough was enough. 'I had taken 13 weeks off work in time spent riding for Britain, or England,' he says. 'I thought, bugger this, so I quit and I went to work for my brother. But within two weeks I got the offer and turned pro with Hercules. So I headed off to the south of France. Sorry Mike!' I presume that Mike is his brother. Sorry Mike, indeed. After 1,300 miles in Egypt through the foment of Suez, a training camp in the south of France must have seemed at least a little bit cushy.

There had long been a question of a British team taking part in the Tour, and in 1937 there was an abortive attempt by two British riders, Charley Holland and Bill Burl, who did not finish due to equipment problems and a broken collarbone respectively. It had been too early. In 1939 Henri Desgrange, while casting around for friendly nations to send teams to the final pre-war Tour, held forth on the difficulties barring their participation: 'An English team would make us very happy, but our allies at this time are slowly evolving towards professionalism and find themselves caught up in industrial rivalries that have no place in the Tour de France.' Despite Desgrange's disapproval, it was more or less a bike industry initiative that got the national team going. As cycling writer William Fotheringham explains in *Roule Britannia*,[25] the plan to launch a serious British dig at the Tour was hatched at the 1953 World Championships in Lugano, where a coterie of British press and VIPs, together with 'Mac' McLachlan, publicity director for Hercules Cycles, congregated in a bar and built castles in the air for a British squad. That year there was a depth of talent that hadn't existed previously, and things were finally approaching critical mass. One of Hercules's riders, sprinter Dave Bedwell, was racing at

25 Which charts in detail the course of British involvement in the Tour de France and is highly recommended.

the Worlds that year; and one of its rival Viking's riders, Ian Steel, had won the Peace Race in 1952, the formidable event between Warsaw, Berlin and Prague in which British clubmen pitted themselves against the best of the Soviet bloc's 'amateur' state-sponsored athletes in a great race behind the Iron Curtain. He had then been invited to the Tour by Jacques Goddet but had declined, saying he'd prefer to wait for a full British team.

Why not aim high and send a team to the Tour? Hercules, for one, took the bar-room schemings seriously. In 1955 the Tour was still raced by national, not trade, teams and the Birmingham-based company reasoned the huge publicity around a British national team would benefit the bike company with the most riders on it. It decided to load the dice in its favour by sending all its riders abroad for an intensive period of preparation. As Tony tells it, though, the time at Les Issambres, in a big pink villa near the beach, was more like a cycling holiday in the sun. 'We'd ride around, in very nice weather down there, and there was no planned training or preparing for anything, let alone for the Tour de France, not that I heard of anyway,' he says. 'I wasn't that interested in long distances, I didn't have to train much.'

The first real test soon loomed: Paris–Nice, the first major stage race of the year. But as the team prepared to go north, they received news it had been cancelled because of snow in Paris. 'We thought, thank Christ for that! You know, we were hardly ready for the Paris–Nice. So we went off for a ride and pretty soon they were scouring the countryside trying to round us all up, asking us to race anyway. So we went up to Paris and started out in the wet snow and the pouring, cold rain, as I remember. But that was normal weather,' Tony says, encapsulating in a couple of sentences the winning combination of naivety, pluck and stoic optimism that would both hobble his efforts and sustain him through what was going to be a very long Tour de France.

Paris–Nice was a useful primer in that it was a taster of how difficult proper continental racing was. It also introduced Tony – and not only Tony – to the concept of elimination. 'I don't know if this is a known fact, but the whole team was eliminated on one stage because of the time limit,' he says, in an off-hand manner. 'You can't just cruise in any time, day or night. You have to stick to the time limit and that's a big problem when you are riding on your own. You're off the back, you've got to keep going as hard as you can because you don't know where anybody else is. It's not like today. Today it would be easier. Those days you had to kill yourself because you had no idea if you were going to make the time limit.'

The British team were given a stay of execution and continued the race from the grey, slushy north to the Riviera sun.[26] 'Of course, Jean Bobet was the designated winner,' Tony says matter-of-factly. 'So we stepped back and let the team do the work for him.' Eventually, Brian Robinson finished a very creditable eighth. After Paris–Nice Hercules continued to race around France and Tony, along with five others from the team, made the 10-man Tour de France selection.

In the French press, despite some good showings by the Brits pre-Tour (Robinson wore the leader's jersey in the Tour du Sud-Est after three days, though the team then faded), there were concerns that their lack of stage-race experience would slow them. Celebrated Tour writer Antoine Blondin was dismissive, describing them as 'displaced persons', and did not stint with the national stereotypes: Tony would have done better 'to return to the pages of *David Copperfield* from where he appears to have escaped'; as for their *directeur sportif* Syd Cozens, his 'learned spectacles, slight portliness and meditative look belong to Mr

---

26 Other historians have it that only Bernard Pusey and Hoar missed the cut.

Pickwick'. Whatever Cozens's outward appearance, he wasn't a very suitable team manager. 'Syd was fluent in French but that was almost the only good thing about him,' Tony says. 'He didn't know anything about road racing, though he'd been a good six-day rider.' Later that season Tony would lose out on a win at the Tour of Holland when, as part of a two-man break, he missed the entrance to the velodrome for the final circuit due to a mistake by Cozens. 'I don't think we ever discussed racing tactics, in any of the events,' Tony says.

Whether or not Cozens was the right choice, the truth was that nobody in the UK had experience of road racing at Tour level; it was a shot in the dark for everyone concerned, and Tony had no expectations going into the race. 'I just thought, Oh well.' He laughs. 'I guess we were new to it and I thought I'll just see what happens. Ride the best you can. We're not stupid, we're fairly talented riders, let's just see what the difference is here. That was my attitude. We'd ridden the Paris–Nice and been given an indication of what it was going to be like – it was going to be hard. But we were well equipped and were probably making more money than most of the pros, even though we were only making 10 quid a week – not bad for those days – but we didn't have any team structure, we didn't ride as a team.'

That final point was exactly what was animating the letters pages of *Cycling*, the UK's foremost cycling magazine; other correspondents feared the team's propensity to go from the gun, which had proved its undoing in the Tour du Sud-Est, did not bode well for *La Grande Boucle*. 'At present our riders seem to take off like a rocket and come down like a stick before the real fireworks start,' one worried reader wrote. But the Tour wasn't the main event: as a measure of how marginal it was, in the month leading up to the start *Cycling* devoted barely half a page a week to the race, far less than the club-level TT results. Finally, the

day before the Tour, there was a two-page spread. It predicted
only four riders might make it to the end (Tony's name wasn't
among them) and the rest would risk falling foul of the time
cut. In France, meanwhile, *Miroir Sprint*'s UK correspondent
Jock Wadley dampened down any false expectations: 'Those of
us who know and understand continental racing will be more
than satisfied if three of our representatives make it to the finish
at the Parc des Princes on the 30th July.'

As it turned out, there would only be two. Partly this was due
to the race route, which was a humdinger. Stage two took the
riders over the notorious *pavé* of Roubaix, the jarring, monstrous
cobbles that the Flemish and northern French love but which
are dangerous and exhausting to ride. There, Bernard Pusey
became the first Briton to abandon, coming in exhausted after
waiting to help teammates with punctures and missing the time
cut. Bevis Wood and Dave Bedwell, meanwhile, had crashed,
and both then abandoned the following day on another cobbled
stage to Namur. On stage seven, two kilometres from the start
in Zurich, Stan Jones punctured and, at the end of his abilities,
abandoned, leaving Tony and Ian Steel, who had dropped back
to help him, to ride 240 kilometres on their own. At the finish
Steel dropped out too, beaten by his lack of race miles beforehand
and dispirited by his lack of French. On the race's entry to the
mountains, therefore, the British numbered only five.

The first day in the Alps brought the Col des Aravis and
the Col du Galibier – the first of them relatively gentle; the
second, the 2,556-metre Galibier, was known for its foreboding
atmosphere and unpredictable weather. Ken Mitchell and Tony
both crashed, but everyone survived inside the time limit. The
next day brought another full menu of Alpine cols. Tony crashed
again and Bob Maitland hit the floor. Though he struggled to

the top of the col, that was the last action Maitland would see. Then a rainstorm made the climb of the next mountain pass, the Cayolle, miserable and treacherous. On a long solo chase to the end Tony crashed once again, in a pitch-black tunnel, and he eventually limped in four minutes and 24 seconds outside the time limit. When I spoke to him, he didn't remember the occasion, but *Cycling* records the grim fact of his transgression. Whether the organisers spontaneously showed some clemency or his roguish team manager argued his case is less clear – but he was reinstated on the excuse that traffic leaving the finish at Monaco hampered his progress to the line.

The crash on the Cayolle was the undoubted low point of his race: 'Oh shit yeah,' Tony says. 'I was going into a tunnel – they weren't lit in those days – and there was another cyclist. It was on a descent too. You couldn't see a damn thing. I heard him come up and I moved over. I guess the edge of the road was gravel and I crashed in the dark. I was ever so scratched up, even though I got away with not wearing a helmet. I slid a long way, I was going fast.' Monaco was a rest day and a chance to take stock. He was *lanterne rouge*, hours behind the race leader, having been hamstrung by the crashes, disorganisation and in considerable measure by the terrible team-issue tyres. 'I lost a lot of time before we were totally decimated, waiting for guys for flats,' he explains.[27] 'We were being sponsored by Dunlop, who said they were going to come up with a special tyre. "Oh yeah?" we said. And what they'd done was taken a Number 6, a grass-track tyre, and put a road tread on it. They were quite fat things. We hoped they had matured them, because they have to have aged six to nine months, to cure the rubber. "Hell

---

27 In 1955 the riders had to mend punctures on the road. Only in 1956 would they for the first time be allowed to take a new wheel.

yeah, don't worry . . ." they said. But then we had so many flats. It was incredible.'

Without being cured, the rubber in old-fashioned tubulars is much more vulnerable to puncturing, and ageing also improves the casing and sidewalls of the tyre. Good racers and teams hoarded tyres until they were ready and Brian Robinson at least had ensured his own supply of his preferred tubs, the sponsors be damned. Dunlop's incompetence was discovered one night when Tony and his teammates cut one of the tyres open to discover a fabrication date of less than three months previously. Stitched up by your tubs! I say. 'Yeah . . . We switched to Vittoria and we didn't have any more problems,' Tony says. 'They still paid us the £200 though . . .'

In his voice the sound of the corners of his mouth turning upwards, and thousands of miles away I can tell he's smiling.

Punctures and crashes aside, Tony had quickly transformed himself into a savvy stage racer. At first the Tour had been simply intimidating: 'When we got a first glimpse of the big teams in action . . .' he is momentarily lost for words as he casts his thoughts back to the Golden Age. The 1955 Tour starred Louison Bobet, the eventual winner and first man to win three Tours de France in a row, who was on the main French team with brother Jean, André Darrigade, a sprinter, and Raphaël Géminiani. The Belgians had the incomparable Rik Van Steenbergen and Stan Ockers, twice a Tour runner-up and 1955's green jersey. Former winner Ferdi Kübler was ageing, but still a threat on the Swiss team, and the Luxembourg team had the Angel of the Mountains, Charly Gaul, who is among the Tour's all-time great climbers. 'The big teams dominated the racing, and the sprints. We'd never seen these sprint finishes in any racing before that. That was quite impressive,' Tony says.

The British riders, coming from a country where competitive cycling was somewhat furtive, were also unused to the festival atmosphere the Tour took with it around France. 'It seemed to me that wherever the Tour stopped for the night there was a big celebration in town, and you'd have trouble getting to sleep because of the sheer noise outside your window, people having a good time. It wasn't conducive,' Tony says. 'I didn't take any sleeping tablets, and just the wear and tear of three weeks of riding slows you down.' The other thing he'd had to get up to speed on – literally – was the descending. 'Oh yeah, the descents were hairy! I had to learn to ride those descents because there was no one to teach me. You'd think we'd have had some training. I don't recall anyone telling us to go out and practise.' And then he sounds touchingly like a fan and not someone riding with these famous cyclists as a peer and equal. 'They were quite exciting! They were really quick some of those guys, they really swooped down those S bends like they knew what they're doing . . . which they did.'

Other than that, he quickly caught on to the tricks of the peloton, and measured his energy to take advantage of the frequent café raids. 'Typically when I saw the *domestiques* stop to help themselves in the cafés, I knew that there would be no breaks while these guys were off the back – there'd be 20 of them. So I'd stop with them, get some drink out of the fridge with the others and then we'd catch back up again. I was in survival mode I guess.'

Being one of the bigger guys in the race ('There weren't that many people taller than me and certainly I had shoulders. Most road riders don't seem to have them!') he had trouble in the mountains. There are no climbs in the UK comparable to those of the Alps or the Pyrenees, and consequently not much chance of training for them. Sometimes Tony stuck with

a beefy Frenchman who was a master of cajoling the crowds
into giving him a push – and didn't mind soliciting one for
monsieur l'anglais either. Sometimes he rode in the *autobus*
and sometimes on his own.

'I know what it is to die – I died several times in those
mountains,' he once said. It was on one very particular mountain
that the darker secrets of continental racing became clear to
him. Two days after the rest day the peloton ascended Mont
Ventoux, the bald peak that presides over Provence and which
is feared by riders for its airless lower slopes and barren, bleak
rocks above the treeline. Tony, however, was having a good day:
'I was riding up the Ventoux, looking around, thinking I'd be
seeing the Frenchman pretty soon or some other guys, and I
was catching a group and there was [Miguel] Poblet in it and a
whole bunch of other top names, and I was thinking this can't
be true. I was thinking, Jeez, maybe I've suddenly improved! And
before I caught them I passed the ambulance, with Malléjac
there, staring up with his dilated pupils – you know you get
that from amphetamines. Then I saw this other group I was
catching up with and recognised all the good riders, and they'd
obviously had the same problem as Malléjac. So I passed them!
Next day, the French team pushed Bobet the whole way. He
was a sprinter, they wanted him for the last stage.'

Not many in the English-speaking world remember the
collapse of Jean Malléjac; our Ventoux mythology centres on
another fallen figure, Tom Simpson, who 12 years later would
fall prey to the same harmful cocktail as Malléjac ('Fatigue,
sun and everything else' pronounced the 1955 *Miroir Sprint*
somewhat euphemistically), only fatally. It was a near miss for
the cycling world, prefiguring Simpson's death only a matter of
kilometres away. But for the caprices of fate we could instead
be mourning a Frenchman who weaved across the road and

fell in the forest, one foot still clipped in, the other continuing to pedal, turning circles in the hot air above him.[28]

Even if they'd wanted it, Tony says, the British team's *soigneur* would not have 'prepared' them in this way: it would have done his reputation as a purveyor of magic potions no good to prepare riders ineffectively, or dangerously. It took more than one madcap adventure around France to enter the circle of trust. But for the British riders it was obvious that many of the peloton were not riding the '55 Tour on water alone. 'The Germans were the best ones,' Tony tells me. 'You were riding along and you could see the mountains coming up and then there was all this activity. The German team would stop by their car and we swore they were getting an injection because about two miles down the road they'd go by like a bloody train. We all knew it.'

It seems weird to be discussing amphetamines with an 80-something-year-old but ho-hum, that's cycling.

Mont Ventoux did for half the remaining UK riders, as Fred Krebs and Ken Mitchell dropped out. Since Brian was still going pretty well (he had at one point been 11th, falling to around 40th after Ventoux before recovering to 29th by Paris) Tony did not see him much on the road, and, though Tony would give him a bottle whenever their paths crossed, they were both now effectively riding unsupported – two lone riders in a race full of powerhouse teams. If Brian was doing his national flag proud, Tony wasn't doing badly either. During the latter stages of the Tour he was contesting the sprints, almost nailing some of the intermediate gallops and finishing 16th in the first stage after the Pyrenees. At one point he was even cautioned by the commissaires for aggressive riding. 'I think the big surprise was,

---

28 Malléjac maintained until he died that he'd been given a dodgy bidon; from his hospital bedside his DS implored police to open an attempted-murder investigation.

don't tell Brian, but I beat Brian by a minute and a half in the TT, you know,' says Tony, referring to the penultimate stage from Châtellerault to Tours. So what was going on with last place? 'It wasn't so much me finishing further down, it was all the people behind me quitting.' he says. 'It was a French plot to keep a Brit in last place! They pay these people off! So I'd move up six places and then those six would disappear, keeping me in last.'

He'd spent the race around halfway down a field of 120 riders, and 69th was where he finished. The problem was the 51 people below him dropped out, through injury or to save their legs for the next challenge. But that wasn't Tony's style: 'I wasn't one to quit a race, but you definitely wouldn't quit the Tour – there was some incentive to finish. To finish the Tour was something!'

His experience tallies with that of other *lanternes* and near-*lanternes*, who paradoxically find that their stamina and persistence see them left in last position. Paul Sherwen, now a respected commentator, was one of the peloton's hard men in the early '80s: 'I remember in my last Tour de France in 1985 I was the last guy overall, because I had a big crash on one stage and I lost 50 minutes in one day. And I didn't want to be last overall, I kept fighting not to be. But every time I overtook a guy in the overall standings, he fucking abandoned,' Paul says. 'I finished 141st out of 144 because I managed to jump over a couple of guys in the last week. But it was horrendous.'

Or, to put it another way, in the words of Wim Vansevenant (*lanterne* 2006–2008) to American journalist Sam Abt: '*Lanterne rouge* is not a position you go for. It comes for you.'

As the race drew to its close Tony was, unbeknown to him, becoming something of a star. As at Paris–Nice, the race organisers had realised the publicity value of the two plucky *rosbifs* (also maybe a factor in the Monaco *repêchage*) and the press were promoting a French v English fight for last place. In the blue corner, Henri Sitek, riding for the regional Ouest team; in the red, Tony Hoar, the title-holder, who didn't even realise he was in a fight. 'When they wanted to do publicity photos they'd get Henri Sitek and myself off the back and photograph us, you know. Then we had to catch up the peloton!' Tony says. Out of the contest a deep friendship supposedly grew between the men, but Tony doesn't remember that, either: 'They said we were fighting for the *lanterne rouge*, which wasn't true . . .' he pauses. 'And we didn't form that good a friendship. He didn't speak any English, and my French writing was awful.' The pair wrote once or twice after the Tour, but then nothing for 50 years or more. 'I didn't ever see him again after the Tour,' he says. 'But the year before last a journalist friend of his started writing to me.' The Tour was scheduled to finish in Albi, Sitek's town, and Sitek had been asked to say a few words on the podium. 'He wanted to know what I was doing so he could tell the people what happened to me in the years that intervened. So I wrote back through this journalist who spoke quite good English and found out that Henri had throat cancer,' Tony says.

Sitek, long retired, had been thrilled to find out what had happened to Tony, whom he remembered and had counted as a friend. As we talk about Sitek Tony becomes more meditative, his voice slowing, sounding as if it's coming from further and further away. He is sometimes hazy on the details of that Tour – given that it's almost 60 years ago he has every right to be – but some things, some emotions, still stand out sharply. Sitek died of his cancer on Christmas Eve in 2011 without the pair ever having spoken again – but something of the solidarity of the tail end of the race had stuck with them.

Paris: a street corner, the early 1950s. A group of kids stand, all facing the same way, expectant. The street is empty. Samuel

Beckett approaches them and asks what they're doing. 'On attend Godeau,' is the reply. We're waiting for Godeau; Godeau, in this story, being the oldest and slowest rider in the race. Implausible as it may sound, the tale has some currency with many Beckett aficionados as an explanation of the origin of Beckett's most famous, most discussed and least seen character, Godeau. It's not true.[29] But for a book on the *lanterne rouge* it feels right. After all, this was the man who wrote, late in life, 'Ever tried. Ever failed. No matter. Try again. Fail again. Fail better.' A group of cycling fans waiting for a rider called 'Godot', who may or may not come, says something about the solidarity and compassion we feel for, even the faith we place in, the last-placed rider. Or as the lesser-known philosopher but better-known and venerable cycling commentator Phil Liggett put it to me: 'Normal people feel an attachment to a guy that is struggling through the Tour just to survive in the race, because that's what normal people on bikes would do. They're not superstars like the guys at the front end of the peloton. It's equally as hard for the guys at the front, but they get results. The guys at the back are suffering like hell just to get to the finish.' Tour riders, in their modern incarnation especially, might almost be a different species from your average recreational rider – impossibly bronzed, stick-insect-like creatures with large, reflective eyes who do not seem to labour as we would with the fantastical distances and impossible climbs of the Tour. Hoar and his friends were human – all too human, in some cases – and *Cycling* hailed his 'grit, bonhomie and laughing disposition in the honourable last position'. To keep a stiff upper lip in a

---

29 Another version has it that the kids are waiting outside the Roubaix velodrome. That is more plausible: Roger Godeau was a track star and twice a national champion in motor-paced disciplines. Beckett was definitely a cycling fan, and in the '30s used to visit the track regularly.

disorganised and disintegrating team takes something special. He was, to use the stereotypes the French had imposed upon them from the start, the epitome of the gallant and gentlemanly British underdog – and, finally, the dignified loser.

Like many of his British professional peers, Tony was not far removed from the 'normal' world. He had been a plumber in the naval shipyards while representing Great Britain prior to joining Hercules, and he would after 1955 fairly rapidly head back that way. However, for the few minutes he cycled his laps of honour around the Parc des Princes velodrome he was a hero. The wily Mac McLachlan presented Tony with a battery-powered lantern and as he rode 'Or-ah, Or-ah, Or-ah' resounded around the stadium: the French public were chanting his name. 'One of the commentators came over and said "I think you really captured the French imagination",' Tony says. 'So I got five or six contracts, mainly in Belgium, and the first one I went to I was getting – it sounds terrible me saying this – I was getting much, much bigger cheers than Bobet. But my contracts dried up very quickly!'

The night of the Parc des Princes, Brian and Tony dined with the Hercules executives at a fancy restaurant in Paris. The next morning Tony rode a 100-kilometre race on the Montlhéry Autodrome near Paris with most of the Tour riders, including his hero, Fausto Coppi. After the criteriums it was quickly back down to earth. He was contracted to work the Cycle and Motorcycle Show at Earls Court, promoting the 'Tour de France Équipe' model on the Hercules stand with Brian Robinson. With a heavy frame, mudguards and a large, frame-mounted pump, it is not clear from the Tour de France Équipe that Hercules had learnt much from its foray into continental racing.

After that, Tony had a contract to ride an Omnium in Brussels, the sort of track event he might have excelled in.

But the combination of the Cycle Show, tricky logistics and a smashed track frame meant that he didn't make it. He'd lost his momentum and he realised that perhaps he didn't have the commitment and drive to persist at the highest levels of professional cycling. 'That was the end of my career, I guess,' he told me. The following spring he set off for the Vuelta a España with Brian Robinson and also Ian Steel – he had, despite their opposing affiliations the year before, forged what would become a lifelong friendship with the Viking rider. The trio were uncontracted riders in a mixed team riding for the Swiss heartthrob Hugo Koblet. But Koblet wasn't the same rider who'd won the 1951 Tour. He was on his way down, and sick to boot. It didn't go well. During a team time trial on the Montjuïc motor racing circuit Tony rode out of the gates, collected his money, quit and never went back.

Many of the *lanternes rouges* are Tour debutants, riders who for reasons of youth, inexperience, injury or simply being out of their depth find themselves propping up the GC. Their goals and ambitions for the first Tour have nothing to do with winning – they are looking to gain experience, perhaps, learn from their teammates, survive, come back next year and do it better. The same also goes for their teams. But without 1955 and the experience gained, Robinson would likely not have come back in 1956 and got third on the first stage and 14th overall, one place behind Charly Gaul, or won Britain's first stage in 1958, setting in motion a chain that can be traced to the Tour winners of 2012 and '13. 'The truth emerges, perhaps, that we were not quite ready to name a full team,' *Cycling* said in 1955. 'But this much is overwhelmingly of benefit to our place in future road classics: that by hard and painful ways a tremendous and valuable experience had been gained.'

Some of the *lanterne rouge* debutants ride only one Tour, but not too many leave professional cycling soon after. Late in 1956 Tony went to Canada, where he already had ties, and played a role – an organisational one – in the fledgling Canadian Cycling Association, renovating a velodrome, organising meets and, for a time, running the BMX World Championships before the UCI took BMX over. He settled eventually on Vancouver Island, also coincidentally now home to Svein Tuft, *lanterne rouge* 2013. So the second-ever British Tour finisher, who took up bike racing again later in life and continued almost until his 80th birthday, now makes bike trailers, racing wheelchairs, kids' carts and anything else that needs a pair of wheels, some welding and a bit of ingenuity. He made his first trailer as a teenager out of a lettuce crate and some pram parts, so that he and his best mate could ride, with food prepared by Mum, to Bournemouth, camp overnight and then ride back. A crash on a steep hill upturned the contraption and dumped the apple pie on the ground (literally upset the apple cart, you could say), but the boys made it safely home. Sixty-something years later his bestseller – and this is very Canadian – is a kayak trailer. Indefatigable, the locals call him, and he's still working away now, till midnight most nights he says, finishing each conversation with the news that he's going back to his welding.

Indefatigability – a quality that will see you to being a *lanterne rouge* and much, much further still.

1955
130 starters
Winner: Louison Bobet, 34.45 km/h
Lanterne rouge: Tony Hoar, 32.91 km/h @ 6h06'01"
69 finishers

Chapter 6

THE ESCAPE ARTIST

I didn't want to be ridiculous any more.

Pierre Matignon, *L'Équipe*, 21 July 1969

What is it about me, the Auvergne and pre-dawn starts? Years ago, when I'd lived here as a student, it had been impossible to wrest me from bed before 11 a.m. unless I was scheduled to teach English to a class of French teenagers. When it came to the 8 a.m. lessons I'd been only marginally more present than they had.

But now, for the second time in little over a year, I was in the mountains of south-central France putting my cycling kit on in the dark.

I was back in the region to cycle up the Puy de Dôme, one of the Tour's holy mountains. Ever since I could remember there had been arbitrary rules restricting the hours cyclists were allowed to hurl themselves at the narrow, precipitous access road – that was to be expected because this was France – but this time I'd arrived to be confronted with a big fat 'Non'. For a couple of years the road had been completely closed while the rails were laid for a rack-and-pinion tourist train to the top.

Now the train was running it had been decided that because the tracks were so close to the road, and the road's width so limited as a result, bicycles would not be allowed up at all.

It seemed unfair – and even less fair that the Tour had been deprived of one of its sacred sites. The road was now too narrow to accommodate riders, spectators and all the Tour entourage, and the newly landscaped mountain top, its car parks grassed over, offered no space for the TV trucks and finish line paraphernalia a modern Tour needs. Christian Prudhomme, the race director, had even discussed the possibility of putting on a special farewell stage, but since that would have meant postponing the construction work for several months the regional authorities hadn't gone for the idea.[30] According to Prudhomme the Tour would never again finish on the summit.

It all just seemed unfair. And besides, the Auvergne, a remote, largely rural and mountainous region, is a long way from the UK. Not climbing the Puy would leave me 1,000 kilometres from home, twiddling my thumbs with nothing to do. Plus I was only 45 kilometres from Issoire, the site of my previous failure in the Massif Central, a failure which, if I was being honest, had been weighing on my mind somewhat in the intervening months. I couldn't come here again and not ride. So I decided to give the Puy a pop anyway, as a kind of homage to the *lanterne rouge* and to stick two fingers up at stupid rules and regulations.

The Puy de Dôme is the largest and best known of the Chaîne des Puys, a chain of extinct volcanoes that extends like a rash of pimples across the face of the Auvergne. The word *puy*, like *poggio,* is derived from the Latin *podium*, meaning high or

---

30 As an aside, the train then went out of service for over six months not long after it opened, owing to electrical problems and a derailment. This is somewhat galling.

elevated place, and many are archetypal volcano shapes, with circular craters at their peak. Think of the volcano on the label of bottles of Volvic mineral water and you're figuratively and literally not far off – that's the Puy des Goules, about three *puys* down from the main event. But the Puy de Dôme is a proper domed *puy*, protuberant and swelling like an angry boil waiting to be lanced. With its communications aerial atop it dominates the landscape for miles around, much like Mont Ventoux in Provence, giving its name to the *département* and looming over the town of Clermont-Ferrand. And like Ventoux it's a grand example of the 'because it's there' school of endeavour: the only reason to ride a bike up it is simply because . . . This feat was first accomplished in 1892, an act of madness that took four-and-a-half hours (and two-and-a-half hours down, accomplished both ways on the steep mule path, the Sentier des Muletiers). Cols, however difficult, are passes that came into being because they were the easiest or fastest way between two places that needed to be connected – donkey tracks that would, with a bit of courage and how's-your-father, get your goods (puy lentils, perhaps) to market quicker than your neighbour taking the valley road. Ventoux and the Puy are different. They exist only as a challenge, the ultimate mirror, says cycling philosopher Paul Fournel, in which riders, stripped bare, confront not only the grandeur of nature but also their essential selves. Climbing it in the dark – which is what I quickly figured out I would have to do – sounded like a marvellously silly idea, a cross between a *Boy's Own* adventure and James Bond.

There is only one proper road to the summit – a fact that led Tour writer Antoine Blondin to call it a 'col-de-sac' – but like the Giant of Provence people have been climbing it for much longer than bikes have been around. At the top are the ruins of a Gallo-Roman temple to Mercury, the messenger god and god of travellers, which were discovered in the 19th century as work began on an observatory. By that time scores of people were going up in carriages or on mules from the spa towns below, to take the air and to eat in one of the several panoramic restaurants. In 1906 the first tourist train to the summit was opened, but not before the first car raced to the top. That was in 1905, when Auguste Fraignac drove to the summit. His attempt was timed to take advantage of the publicity surrounding the Gordon Bennett Cup,[31] which was taking place on the roads below, and was one in the eye for the local industrial giant Michelin (whose factories still sit in the shadow of the Puy) since Fraignac's car was shod with Continental tyres.

At 1,464 metres, with about 1,100 vertical metres of climbing from the town below, the Puy is not that high, but its stature in the minds of many is much greater. Vialette, an Auvergnat writer with that peculiarly French attribute of having only one name, talked of its 'moral altitude' and leapt to its spirited defence when some Alp-dwellers suggested that, in the case of mountains, size did in fact matter: 'As I've already written, the bride can never be too beautiful. As far as I'm concerned, the Puy de Dôme has been too small for too long now,' he wrote. 'In the case of mountains the altitude is a "moral altitude", and morally, the Puy de Dôme is far higher than itself. Morally, the Puy de Dôme is bigger than Mont Blanc.'

For cyclists, this moral rigour truly manifests itself in the last four kilometres, which take you from the old tollbooth, now the site of car parks and the train station, to the top – they are a

---

31 For transatlantic playboys, the Gordon Bennett Cup was the first truly international motorsport competition, held at the behest of a newspaper baron whose name, some say, is the origin for the expletive. From the pictures, the major qualification criteria appeared to be a solid collection of tweeds, handsome facial hair and, probably, more money than sense.

steady, unremitting 12 per cent gradient. When race director Jacques Goddet introduced the Tour to the Puy in 1952, he wrote: 'Our good father surely did not think, when extinguishing this old volcano, that its flames would become a velodrome, an Olympic velodrome with a single curve climbing ceaselessly.' His hopes for the peak had been realised that year when Fausto Coppi took flight, distancing his serious rival Jean Robic; only Jan Nolten, a Dutchman, was able to come anywhere close. In 1988, meanwhile, Johnny Weltz was 26 years old and riding for Fagor when he inched ahead of his breakaway companion Rolf Gölz on its slopes to become the last winner at the summit. 'At that time we'd climb in a 41×23 or 41×22, while today riders want a 39×25,' Welz said, explaining the hardmen gears that Tour contestants used to use.[32] 'The slopes of the Puy are very steep. The top a little less so, but you've already given everything by the time you get there. There are no hairpin bends on which to recover. The climb makes me think of Ventoux. When it's hot, you suffocate. In the Alps, the cols are less hard. Even Alpe d'Huez is easier.'

In between Fausto and Jonny, one of the Tour's most famous battles was waged on its slopes. In 1964 two French heroes, the smooth, stylish Jacques Anquetil and rough-hewn Raymond Poulidor, duked it out, elbow to elbow. Jacques had won four Tours already and was in the yellow jersey; Poulidor, the Tour's eternal nearly man, was 56 seconds behind him in the GC and was the better climber. Belying his aloof public image, Anquetil got fully involved in the fight as each tried to best the other, leaning and pushing for the advantage. It was Anquetil who eventually cracked, though he managed to hold on and not be distanced

---

32 The first number is the number of teeth on the chainring, so the higher it is, the harder the grind. The second is the teeth on the biggest cog on the cassette at the back – bigger cogs make life easier. Your average amateur sportive rider might want a 34x27 for the Puy.

until the pair were 900 metres from the line. So cooked was he, Poulidor put 42 seconds into him in these final few hundred metres of the ribbon road up the mountain. Actually, Anquetil was on the point of blowing the whole way up, his aggressive riding next to Poulidor was a bluff: he knew that by staying level he'd sow doubts in his rival's mind. For his part, Poulidor had lied to his DS about reconnoitring the climb (he was still racing criteriums for cash three days before the Tour) and had fitted the wrong cog – a 24 instead of a 25 – and consequently was turning too large a gear to accelerate away. Or maybe he was bluffing too, only bluffing better. 'We were both cooked,' Poulidor admitted in a 2013 interview with *L'Équipe* magazine. On his deathbed Anquetil told Poulidor that battling his cancer was like climbing the Puy de Dôme all day every hour of the day.

The Puy made 13 appearances in the Tour, and was the privileged battleground of some of the sport's best climbers. Federico Bahamontes, Julio Jiménez and Lucien Van Impe won there. Luis Ocaña and Joop Zoetemelk both won twice. Later in its lifespan there were lesser lights. And in 1969 there was a certain Pierre Matignon, who went into the Puy stage a hopeless *lanterne rouge* and came out of it a cannibal-beater.

So. How to break into – on to? – a mountain? Going up in the dark before the first train, with a chance of hiding from any security, seemed like a safe-ish bet. Coming down in the light with the trains running would be a different thing. A *Mission Impossible*-style recce was in order.

The first thing I needed was a layby, a base from which to launch my night-time sortie. Car duly parked up a dirt road, nose poking towards the tarmac for a quick getaway, I walked down to the foot of the Puy and realised it was not a promising day for a snoop around. Clouds hung at 1,100 metres, obscuring the top and many of the other ancient volcano peaks. If I was going to gain any intelligence at all it wouldn't be visual, more the reassurance of treading the paths, tasting the atmosphere, feeling the rack-and-pinion train labour its way up to the top.

The new train terminal, made of glass and raw, pungent pine, stood in a clearing; the platform was full of tourists and 'hikers' (does taking a train up a mountain count as hiking?) with a curiously expectant air, as if hoping that during the journey up the gloom would lift, the sun come out and glorious views be revealed. The train, which looked much like an ordinary suburban tram, scooped everyone up and we began our journey into the clouds. Just above the car park I saw the start of the access road, with a barrier across it and a security camera or two . . . then we trundled past the crucial control point and on to the Puy and within 500 metres the world had reduced to the inside of the train and a small fluffy space of tarmac and rock around it. The train hugged the sheer rock wall, taking the inside line as it headed clockwise up the Puy. What remained of the road, and it was narrow, was only separated from the rails by a small border of aggregate. To the left, forest. A dark wall of trees sloping away to the farmland below. Further up, as the gradients steepened, the land fell away more suddenly and became cliff-like, a metal guardrail appeared. The drop on the other side looked substantial. This would be a problem: on the lower slopes if a car were to appear – I was assuming any transport would be security – I would try to leap off the side of the road and hide in the trees until it passed; on the upper slopes there was a good kilometre or two where my only options would be a rock wall or a large drop. I'd be a sitting duck, game over. Near the summit the train left the road and disappeared underground into the bowels of the new glass and dark volcanic rock visitor centre that, despite the preponderance

THE ESCAPE ARTIST   111

of old women in flowery macintoshes and men with knapsacks
and sensible shoes, had the air of a Bond villain's hideout.
Outside, I made my way around the short paths that circled the
site but navigation was by signpost alone: the thick cloud was
impenetrable, almost claustrophobic. People walking towards
me would emerge suddenly only a metre or two away before
disappearing equally quickly into nothingness. Voices drifted
through the clouds and a little birdsong followed me around
the desolate peak. A few baaas and the sound of bells, sheep
somewhere nearby. The overall effect was anaesthetic.

Having fixed the location of the Sentier des Muletiers in
my mind (the plan was to walk back down, to avoid daylight
encounters with trains and cars), I went back into the visitor
centre where I partook in a little *son et lumière* edutainment
and bought a tuna baguette and a Coke, my outrage at the
exorbitant €8.50 bill mitigated somewhat by the thought
that I was somehow obliquely getting one over on them. No
sew-on patches for cyclists in the boutique, although there
were, somewhat mockingly, those little roadside mile-marker
ornaments with the road number and height of the summit
upon them that cyclists like to purchase. I scorned one of those
for a copy of *Known and Little Known Volcanoes of the Massif
Central* (Éditions Débaisieux, 2004; highly recommended), and
then it was time to go.

To go by the results, 1969 was a landmark Tour. A young Belgian
hotshot called Eddy Merckx made his debut, riding for the
Faema team. It almost wasn't to be: Eddy had been chucked
out of the 1969 Giro for failing a drug test in questionable
circumstances – papers at the time discussed Italian prejudice
against a Belgian winning the Giro, a vendetta against Faema,
or even against the Tour de France itself – which put his Tour

appearance in doubt. But his participation was ratified at the 11th hour and his indignation at being ejected from the Giro, wearing the *maglia rosa*, no less, fuelled a comprehensive demolition of all-comers at the Tour. He won the yellow, green and polka-dot jerseys – almost certainly the only time this will ever happen – as well as the now defunct combination jersey and, with Faema, the team classification too. It was a whitewash and the papers coined a new term, *le merckxisme*, to describe the steamrollering counterpunch style he inflicted on anyone who dared attack him. Have a dig off the front and if you were worthy of his attention he would come to get you himself – no sending *domestiques* to do the grunt work – and then simply ride away to win, leaving the field in smithereens.

Future stars Lucien Van Impe, Luis Ocaña and Roger De Vlaeminck also made their Tour debut in 1969. And then there was Pierre Matignon. Pierre was riding for the Frimatic-De Gribaldy team, which was partly bankrolled and fully under the control of ex-rider and lifelong Vicomte, Jean de Gribaldy. An indifferent cycling career behind him, De Gribaldy had become a crack manager, *directeur sportif* and talent spotter; later, he would bring legends Bernard Thévenet and Sean Kelly to the sport, but his first great find was Joaquim Agostinho. Agostinho only came to cycling at the age of 25, a prodigious talent and ball of muscle, though he was never completely at home on a bicycle and the peloton frightened him. He crashed frequently, and eventually fatally. The crash that killed him seemed innocuous: during the 1984 Tour of the Algarve, he hit a dog only a few hundred metres before the finish and, though he was helped back on to his bike and across the finish, he fell into a coma in the ambulance taking him to hospital and never regained consciousness. Agostinho was 27 when he turned pro at De

Gribaldy's urging, and won two stages of the 1969 Tour in his first year with the team. Eddy, on the other hand, took the yellow jersey in stage 1b,[33] a team time trial in his home town. Though he ceded the jersey to his teammate Julien Stevens after his first win, Merckx's dominance saw him lead from the sixth stage to the end, winning seven stages including time trials and mountain stages.

Agostinho was the only man he feared going into the Tour de France, but their attitudes could not have been more different. 'Agostinho,' wrote *International Cycle Sport* in tribute after he died, 'loved the Tour de France. There were few other races which he took seriously, indeed he raced relatively little during an average season – enough to pay for and maintain life's dream, but no more.' Merckx, on the other hand, seemed to feel the need to win everything, and his sorties in the mountains, notably in a colossal 214.5-kilometre Pyrenean stage from Luchon to Mourenx, regularly blew the 1969 race to bits, leaving even the finest of his rivals – that year, Roger Pingeon, Raymond Poulidor and Felice Gimondi – more than eight minutes behind him in his wake.

It might be heresy to say it, but the urge to win at all costs, to dominate totally, arguably created a boring race. The Merckx show of clinically picking off his rivals had, by the Pyrenees, completely killed the spectacle. On stage 21, Tour director Félix Lévitan reportedly asked Rini Wagtmans to make an early break, to liven the proceedings up. Wagtmans duly attacked in the neutralised zone and, when sufficiently out of sight, hid behind a van before re-mounting after the pack had passed. But the plan backfired since the peloton, fearing Wagtmans had got away,

---

33 1969 featured many days split into stages, which increased the number of stage-start and -end opportunities for the organisers, a lucrative move.

continued to ride at full gas and the Dutchman was forced to chase them the whole stage, simply to stay in the race.

There may have been predictability, a kind of stultifying awe at the top of the rankings; but there is much more to any Tour than the top of the GC. It is composed of myriad stories and many races – the daily fight to be first, first up the hill or at the sprint *prime* – and the numerous personal rivalries and jostlings for position that take place in teams, between teams and up and down the standings. And the De Gribaldy team, though talented, was a small and young squad, so it was probably looking for stage wins to make its race.

Lining up for the Tour presentation Pierre Matignon looks mild-mannered and apprehensive – and well he might. He'd been a very good amateur and had wanted to turn pro at 19, but in those days that wasn't allowed, so Pierre instead went to do his national service and in his own estimation was never the rider he'd been before. He'd taken a long time to turn pro and had been an amateur national champion in '68 before being picked up by De Gribaldy at the age of 26. By contrast Merckx, in his team photo, is leaning over his bike at the end of the row of Faema men and seemingly giggling, as if he'd just been notified that his doping suspension would not stand and, like a naughty schoolboy, had rushed to get in the photo.

Matignon was riding his first Tour in support of Agostinho, playing *domestique* to one of the Tour's undoubted threats, and though his leader, with two stage wins, was doing as well as anybody else, Matignon's own race was not going well. After stage 14 he had been penalised with Rudy Altig and three others for a doping offence, a 15-minute penalty that put him in last place. It was ignominious. He had begun to engage in a slow bicycle race with fellow tail-ender André Wilhelm to win the *lanterne rouge* – no doubt with the criterium circuit in mind.

Yet it can't have been all about the money. Somewhere in there was pride and the feeling perhaps that if you had a chance to make a mark, however small, on cycling history then you should take it. To ensure your name would not be swallowed up completely, just one more in a forgotten list of unfancied starters and middle finishers.

By the 20th stage Pierre would have been justified in being pretty fed up. He was 86th and last. 'This could be a profitable stage today,' his Tour DS, Louis Caput, said at the start in Brive, south-western France. Though Pierre can't have thought it would be for him. The day's events take a turn for the worse when, not far along the 198-kilometre road to the finish atop the Puy, his rival Wilhelm – inexplicably – attacks, and unlucky Pierre simultaneously punctures. Heaping on the indignity, his DS does not consider him important enough to be paced back and tells the team to continue riding for Agostinho and the reputable climber Paul Gutty. But the mechanic, perhaps taking pity, gives Pierre one of the better wheels on the rack. 'I'll give you a light one, but I want a stage win, eh?' he jokes. He leaves Pierre to slowly, painfully, fight his way back to the peloton alone.

Maybe 100 kilometres later, on the Côte de Chavanon, 66 kilometres from the end, Frimatic-De Gribaldy attacks the pack – and it is Matignon, not Agostinho or Gutty, who makes the solo move. Nobody from the peloton follows him and by the top he has a decent gap. He works and works, and with 20 kilometres to go he has more than seven minutes on the chasers. He has been allowed to get away since he is so far behind in the overall standings he is insignificant, but with the Puy ominously in sight the peloton wakes up and Peugeot takes up the chase. It is the first attempt to seriously try to bring him back. The time gap begins to fall, but Pierre is already on the Puy when Merckx realises that a pipsqueak might just be about to steal a marquee stage from him. With his lieutenant Martin Van Den Bossche, the Cannibal goes all out to try to reel him in.

Was I thinking of Pierre as I left the car on the dirt track, freewheeled down the hill in the dark, half cycled, half walked a forest path cutting past the entry road, car parks and station, and then made my way around the clearing to the road just above the barrier and the CCTV camera? Not really. I was thinking that I needed to pee, that it was warm and muggy, yet clear, at the bottom – therefore hopefully not freezing at 1,464 metres – and that while my cycling kit was completely ninja black, the musette I had slung over my shoulder containing a pair of plimsolls ('rubber-soled shoes' they'd be called in the Hardy Boys or the Famous Five) was a glaring Persil white.

I really needed that pee.

After a short comfort break, I was off, chasing Coppi and Bahamontes, Jacques and Raymond, Eddy and Pierre up a hill into nothingness. Riding through the pitch-black night is a weird, disorienting experience. It transforms gradients and efforts so that, depending on your frame of mind, it can feel either that you are floating in space or entangled in treacle. Here, with just a small V of pre-dawn sky above the Puy and the forests, and the dim silver trace of the train tracks to my right, the percentages ceased to have meaning and I felt I was ascending not on a bike upon a road but into the air, dream-like, extra-terrestrial, paradoxically at ease but also with a great weight pushing down on my shoulders. I stood up and turned the pedals smoothly, and tried to keep my breath and heart under control for fear of them smothering the sound of a car coming up behind me. Every few seconds I looked back to check, but you can't climb a mountain, any mountain, half-heartedly; I accelerated, to get it over with as quickly as possible. Suddenly I saw light, headlights, searching through the black, not from behind as I'd expected but from above, the car hidden by the rock of the Puy, its beams falling down from the right, angling closer as it descended, dispelling my breakaway companions, the peloton of famous riders I had surrounded myself with. Thank God I'm still in the forests. I jump off the road, down into a pile of leaves and crouch below the level of the tarmac. Gordon Bennett.

Why did Pierre attack on this stage of all stages, with this monstrous mountain ahead of him? If his goal had previously been the *lanterne rouge* and the financial security it brought, what kind of gamble did he make, what kind of cosmic pact with St Jude, the patron saint of lost causes? I could only suppose that he was fed up with the beating Merckx had been dispensing, wanted to salvage some dignity after the punctures, the 15-minute penalty (at a time when doping had been illegal only for two years, still considered routine and rarely punished) and the bad luck. That something in him had snapped, and he'd taken his meagre stack of chips and put them all on number 20, to hell with the consequences. And when he knew that Merckx was coming, could he feel the hot breath on his heels? Did he feel at his lowest and most vulnerable the moment just before he realised he was safe? How did he travel through that dark night before the glorious dawn at the finish above?

Watch the race footage and you can see Pierre escape, an extra bottle stuffed into his back pocket, cap worn high, brim bent. Despite what the papers said in tribute afterwards, he looks an untidy rider. He struggles with the bike – stomping on the pedals is his default position in this clip. We cut away and cut back and his cap has gone, revealing dark, tightly curled hair. His face is young and worried. The camera pans down to his rider number: 88. The Puy hoves into view, squatting over the monochrome landscape, and now Merckx is chasing in his HD-monogramed yellow jersey, the hound behind the fox, other riders trailing behind him. While Merckx sails through they are labouring; it is pig hot. The tarmac is melting beneath them. Back with capless Pierre and the extra bottle in his middle jersey pocket is gone too. He is discarding everything, stripping himself bare. They're on the lower slopes, instantly recognisable by the steep rock wall on the riders' right and Paul Gutty, Matignon's teammate, has joined Merckx, who is pulling Poulidor up the hill. Felice Gimondi is behind, alone, as is Roger Pingeon of Peugeot-BP . . . nope, he's there with Gimondi, who looks desperately like he might cry . . . is going to pull past him. Little matter: they are both in trouble and will finish well back, Merckx's pursuit of Matignon yet another nail in the coffin of their Tour. Poulidor, though, is a sucker for punishment on this climb and stays with the chase. A fat man in a white vest and slacks runs up the hill clapping Merckx and now Poulidor is getting dropped (it is his turn to lose an improbable amount of time in a short distance on the Puy: 37 seconds in 600 metres) while Gutty still rides next to Merckx, desperately willing Merckx backwards. 'I knew the steep slopes of the Puy well enough,' Gutty said afterwards, 'to know that even the best lead can melt like snow if you tire and lose hope of victory.' Gutty is bluffing, taking a lesson from *Maître Jacques* on these same slopes five years back and staying level, trying to psychologically damage Merckx. And where is Matignon in all this anyway? Two fat ladies, 88. The cameras are sticking with Merckx – it is not worth wasting precious celluloid on Matignon, the back of the race, even when it's at the very front. Why watch the *lanterne rouge* when Van Den

Bossche and Pingeon are coming up on Poulidor, passing him, cleaving to the cool shadows in the lee of the hill, and I wonder as I sit forward, straining for, hoping for, a view, if Matignon is going to be denied the public recognition of his glory. But no: the film cuts to a static expanse of empty road at the finish line and a head swinging around the corner, rising, revealing a body heaving from side to side, a motorbike with aerials and a commissaire riding in a Citroën DS (what class). And Matignon glances behind as the Citroën peels off, sees there's nobody there, raises a hand in triumph, swerves and almost falls off. He's exhausted, his head rocks to one side. Tries to loosen his toe straps, can't, is swallowed into a crowd of well-wishers who hold him up, won't let him fall. Two fat ladies. Bingo.

Matignon has 85 seconds on Merckx, who has chased him all the way up the infernal spiral and who finally breaks free from Gutty once Matignon is safe. Merckx cruises in, serene and displeased; Gutty five seconds back is doubled over in pain. Van Den Bossche is next, overtaking Pingeon at the last, while Pierre is kissed by his trainer and given a commemorative plate by a man with a severe fringe and a pair of Ray-Bans.

If looks could kill, Merckx's would flatten the crowd, raze the vegetation, incinerate the film in the camera. He knows he has missed a trick at one of the most prestigious finishes. He flips up the brim of his cap, paces back and forth like a lion in a cage, scowls. He is terrifying. The former Tour winner Antonin Magne calls this Merckx's only mistake in the 1969 Tour.

'I felt ridiculous,' Pierre said in an interview after his win. 'I wanted my name at least once to appear on the race reports – for sporting reasons, it goes without saying. I will not make the same mistakes again, I'm decided on that' – [he's talking about his dope bust here] – 'and I wanted to try. It felt miraculously good after so many days running on empty to play a part in an attack.

'Let me tell you frankly, I hadn't planned anything. But climbing the Côte de Chavanon, I told myself the time was right, and that since I was at the front I should accelerate and try something. I was sure I would be caught, but that I'd make it to the end as part of a front group. When I saw nobody was coming I kept going, cautiously at first to save my reserves for climbing the Puy de Dôme. Never did I think I'd cross the line in victory. I was sure, even though my lead was comfortable with five kilometres to go, that I'd be caught in the final kilometre.

'Really, I was lucky, very lucky that the big guys didn't try anything behind me before the final climb of the Puy.

'It was hard. I started tapping into my energy reserves on the long climb of the Col de la Moréno, and I recovered a bit on the descent, but I'll remember this Puy de Dôme.

'Never have I suffered so much on a bike. I couldn't see clearly in the final kilometre, and several times I was tempted to get off, but I shook myself out of it, saying to myself: "Come on, one last effort. This time luck is on your side."

'I don't know how I found the strength to finish. I zig-zagged on my bike, my head hurt terribly.'

His gamble had paid off. Arguably the least important man in that year's race had won one of its most important stages. For that he will be remembered – and for the right reasons – a lot longer than if he had come last. His brave act catapulted him out of last position. The previous day the Tour's photographers had stopped to buy a paper lantern for Pierre, for the obligatory publicity shots. Now, the lantern was destined for the saddle of André Wilhelm, who on the Puy lost 12 minutes to Pierre and found himself, two days before Paris, definitively last.

As for Merckx, the greatest cyclist who ever lived had to content himself with being beaten by a minnow. The Puy de Dôme was not a lucky place for him. He would never win there and in 1975 was punched in the stomach by a spectator on its slopes, which many people think led to him cracking on the Pra Loup the next day and Bernard Thévenet winning the race. An epoch-ending punch, in other words.

But the day after his first beating on the Puy, Merckx was still huffing and puffing. 'The Puy de Dôme? Less hard than I thought,' he said.

Back on the side of the mountain in the darkness, the car has passed. I wait and wait some more . . . nothing . . . so, assured that I am inhabiting a land of silence and darkness once more, I pick the dirt out of my cleats, remove the leaves from my behind and get back on my bike. The darkest night comes before the dawn, I think.

The rest of my ascent is undisturbed save for the bats flying round near the top, pipping and squeaking. I stop to take a few pictures of the Auvergne spread out before me in the night but it's too dark to mean much. Up across the train tracks, past the visitor centre and the subterranean terminus of the train, past the point where the road turns to mud and a solitary traffic light winks. Up again, on to tarmac once more, to the ruins of Mercury's temple, then along the Chemin des Conquérants – the conquerors' path – to my escape route down, where I stash my bike, put on my plimsolls and casually start to walk around, just another Lycra-clad foreign tourist on a desolate mountain at dawn, taking in the view.

There are bells again and then baaas, then dogs and shepherds, numerous shepherds in fleeces and sensible shoes moving their sheep from one part of the mountain to another as the sky lightens. They're friendly, we chat, and I begin to feel the cloak and dagger was maybe a little foolish. The first hiker of the day arrives, a middle-aged man with a classically French moustache and a big camera. A sliver of deep red sun appears over the horizon bathing the view of the line of extinct volcanoes in an extraordinary soft light. It's time to leave.

Walking down with the bike slung over my shoulder, I can hear the first train of the day going up, its pinions singing in the morning sun. I meet a mountain biker illegally cycling up the narrow path. We give each other a look, both caught in the act, and then pretend there's nothing amiss. It is very steep and rocky with loose gravel. Chapeau to the man. Now a race to get back to the hotel in time for breakfast.

Back in Le Mont-Dore, a careworn spa town between its summer season and the first dumps of snow that signal skiing, where the only guests except me are an unhealthy looking bunch who have been sent on a State-funded 'cure' to take the waters, there is a bicycle race going on.[34] It is 8:30 a.m. and the main streets are already shut off, but the marshals patrolling the barriers see the bike in the back of my car, assume I am here to race and let me through. It's not the first barrier I've been through today. I drive slowly on to the course and duck neatly into the hotel car park.

Later, as the clouds lift from the deep cleft in the rock Le Mont-Dore occupies and a hot sun dries the roads making everything muggy, I drink a beer in a café 500 metres from the finish line and watch the *kermesse*. The finishing straight is somewhat desolate, a long stretch of bumpy tarmac at

---

34 What is this affinity, anyway, between cyclists and spa towns? All over France they are full of both *curistes* and *cyclistes* – two groups searching for something healing in the mountains.

about a 6 per cent gradient, up which a string of aged and not-quite-so-aged third-category riders are toiling. On the third-to-last lap there's a tough break for Daniel Barthélemy of local team Alcoolo Vélo (kit: fluoro pink, adorned with a comic-book illustration of a cyclist leaning forwards as a wine bottle suspended from a stick – a rod for his own back? – hangs in front of him). Somebody at the finish line has a spare wheel, but the change is fumbled and Daniel loses all contact. No fighting back: unlike Pierre his race is over. Nevertheless, he gets back on his bike and I see him come round two more times on his own, doggedly making it to the finish, where nobody much even cares.

And really, that's the point, I think. You just have to get to the damned end. Whether you're racing with a Cannibal hot on your heels and one of the Tour's most fearsome mountains ahead of you, or if you're racing for the bottom because there is nothing else left to try for. My mind wanders back to that day in the hail the previous summer and the finish line I did not cross, only a few kilometres from here, and I wonder how long it will be before I am back in the Massif Central again.

1969
130 starters
Winner: Eddy Merckx, 35.41 km/h
Lanterne rouge: André Wilhelm, 34.27 km/h @ 3h51'53"
86 finishers

Chapter 7
THE *DOMESTIQUE*

Second-rate men are very useful, provided they know, like zeroes placed after real numbers, to keep themselves out of the limelight.

Paul Masson

I am staring at a couch. More of a chaise longue, in fact. It stands on a parquet floor in the corner of a large room full of books, dark wood, statues and trinkets from around the world – mahogany busts from deepest Africa, ivory heads from the Orient. This is no ordinary chaise longue: it is covered in velvet cushions and a dusty Persian rug, it is heavy with the repressed desires of a civilisation. It belonged to Sigmund Freud and is the one upon which we revealed to him that we all lust after our mothers and want to kill our fathers – or vice-versa if you're female – opening a Pandora's box of dreams, desires and fears on to an unsuspecting 20th century.

The search for the meaning of the *lanterne rouge* has taken me to Freud's house in Hampstead, north London. Rather than delving into my own unconscious, I'm hoping to learn something from a day of talks on psychoanalysis and sport put on by the Anna Freud Centre in honour of the London Olympics. First on the bill are my main targets, Alastair Campbell and Mike Brearley, who are appearing 'in conversation': the idea is the two men will share and discuss their experience of teamwork and leadership from their respective fields.[35] As their bonhomous conversation advances – peppered with great anecdotes and insider jokes including Tony Blair's nickname for Campbell (Keano, after the hard-tackling Manchester United midfielder) – I realise I may have harnessed my cart to the wrong end of this horse. I'm interested in their opinions on motivation and how someone, who may well be in last place, keeps their chin up in the face of back-breaking work and guaranteed, often fruitless, suffering. They are looking at the issue from the perspective of leaders used to guiding men through a crisis; it is what they'll always be. I, meanwhile, am trying to see things from the other side, from the point of view of a bike rider who will sacrifice his energy, his chances for personal glory and sometimes his skin for his team leader, someone who is often unrecognised and unthanked in the wider world. The *domestique*, in other words.

In the break after their onstage chat I catch Brearley and Campbell over coffee and Hob Nobs. What advice would you give, I ask, to a leader who has to inspire his team in a situation in which all hope is lost and there is absolutely zero chance of winning? To which they both stop dunking and look blank for just a microsecond. Then they look at each other and agree that however grim the situation there is always something to be saved, always something to shoot for. It's not as if I'd been

---

35 Brearley captained the England cricket team in the '70s and '80s, wrote *The Art of Captaincy* in 1985, qualified as a psychoanalyst and was president of the British Psychoanalytical Society. Campbell, a former journalist and once known as 'Blair's Rottweiler', was Tony's director of communications and one of the key architects of the New Labour project.

angling for juicy gossip on Botham or Blair, a catastrophic lower-order collapse, or a beleaguered election campaign, but their response is illuminating: success is an all-encompassing mindset, failure is inconceivable. It is not an option. Whereas I suppose the point I was obscurely, perhaps too obscurely, groping towards is that despite the overriding focus on the war and not the battles, on positive thinking and salvaging what you can, that there is a lot that happens in sport outside of winning and losing. Especially so in cycling. Losing in cricket, say, is very palpable. You get caught or bowled and you leave the field. That long lonely trudge back to the pavilion. Your loss is compounded by those of your teammates until they all add up into one big, insurmountable loss and your team is defeated. In football, the ball billowing the back of your net, the numbers high on the scoreboard and 10,000 jeering fans.[36] In boxing, an unseen blow to the temple, the back of your head hitting the canvas insensibly, the referee leaning over you and counting to 10 as your consciousness spirals up into never-never-land. Not many ways of spinning that one, are there?

In cycling, the team sport won by an individual as the axiom goes, it's not so simple and Campbell, who is a big cycling fan and has ridden in many a team car, is no doubt aware of the complexities and the nuances that make the GC meaningless to many riders in a Grand Tour. If I were a French philosopher I would call the competing pressures something like '. . . the meditation between the pure ethic of sacrifice and the harsh law of success'. That's how they were described by the Tour-loving Roland Barthes, that master of cramming a whole heap of abstract nouns into a sentence. More plainly, for many riders

---

36 Let's not think about the draw, which is sometimes a win, sometimes a loss and sometimes simply itself.

their job is self-sacrifice and denial, and the harsh law is that they must work for another's success. It is simply *not their job* to win. And for some it is specifically their job *not to win*. Think of Chris Froome holding himself back to support team leader Bradley Wiggins in 2012.

Once you realise that many are dancing to a different beat another world opens up. 'I like to win but I'm not motivated to win. I never go into a race saying "I want to win this",' said Sean Yates. 'The thing that motivates me is riding for someone, either leading out a sprinter or helping a climber or defending a jersey. And when I'm in that situation, in any of those situations, then I perform much better because I'm motivated.' Yates was the British *super domestique* who bossed around the peloton in the 1980s and '90s. And if a rider does all that well, who's to judge that's less of a success than what the guy he has worked for achieves?

Looked at from a certain angle, the *lanterne rouge* could potentially be the second-best rider in the Tour.

Let me explain. In a perfectly efficient (theoretical) situation, a team leader would in his journey towards the yellow jersey profit fully from his *domestiques*' energy and then discard them, spent, along the way, as a space shuttle sheds its empty rocket boosters passing through the stratosphere and into outer space. No longer useful, they fall back to earth, and all the *domestiques* finish towards the bottom, if they finish at all. Perhaps, to fatally muddle the already overstretched analogy, the yellow jersey would be the only one to make it to the moon. That would please old Henri 'ideal Tour' Desgrange. But if at the end of the Tour the *lanterne rouge* is the yellow jersey's *domestique*, and can claim to have played a crucial part in this victory, doesn't that qualify as a great success – maybe even the second greatest in the race?

I make this point to ex-*domestique* and *lanterne rouge* Wim Vansevenant, who is sitting across his kitchen table from me as his young teenaged son shovels down a huge plate of pasta with a meagre coating of Bolognese. It is before 10 on a Saturday morning and the family is preparing for a junior cyclocross race, among the other routine tasks that fill the Belgian weekend. Wim is a compact, fair-haired man who, unlike many former pro cyclists, does not look older than his years. His weekend will involve a lot of farm work. The first time I speak to him on the phone he is in a field, one of those huge, rutted, glistening, brown expanses of Belgian mud that look, from the safety of my car as I drive through the endless suburbs and Andreas Gursky-esque landscapes of Flanders, like extremely stiff and chocolatey fudge icing being folded into itself.

'How are you?' I ask on that first call.

'OK,' comes the reply, then the static roar of wind obliterates any other sound through the earpiece for a good few seconds. Another pause and then, deadpan: 'Cold.'

When I get to his house Wim is slightly unimpressed by my abstract and tendentious conceptifying about the *lanterne rouge*'s worth. His eyes imply that if I had raced through that Belgian mud, in February perhaps, or toiled as a *domestique* for a decade or more at the highest levels of professional road racing, then I wouldn't be having such thoughts. I cannot rebut this. I have never raced through the chocolate mud, ferried bottles from the car to my teammates or helped Robbie McEwen beat elimination after being dropped with 205 kilometres to go. I have frivolous and misguided thoughts about the Tour, a race that I watch and do not take part in, which have nothing to do with tarmac and sweat.

Hold up a minute, though. The situation has actually happened. In 1950, as the mighty Ferdi Kübler took yellow for the Swiss, his teammate Fritz Zbinden was *lanterne rouge*. Does that make Fritz the perfect *lanterne*? Not exactly, since there were strange circumstances involved. The Italian team had dominated in 1950, winning five of the first 10 stages, but during the 11th stage, on the Col d'Aspin in the Pyrenees, the hustle of the crowd knocks Jean Robic and Gino Bartali off their bikes. While on the ground, Bartali, the captain of the Italian team, is threatened and assaulted by spectators, who perhaps believe that he has taken the Frenchman down deliberately. A knife is briefly flashed in his face.[37] Incensed, he races to Saint-Gaudens, winning the stage, and withdraws the entire Italian team in protest. It has dramatic consequences for the Swiss. Since Firenzo Magni, an Italian, had been leading the GC, second-placed Ferdi Kübler is propelled into first. Kübler did not wear the yellow jersey the next day out of respect for Magni, but wore it to Paris from then on. He had been training 1,100 kilometres a week before the Tour and was a class above all his compatriots: 'We were the weakest team in the 1950 Tour, with only five riders,' he explained to cycle historian Bill McGann. 'After 5,000 kilometres, all my teammates who arrived in Paris were between two-and-a-half and three hours behind me in the general classification. Practically, they could never help me.' Poor Fritz, who consequently was unable to be of much assistance to his leader, felt this truth only too sharply: when Bartali withdrew, the two Italians propping up the overall standings also went, so he was cast down into last place, whence he never escaped.

In 2011 too, in the Massif Central on that fateful stage nine from Issoire to Saint-Flour, the *lanterne rouge* and the *maillot*

---

37 He claims; some theories say it may just have been a picnicker holding a sandwich knife.

jaune were on the same team. Vincent Jérôme, more of a one-day rider than a Grand Tour racer, was a 26-year-old teammate of Thomas Voeckler. Jérôme had been caught in a big crash in the first stage and had lost 12 minutes. *Lanterne rouge* from stage one, he had hung on in the team time trial but otherwise come last or very close to it for the first six stages, struggling on with cuts and bruises and significantly less skin than he'd started with. In stages seven and eight, his performances had picked up and on stage nine he had helped Voeckler break away on the Côte de Massiac, the first climb on the day's long menu. Voeckler, Juan Antonio Flecha, Sandy Casar, Johnny Hoogerland, Nicki Terpstra and Luis León Sánchez would stay clear from then on, their lead ballooning after the carnage on the descent of the Puy Mary that knocked out Alexander Vinokourov and many others. Eventually, Sánchez would best Voeckler on the steep slopes to the hilltop square of Saint-Flour but Voeckler would take second on the stage and yellow overall. 'The last time I wore it, it was said they let me take the yellow jersey. But this time I went out looking for it,' Voeckler told *CyclingNews*. 'I made a clear choice. I sacrificed the stage to win it.'

So the *lanterne rouge* on this occasion did help his leader capture yellow. Does this make Jérôme the perfect one? No: he did not hold on to his prize, and neither did Tommy, who wore yellow for 10 days until stage 18; Jérôme had climbed off the bottom spot by stage 12.

Maybe the greatest *lanterne rouge* is Wim. Wim is also one of the modern masters of the art of the *domestique*. Those first *lanternes*, including Arsène Millochau and Jules Nempon, were lone wolves. Any alliances they made would have been fleeting and transitory, forged in the camaraderie of the road and soon forgotten. But the role of the *domestique*, despite the emasculating nickname, has become a complex and honourable one. His job is

THE DOMESTIQUE   131

Sisyphean: to do everything in his power to achieve the team's goals and propel one of its number into the limelight, day after day after day. If that's a GC contender, every man will work to put him in the best position possible for the overall win; if a sprinter, they'll manoeuvre him into a prime spot from which to launch himself at the finish line in the flat stages; if a climber, they'll climb before him to the point where he chooses to take flight solo for the stage win; everything in their power to prevent their leader expending energy unnecessarily – which means, the laws of physics inevitably dictate, expending more themselves. They will shield him from the wind, bring him water from the team car, set an unforgiving pace to tear the air from his opponents' lungs, stop with him when he needs to pee and ride him back to the bunch, and a hundred smaller tasks. *Domestiques* may well be less talented, and less capable of stamping their personal mark on the greatest races, but without them cycling's greatest names would not have the *palmarès* they do. And if the *domestique* finishes last after he's done his job, so be it.

Wim holds the dubious honour of more *lanternes rouges* than anyone else, taking a clean sweep from 2006 to 2008. Only four other men have held it twice – the Frenchman Daniel Masson (1922 and 1923),[38] Austrian Gerhard Schönbacher (1979 and 1980), Dutchman Mathieu Hermans (1987 and 1989) and Frenchman Jimmy Casper (2001 and 2004).

As we sit there in his kitchen, I gather that Wim is not completely disapproving of my tenuous logic of perfect economy. But he is an immensely practical, roll-your-sleeves-up kind of

---

[38] If Masson was Belgian (as many sources have him, though the truth is unclear) he was the first non-French *lanterne*; Richard 'Fatty' Lamb of Melbourne was the first non-European in 1931, and Zaaf in 1951 the only African. Otherwise, save for Yauheni Hutarovich, a Belorussian, they have all been canonically Western European. In 2013 the Canadian Svein Tuft was the first North American *lanterne rouge*.

guy, not prone to such flights of fancy. He's loud, too, and keen on the Belgian shrug, a violent rushing exhalation of breath accompanied by raised shoulders and raised eyebrows, which can mean many things but which is always clear in context. I'd read about it previously but nothing prepares you for the real thing. When I listen back to the tapes, it comes out as an eruption, 'Hoh', twice as loud as any of my conversation.

Wim retired in 2008 and has been back in civilian life for four years when I see him. It doesn't entirely suit him. For one thing, he consistently underestimates the amount of time it takes to get anywhere. Hoh, it's 45 minutes from where you're staying (it's an hour and 10); hoh, it's 20 minutes from his farm to Koksijde, where the UCI Cyclocross World Cup is being held on the sand dunes later that day (it's 35). I think he just lives a lot faster than we do. He is also handy with home truths that punch sense through the bullshit and chaos of the cycling life. Take this: 'When you are a cyclist, and you are thirsty, you have a *soigneur* who will get you a Coke. But in normal life, you have to supply your own Coke. Otherwise you won't get a Coke. It took me a few years to . . .'

Figure out how life works again, I offer.

'Yep, and I've already said: life sucks. Normal life sucks. It actually does. When you are a cyclist you don't have to think you just pedal. As fast as possible. That's all, the rest is taken care of.'

Try another one: 'Oh yes, 2006 was the year of Ullrich . . .' We're talking about his first *lanterne rouge*, the year the Tour was blown wide open by the Operación Puerto drugs investigation and favourites Jan Ullrich and Ivan Basso were forced to withdraw because of their links to the dodgy doctor Eufemiano Fuentes. Alberto Contador and Francisco Mancebo were also implicated, and Alexander Vinokourov did not start because his Astana-Würth team could not field enough eligible riders to meet the six-man minimum.

Says Wim: 'I didn't have much time to think about all the shit that was happening because I was buying my farm on the telephone!'

Talk about down to earth. A final one: 'It's always fun to race in the Tour when you win victories, otherwise it's shit. If you don't win, or have a GC rider, the Tour de France sucks.'

Killer.

Wim's wearing an old Lotto-Domo fleece, which clearly now has a second life as premium agricultural wear. It's from 2004, the year after he joined Lotto and was reunited with his friend and Classics specialist Peter Van Petegem. Van Petegem was Wim's first leader, the man to whom he devoted his services after he had made a very clear-eyed choice at an early age to be a *domestique*. I ask him what his ambitions and strengths were when he started out.

'Hoh. My strengths! . . . Actually I was a poor cyclist,' he says, obviously lying through his teeth. 'I tried it for a couple of years and I realised if I continue like this – a little bit of climbing, a little bit of sprinting, a little bit of time trial – my career wouldn't last very long.'

So you were conscious it was a sacrifice, I ask.

'It was a sacrifice, but it was quite easy: if I didn't do it, my career would probably end within a couple of years.'

He met Van Petegem in 2000 at the Dutch Farm Frites team and worked to become his indispensable helper. He explains the self-abnegation: 'Don't think about yourself: just think what you would do if you were Peter Van Petegem,' he says. 'If he said: "Go left", I went left. If he said: "Right", I went right. If he said: "Stop", I stopped. Even if I was dropped I didn't care. The rest, I didn't bother.'

For years Vansevenant sheltered and shepherded Van Petegem, deciphering every centimetre, every cobble of the course so Van Petegem, multiple winner of the Ronde van Vlaanderen, Paris–Roubaix and several of the minor Classics, could take best advantage of the terrain. Being Belgian, the spring Classics were Wim's first love, and it was there he first applied his craft. 'I know the Classics. I live close by. I know all the roads, all the climbs and all the holes in the roads,' he says. 'When you end this street, I know where the wind is going to come from, from there or from there. It's very important to know everything, to know the route by heart.'

He continues: 'I was his left and right hand. Both. And after a couple of years he didn't have to say anything any more, I already knew what he was thinking. In the Tour of Flanders, I was sitting second last and he was always sitting last. Just before the Kwaremont,' – one of the race's decisive cobbled hills – 'he looked at me and' – here Wim extends the Hoh-shrug into an extended eruption like a rocket lifting off on a spaceflight to the moon – 'we went to the front. It was like an interaction between two persons without words.'

I don't think I'd understood before talking to him how personal the relationship must be, how important that understanding and mutual respect. 'They inspire you, that's the thing,' Wim tells me. 'If you work like in the Tour de France for three weeks there has to be a personal connection between the riders, if not they won't go 100 per cent for each other in the race. It's all about loyalty and respect . . . like in normal life I guess,' he says.

The two men became good friends. They roomed together. Van Petegem married Wim's wife's friend.

In 2004 Wim's loyalty was rewarded. Lotto-Domo asked

him to take a rest after the Classics and to ride the Tour.[39] In 2005 it was the same. That year the team had dual objectives – yellow for Cadel Evans and green for Robbie McEwen. The two goals would stretch the team's resources to the limit, and mean each man would need to use his strength wisely. Four or five riders had been allocated to Cadel, and the team wanted to know who was going to ride the first 120 kilometres of each stage, thwarting dangerous escapes and bringing the gap down to set McEwen up for a sprint finish – be Robbie's right-hand man, in other words. 'I said, no problem, I'll do it,' Wim says. 'If you want me to ride three weeks I'll ride it, even if it's going to see me out of the race. I want to ride as long as possible. That's how it started. I did three weeks, and I rode for Robbie in the sprint, while the other guys were waiting for the hills to help Cadel. And the team management said, "Thanks for saying that, because it also opened the eyes of the other guys." At the Tour de France you can't think for yourself, you can only think for your leaders. And in between we are all *domestiques*.'

Aad van den Hoek tells me something similar, over coffee in a café in Vlissingen, in the extreme south-west of the Netherlands. In the 1970s he was with Ti-Raleigh under the watchful eye of DS Peter Post, a famed disciplinarian. 'He was always tough, you were afraid of him,' Aad says. 'I had no speciality. I was not good in the sprint, I was not a good climber. In a few races I could go for first place, but . . . I was always at the back, always a helper.' Nevertheless, Post had invited him personally to the team, which he had set up with

<hr>

39 Van Petegem would later move to QuickStep, but Wim stayed with Lotto until his retirement.

the UK-based bike and tubing company in 1974. The team registered in Holland in 1975, and was the stable for an array of Dutch talent – Hennie Kuiper, Gerrie Knetemann, Jan Raas, Peter Winnen and more – as well as German sprinter Didi Thurau and the *domestiques* to support them. Aad's particular friend was Knetemann; it was Knetemann he usually rode for, whose prize money he received a share of and who, when renewing his contract, guaranteed Aad's place the next year. But for the team's first Tour de France, the real hope was Kuiper. Kuiper was world champion and had just won the Tour de Suisse, a strong all-rounder who was capable of attacking, attacking and then attacking again. The 1976 Tour was heavily weighted in favour of the climbers, with eight straight days in the mountains and four summit finishes, including the Puy de Dôme, and Post put his rigorously drilled squad at Kuiper's service. Aad says the expectations weren't high, but the talent and the organisation were there and it was obvious that even in their first Tour they were going to grab a few stage wins. Kuiper won the flat stage four (in later Tours he would win on Alpe d'Huez twice) and Ti-Raleigh took the next day's TTT, but in stage 14 it all fell apart.

Kuiper had been struggling with illness and was suffering a little from a crash. In the Pyrenees he was losing time to the favourites as Joop Zoetemelk, Lucien Van Impe and Frenchman Raymond Delisle traded blows in the high mountains for the yellow jersey. In stormy weather, only a few kilometres along the road towards the summit finish at Saint-Lary-Soulan, he crashed again. 'We waited to see if he could stand up and go on,' says Aad. They waited and waited as Kuiper, his world champion's stripes muddied, sat dazed by the side of the road, collecting himself. But there is a certain way a rider holds himself when he cannot go on and in the photos Kuiper has

last-placed man is traditionally given a mock lantern to celebrate his *lanterne rouge*. This is
ues Pfister (left) and Pierre Claes in 1927 with Pfister's tin-can prize.

Left: The first last man: an eighty-one-year-old Arsène Millochau – *lanterne rouge* in 1903 – bashing away in his kitchen-workshop and on his bike in Paris.

Right: Henri Desgrange, father of the Tour: 'The ideal Tour would be one in which a single rider succeeded in completing the challenge'.

les Nempon (*lanterne rouge* 1919) pictured on the front of *L'Auto* just before the race.
the end he would be the winner, loser and sole survivor of his category.

1939: after the ordeal of the Pyrenees, Amédée Fournier takes a little nap in a hay field somewhere nea

Daniel Masson (top middle) was the first two-time *lanterne rouge* (1922/23).
Richard "Fatty" Lamb (below), an Australian, was the first non-European, in 1931.

ABDELKADER ZAAF

Was it something he drank? Abdel-Kader Zaaf under a tree after collapsing in 1950, and subsequently advertising Saint Raphaël tonic wine. By the 1951 Tour he was a fans' favourite.

Tony Hoar (right), the first Briton to come last in the Tour, is handed his paper lantern by Henri Sitek, his companion at the bottom of the general classification.

er have I suffered so much on a bike.' Pierre Matignon nears the top of the Puy de Dôme at the of his great Eddy Merckx-beating escape in 1969.

Aad van den Hoek was a loyal *domestique* whose 1976 Tour hopes were scuppered when his leader Hennie Kuiper crashed and abandoned. With nothing else left to play for, he went for the *lanterne.*

ove: Bernard Hinault and Gerhard Schönbacher, first and last in 1979.

low: Mathieu Hermans heading for last place in 1987.

Aad van den Hoek

Gilbert GLAUS

Hermans Mathieu

COFIDIS

Philippe GAUMONT

JACKY DURAND

Jimmy CASPER

hat's the collective noun for *lanternes rouges*? Autograph cards of some *lanternes* through the years,
ckwise from bottom left: Mathieu Hermans (*lanterne rouge* 1987, 1989), Aad van den Hoek (1976),
bert Glaus (1984), Philippe Gaumont (1997), Jacky Durand (1999), Jimmy Casper (2001, 2004).

Top: The late Philippe Gaumont winning Gent–Wevelgem in 1997. This photo was the only piece of cycling memorabilia he kept in his bar in Lens.

Bottom: Jacky Durand, *lanterne rouge* 1999, bothers that year's winner, Lance Armstrong, towards the end of their 3,690km journey to Paris.

ft: Wim Vansevenant, *super domestique* to Robbie McEwen and Cadel Evans, and triple *terne rouge* (2006–8).

ght: Iker (left) and Igor Flores: the only brothers both to come last in the Tour, training in eir native Basque country. Illness did for one, bad management, in part, for the other.

2000: a year after his *lanterne rouge–prix de la combativité* double whammy, Jacky Durand shows he is still a master of the art of the break.

that air. He is holding his left elbow awkwardly, a man in a white shirt has a protective arm around him. Meanwhile, up the road the decisive battle of the Tour is going on. Van Impe is attacking on the Portillon, several cols from the stage finish, Zoetemelk is cracking and Luis Ocaña, who is making his own bid for glory, will not last the course. It is all happening, and Ti-Raleigh is going nowhere.

I can picture the team members standing there on that mountain road in the gloom, each one going down with the captain on this sinking ship.

Eventually they get going again, but without a leader. Every man comes in outside the time limit, but they are not alone. Van Impe has exploded the race and 45 of the 93 remaining riders miss the cut. Peter Post asks the Tour management to waive that day's elimination, which they do. But what now? The team is stuck in the mountains with no competitive rider and with seven days of racing left. For Aad the answer is to go for the *lanterne rouge*. Before the crash he was mid-pack; now he is second last, above Super Ser's José Luis Uribezubia, who has been diligently losing time the whole race. Two days later, on the stage to Fleurance, Aad drops from the peloton: 'A few kilometres before the finish I stopped and hid behind some cars,' he said. 'Uribezubia passed and I waited a few minutes, and I got on my bike.'

Through that sleight of hand, the *domestique* without a leader came into Paris last and received the small recompense of the *lanterne rouge*. Post, however, reckoned it was a disgrace and rowed with Van den Hoek. But Aad stayed on the team until 1983 because he was simply too good at his job to let go. Besides, Gerben Karstens, another Ti-Raleigh rider, won on the Champs-Élysées – those extremes of first and last again – which provided some comfort.

Wim was not, or so he says, aware of his GC position most of the time. It just didn't mean anything to him. Towards the end of the 2005 Tour a journalist told Wim that he was second-to-last, and he thought then to drop off the back and go for the *lanterne rouge*, but 2005's *lanterne*, Iker Flores, was, as we shall see later, unbeatable. Before that, it hadn't even occurred to him, Wim tells me. 'You're there to compete, to be with your team. That was the main object at the Tour, not to go and be the *lanterne rouge*. My goal was to win stages and win a jersey, that's the thing: you have to go with that attitude otherwise you better stay home, because it's a crazy race, it's too hard.'

Maybe the seed had been sown in 2005, but through most of the 2006 edition he similarly paid no mind to the back of the race. He explains: 'Robbie was in the green jersey, I didn't notice or care that I was close to last. In the flat stages I was already saving energy for the next day, because I knew that I would have to do the same job again! And after my job was finished I would just sit back in the peloton and let myself drop and pedal easy to the finish,' he says. 'I remember one stage, in the last five kilometres I was riding next to the second team car, and I saw a big television screen and I stopped. And the car stopped, and I saw Robbie winning in the last kilometre or so. So I was already cooling down when the guys were going 200 per cent for the finish. I took a little rest, and tomorrow we went again for the same goal.'

Wim's professionalism and race savvy, though often invisible to the general public, did not go unnoticed by those who mattered. In a *Wall Street Journal* article by cycling writer Bill Strickland, Wim's *directeur sportif* Marc Sergeant made almost exactly the same point: 'He can ride at the front all day when we need him to,' he said. 'But when his part is done, he has the intelligence to know he should relax so he can come back strong the next day.'

Somewhere along the line, however, the *lanterne rouge* became a target. 'I wanted to be the next Belgian after Hans De Clercq to be last in the Tour,' he told journalist Sam Abt towards the end of the 2006 edition – with De Clercq, *lanterne rouge* in 2003 and by then working for Belgian TV, looking on and smiling.

So how do you go for the *lanterne*? Work for the team's goals first, Wim says, because otherwise you'll find yourself not selected for the major races, or even out of a job. Next, lose as much time as you can on the flat stages. Any lump of a rider can lose time in the mountains; it's the flats that you can make dropping back count. And leave it to the last 10 or 15 kilometres, since by that point you can be assured of finishing within the time cut and can judge your losses to perfection.

Jimmy Casper, a sprinter, was his main challenger for *lanterne rouge* in 2006. Casper was going for his hat-trick, yet he had one major handicap, Wim says. 'He had to sprint. In the climbs he couldn't drop back because otherwise he'd be outside the time cut. But he had to sprint, that was his role, he couldn't sit back. That was my luck, as I was already sitting back.' In the mountains, Wim could sit in the *grupetto* with McEwen and nobody would be able to risk going slower. Then, on the Champs-Élysées, his main rival was racing for the win. Fans on Internet forums commented avidly on Wim's 2006 battle for the bottom, reporting it as if each contender were vying for the top spot. The Basque rider Aitor Hernandez had been forced to defend the *lanterne rouge* in the opening stages and make much of the running, which no doubt tired him out, and Wim stayed cool, biding his time, letting the

Spaniard absorb the pressure. Hernandez soon dropped out of contention. Gert Steegmans, a QuickStep *domestique*, would make a threatening late lunge, but Jimmy Casper, who was motivated and fit, was the serious *lanterne* threat throughout the Tour. Finally, Wim held on for last. He was 16 seconds 'ahead' of Casper after the penultimate stage, and lost almost another two minutes on the Champs-Élysées, just to make sure.

It was a great year for Lotto.

'It was, it was, it was,' Wim says. 'We were one of the lowest budgeted teams. We were very small. And we won the green jersey and we won three stages. And we had a rider who was in the top 10 GC. It was perfect.'

The following year was even better. Wim, working for McEwen and Evans, wrapped up the *lanterne rouge* with six minutes to spare over Briton Geraint Thomas. And in 2008 there was an expectation, a buzz, as he launched himself for the historic third title. It was good publicity for the team and they welcomed it. Wim had also announced that the 2008 Tour would be his last.

Did that change your attitude to the race, I ask. 'Yes for sure. I wanted it to be three years in a row, because then I would have the record. That was my objective: to try to win the Tour with Cadel, and then to try to take the record. That was the main thing for me.'

Evans took the yellow jersey on stage 10 and held it until stage 14, but Carlos Sastre took more than two minutes from him on Alpe d'Huez and, despite a strong final time trial, Evans could only finish 58 seconds behind the Spaniard. At the same TT, Wim had a quiet word with Bernhard Eisel, who had been running him close at the bottom, and Eisel agreed to let him have the *lanterne*. But, on the final circuit, a surprise: 'He put on his brakes on the Champs-Élysées. Even two kilometres before the finish. I saw Bernie braking and I also had to stop! Otherwise I would lose my GC,' Wim says. 'Fuck!' He doesn't remember exactly the details of the pact, but he's not surprised that Eisel thought about breaking it. 'In races you cannot trust anyone because it's all about the money after all. Every year you have to sign a new contract so you have to work for yourself, you use everything you can in your powers to obtain a contract.' Eventually the two men rolled in together, a minute behind Gert Steegmans, who won the stage, and 30 seconds in front of the day's last place, a certain Christopher Froome.

Wim had won his historic third *lanterne*. The team's record over his *lanterne rouge* years stands thus: three stage wins and the green jersey for Robbie McEwen plus fourth overall for Cadel Evans in 2006; a stage win for Robbie and second overall for Cadel in 2007; another podium, second again, for Cadel in 2008. Wim allows that his work played a part in his team's victories between 2006 and 2008, that he has a share of the success. 'Yes, it is partly mine,' he says. 'It's fun to work in a team when it is going well. A *domestique* is as strong as his team leader. If the leader doesn't perform, the *domestique* doesn't do well.'

Wim won only once in his professional career, the second stage of the small-fry Tour du Vaucluse in 1996. How did that feel, I ask. 'HOH! I think that was in my second or my third year as a professional. It's when I was attempting to win races, not like the end of my career when I was helping people to win. That was a big difference. At that moment for me it was a very nice victory because also the way that I won – I escaped two or three kilometres before the finish, and it would have been a bunch sprint for sure if I hadn't got away on my own,' he says. '[In the amateurs] I always won finishing solo. Vaucluse was a very good result because winning on your own in a stage race is not easy.'

He does, however, laugh and pick me up on the idea that any race is small fry. 'It's all the same, it's all about racing and suffering! It doesn't mean at a small race that they don't go hard or try to do their best. It's a race like another.' Nevertheless, like Aad, he realised he wasn't winning enough to make a career, and switched focus.

'In the racing there's only one result that counts, and that's the first. Second hasn't any importance.' It's one of the final things Wim says to me.

One win for Wim. Unless you also count his win at windy, rainy Eernegem one Sunday afternoon in October 2008. That day many of the biggest names in pro cycling descended on the town to pay their respects in a testimonial criterium to one of their hardest working, Wim Vansevenant, on his retirement. Peter Van Petegem was there, as was Robbie McEwen; Gert Steegmans, Jurgen Van De Walle and Nico Mattan also all lined up behind the bike-riding townsmen with trumpets, who set the first lap off to a fanfare. And Cadel Evans, who gave a speech to the sizeable umbrella-toting crowd.

'First of all I want to say sorry to "Sevi" that we couldn't complete the double in the Tour de France this year. The plan was to be *lanterne rouge* in the Tour de France and yellow jersey in Paris and I let him down,' he joked. 'Beyond that, I value every rider who contributes to the team whether that's with results or with the work they do for the team. Wim is one of the riders who you always want to have in your team, in every race you do. He's a real team player in every sense of the word and he's only going to be missed in that way.'

*

Even buoyed by the acclaim of his peers it must have been a tough life, and the disjunction between being invisibly successful in his work and the public perceptions of failure can't have helped. The difference between the Tour on TV and being there, on the side of the road or following the riders in a car, is immense. Even at that remove you see the realities the TV hides: the guys struggling to hold on, the sweat, the blood, the hollow cheeks and the blank, lost stares halfway up the third mountain of the day; then the poor guy, or two, or three, who is having a bad day and is left behind and must do his climbing in the 30°C heat surrounded by the suffocating exhaust fumes and burning clutches of the team cars following the *grupetto*. And to be inside it must be unimaginably worse. I ask Wim what we don't understand, as followers, about everyday life in the peloton. He comes back with this: 'There is a lot of suffering at the back. Even in the *grupetto* you see riders who are close to collapsing, who are mentally completely finished,' he says. 'Certainly the last week, everyone is hoping to finish the race and go to Paris, but in between there are hard mountain stages. You have riders who are too weak and too strong. Still, there is competition. Sometimes you see terrible things: suffering and pain.'

Wim lived with this for years. He seemed to find a freedom in the servitude of the *domestique*, loved the routine, the simplicity and camaraderie of it. Eight or nine men, a team, a defined goal, a Classic in the spring, say. 'That's a feeling you don't have in normal life. Everyone is working for the same thing. It's the same with the Tour de France, all for one special thing,' he says. 'In normal life you don't have it, everybody is selfish and living in his own small world, trying to survive in this fucking world, because he has to pay his mortgage, pay his telephone, and he has to do this and this. When you are a cyclist you don't have to think about that [...] So you are very relaxed and free.'

What happens to old racers? The French talk of *problèmes de la reconversion* when a rider retires. Philippe Gaumont (*lanterne rouge*, 1997) says he 'kept a few contacts, mainly with riders who were finishing their career. They know that re-conversion is not easy.' 'Re-conversion' suggests something of the difficulty demobbed soldiers experience returning to civilian life in American films about the Vietnam war. Redeployment is a pitfall for many sportspeople, who as they grow older find themselves eventually refused entry to the very specialised world to which they have dedicated themselves since an early age. And perhaps since pro cycling is all-consuming, and only recently paid well, it seems particularly difficult for cyclists. The military analogy seems apt – 'peloton' does, after all, mean 'platoon' – and Wim started his cycling career with national service and ended it, at 37, after 14 years of service as a loyal foot soldier, often overseas, back on civvy street, with an agricultural degree he'd taken 20 years previously and a farm to run.

'After I stopped cycling it took me two years to turn normal,' he says. 'Certainly the first year was like hell. You have to find your way again in normal life. It's not easy. But I found my way. You have to adapt.'

Aad van den Hoek makes the point that in his era – a time of 300-kilometre days and split stages, restricted bidon opportunities and steaks for breakfast at 6 a.m. – barely any rider had the luxury some have today of a large financial cushion. After retirement, he had to find a new business and now, 30 years after the end of his first life as a bike racer, he has mellowed. He is a security consultant, selling CCTV and other devices to towns like Vlissingen, and comes to meet me in between duties loaded with armfuls of scrapbooks, magazines and mementoes of Ti-Raleigh. He still cycles, he says, still has that sense of competition. 'When I go with younger riders I try to lose them, I push them,' he says. 'In the final I try to win also. It's always in me.'

Wim on the other hand has left that behind, for the time being at least. 'I've ridden 10 times around the world,' he says. 'I don't feel like it any more. It's enough. My body suffered enough. I don't have any more competition in myself any more. I killed that during my years as a professional.' His parents arrive, to help out with the childcare and the cyclocross arrangements, and it's time to get on, so I leave them to it and head to watch the World Cup cyclocross racing in the sand dunes nearby.

I think back to that perfect row of Belgian houses and the chat with Wim many times, not least when I'm sitting listening to Alastair Campbell and Mike Brearley talk about loyalty, inspiration and belief in your leader's abilities – all of which rang true with the *domestiques* I'd spoken to. After their onstage conversation, when they drew a blank on how to keep on going when all hope is lost, I thought of Aad on that mountain road, and the beheaded Ti-Raleigh team. And I realised that in a way they are right. There is always something to shoot for, even if you've buried your personal ambitions and dedicated yourself to an impossible task. But the force of will needed to do that, to see it through, might well be much greater than they, as leaders, imagine.

Did he mind being remembered for being last? I asked Wim.

'It's one of my main achievements in cycling,' he said. 'If someone hears my name they say, ah! It's the *lanterne rouge* of the Tour de France. I think it's the most important thing in my whole cycling career.'

1950
116 starters
Winner: Ferdi Kübler, 32.78 km/h
Lanterne rouge: Fritz Zbinden, 31.87 km/h @ 4h06'47"
51 finishers

1976
130 starters
Winner: Lucien Van Impe, 34.51 km/h
Lanterne rouge: Aad van den Hoek, 33.59 km/h @ 3h12'54"
87 finishers

2006
176 starters
Winner: Óscar Pereiro, 40.78 km/h
Lanterne rouge: Wim Vansevenant, 39.03 km/h @ 4h02'01"
138 finishers

2007
189 starters
Winner: Alberto Contador, 39.23 km/h
Lanterne rouge: Wim Vansevenant, 37.62 km/h @ 3h52'54"
141 finishers

2008
180 starters
Winner: Carlos Sastre, 40.5 km/h
Lanterne rouge: Wim Vansevenant, 38.76 km/h @ 3h55'45"
143 finishers

Chapter 8
THE SHOWMAN

A trophy means nothing to me.

Gerhard Schönbacher

After that consideration of the hidden art of the *domestique*, this is perhaps a good time to remember that professional cycling is all about publicity. The Tour de France began as a publicity stunt for a newspaper, as did almost all the historic races, and the commercial forces behind cycling's competitive elements are pretty transparent. Ask a football supporter to sing for Aon United or Samsung FC and he or she would look at you funny, but cycling fans know their teams by their sponsors' names, not their regional affiliations. Cyclists are moving billboards, there to sell, and in each team's portfolio of sponsorship opportunities certain spots – most obviously the top of the buttocks – command a premium price since they get the most on-screen, ahem, exposure.

It is something riders know. 'Fundamentally my job is to display the sponsor's logo as predominantly as possible, preferably crossing the line with my hands in the air.' These are the words of Mark Cavendish, speaking to the BBC in London just before the Olympics (that hymn to amateur sport's

Corinthian ideals, brought to you by Coca-Cola, McDonald's, Adidas, Visa and many more). 'It is a commercial thing – it is about displaying sponsors' logos,' Mark continued. 'That is where the money comes from.'

This is not to single out Cavendish – he's an exemplary professional sportsman in many more ways than that – but to underline the level of acceptance of the commercialism of the race. The Tour is a show that can be enjoyed without caring too much about what's going on at the front of the race, and in the publicity caravan, the gaudy pageant of floats throwing out keyrings, sunhats and madeleines to the roadside crowds, the Tour very early on achieved the trick of making the advertising an attraction in its own right.[40] Indeed, for a big portion of the roadside audience, the peloton is but an afterthought, a necessary and sufficient condition for the real show – women dressed up as baguettes chucking out worthless free tat.

The unintended consequence of the publicity imperative is that people soon work out there are easier ways of achieving it than crossing the line with your hands in the air. Some riders, for example, have clauses in their contracts stipulating they must spend a certain amount of time in a break, to make sure their kits get airtime on the TV broadcast of the day. Or how about walking the last 100 metres of the Champs-Élysées with a group of journalists, bending down and kissing the line? It's not a winning move, but Gerhard Schönbacher, a young Austrian, pulled it off and it seemed to keep the sponsors happy. Less so the organisers of the Tour de France. Think back to Jean-François Pescheux and *le fair-play*, and it's easy to see why. In 1979 Schönbacher, guerrilla marketeer

---

40 Nine tons of mini salamis were distributed by the Cochonou girls from their gingham 2CVs at the 2013 Tour. That's 2.64kg per kilometre. Do not tell me that is not a significant draw.

extraordinaire, precipitated an extraordinary fight for the soul of the Tour.

His perceived lack of respect for the race and its ideals so incensed Tour director Félix Lévitan that, in 1980, Lévitan went to war with the *lanterne rouge* and the Devil takes the Hindmost was back.

Gerhard Schönbacher was nicknamed 'The Boxer'. In his youth he was a welterweight, he says, and pretty handy: 1.82 metres tall and 67 kilograms, with a long reach. But middleweight was a different game, full of proper tough guys who were larger and more solid and didn't find his reach so convincing. 'I trained only in the winter,' Gerhard says. 'I played ice hockey. Several of my teammates boxed, because in hockey you need to know how to fight. So we all joined a club.'

Later, as a cyclist (again, something he only took up to help his hockey, but to improve his cardiovascular endurance this time), his boxing skills came in handy at an Italian training camp, when one of his teammates heard there was a decent boxing club nearby that was more than happy to line up their prize fighter for an exhibition match against the cyclist. 'Because I'd always had a big mouth, he wanted me to fight,' Schönbacher says. 'And I said I hadn't boxed in three years, you lose the speed and coordination, everything. But I couldn't get out of it!' Schönbacher laughs, his voice crackly over Skype. He's sitting in his office in Austria, spectacles on and a smile in his eyes, looking less like a boxer than some kid's favourite grandfather. He finishes his thought: 'Eventually I did go, and I knocked that guy out.'

A sporting polymath, his insouciance took him from brawling hockey player to boxer to a decent cycling career. At 25 years old he was a Tour debutant, a cocky, combative sprinter with DAF Trucks-Aida, a Belgian team full of young riders. 'I always dreamed of going to Belgium,' he says. 'I was one of the best amateurs in Europe. It was never really hard, I didn't enjoy training too hard. I just went around winning on talent, but it did get a bit more difficult when I was a pro. The year I became professional I had a skiing accident and I damaged my hip, and from that point on I couldn't sit on my bike straight. I think that hindered me a little bit. But I don't want to use that as an excuse, that I would have won the Tour de France otherwise, definitely not.'

The roots of his notoriety lie in 1978 when a young Frenchman, Philippe Tesnière, was crowned *lanterne rouge*. Tesnière, who died of cancer in 1987, was 'one of the most charming guys in the peloton' according to the papers. 'He was a teammate of mine for two years at Fiat,' Paul Sherwen told me. 'I raced with him in the amateurs, too. I believe he was from Normandy.' A year or two after their time together, Sherwen and Tesnière found themselves competing against each other, in a long two-man breakaway at the Tour du Loir-et-Cher. 'The one thing I do remember about him was he had these flipping huge calf muscles,' Sherwen continued. 'I got beaten by him in that stupid race by a couple of centimetres. I got beaten by a bloke that I knew and I didn't feel so disappointed because he was a bloody good sprinter, but I remember my team manager was really pissed.'

In 1979 Tesnière turned up at the Tour de France very much in a mood to win the *lanterne rouge* again, since the money he'd earned the year before at the criteriums had saved him from going back to his job working on electricity pylons. But he hadn't counted on Schönbacher and DAF. 'After the first rest day, the sponsor arrived at the race, and he said, "Well, you're doing a good job but I don't see much on the TV or publicity going around",' Gerhard says. 'And there was an old Belgian journalist who said: "Why don't you just try and come last every day? That's publicity. The TV get tired of showing winners all the time, because they need other pictures, too."' It was agreed that to maximise exposure it should be someone who spoke several languages; Gerhard spoke German, a bit of English, Dutch and French, so all eyes fell on him. Initially reluctant, he slept on it, agreed and began to finish last, while the Belgian journalist seeded the story in the press corps. 'Journalists kept coming up to me asking, "Is it true that you want to come last?" and I kept saying, "Yes, I want to come last!" I kept dreaming up these stories about how I would do it: that I would hide 30 kilometres in behind a bridge, or whatever. I made up stories. Every day I was in the media. I just made things up. I was provocative when I was younger.'

His attention-seeking had the desired effect, all the more so as his stories became increasingly outlandish. 'The Tour really isn't difficult, we're just pedalling through France,' he told one French TV station. To another he said that the Tour was a circus. But that got him into trouble. 'I had a couple of days before I had a dispute with Lévitan,' he said. 'I can't remember 100 per cent what I said, but something like the Tour is a show, Lévitan is the circus director and we are his apes. We're battling like idiots and they make the money. He was not amused.'

Félix Lévitan was not a man to cross, but Gerhard had not yet gone too far. That moment would come on the Champs-Élysées; first he had to negotiate his way there safely, and in last place. Gerhard knew he wasn't talented in the mountains but he could keep a rhythm and push his way through within the time cut – earning himself something of a reputation as the wheel to follow in the *autobus* in future years. And he was still doing his team duties. 'No one in the team complained that I wanted to come last, because they got so much publicity through me,' he says. 'I still worked for the first 100 kilometres or more – getting bottles for the leaders and helping. But then in the last 50 kilometres I could run my own show.' Other teams were not so happy and Gerhard remembers a manoeuvre orchestrated by a rival DS: four guys sent back to bother and block him, also in a bid for publicity. The intention was to force him outside the time limit: 'I remember I dropped them 10 kilometres before the finish. I made it and one or two of them didn't,' he says.

Philippe Tesnière was a constant presence, the two men at the bottom of the GC marking each other carefully in their race within the race. 'They were a long way behind the third-last rider and they both wanted to be last,' Paul Sherwen told the journalist David Walsh in 1993. 'On one stage Tesnière, I think, stopped for a pee and Schönbacher stopped with him. They were both left behind and they finished together 15 or 20 minutes behind.'

The final significant obstacle for both men was stage 21, a 48.8-kilometre individual test against the clock in Dijon; as such, the cyclists went out one by one, and in reverse order. Tesnière was the *lanterne rouge*, so he was off first; Schönbacher, about a minute above him, second. To avoid elimination each had to gamble on what the winning time might be and judge their ride accordingly, to be as close to the cut-off as possible but without crossing that unknowable threshold. Gerhard sought advice on the roads from Bernard Thévenet, who would later be his captain and who had raced and won a very similar TT in Dijon in 1977. Suitably primed, Gerhard set out at a leisurely pace. 'If you go 100 per cent you'd still lose 15 minutes anyway, so you might as well go slower,' Gerhard says. 'But about halfway I got nervous that it was too slow, so I sped up a bit.' He retired to his hotel to watch the rest of the field come in over the afternoon. At the top of the bill, Joaquim Agostinho,

Knut Knudsen, Gerrie Knetemann, Joop Zoetemelk and then Bernard Hinault, the first man out last, tearing up the road to put the seal on his second Tour win. TV pictures can be cruel: the flattening effect of the telephoto lens made Gerhard think, as Hinault ate up the final few 100 metres, that Hinault was closer to the finish line than he really was and that he, Gerhard, would be eliminated. On the edge of his bed, he waited for the time cut to be announced. Hinault completed the 48.8-kilometre course in one hour, eight minutes and 53 seconds; Gerhard was 12 minutes and 59 seconds slower, some 30 seconds safe; Tesnière was 53 seconds too slow. He had misjudged and was eliminated. 'The brave lad from Fiat was in tears, and he couldn't sleep all night for thinking about what he has lost in this adventure,' the paper said. 'One might even wonder if it wasn't to conserve this *lanterne rouge* that he dropped so far back and committed this error of judgement that has cost him dear.'

As soon as Tesnière's elimination was ratified, his manager, Raphaël Géminiani, complained to the jury that a pitiless Hinault had gone unreasonably fast; but since there was only one casualty of the great champion's fury the argument did not stand up. And the elimination did.

'I'll come back to the Tour next year without the idea of coming last – but to win a stage,' were Tesnière's parting words.[41]

His departure left Schönbacher safely in last. And on the last day he had a word with the journalists before the start. '"When everyone goes over the finish, don't turn your cameras away, I'm going to do something silly." So, 100 metres before

---

41 He did come back in 1980, as part of the Boston-Mavic-Les Amis du Tour team, which was partly comprised of unsponsored riders like him. He escaped on the first stage and, though he didn't win the stage, collected enough KoM points to wear the polka-dot jersey for two days. In 1981 he came 120th – second last.

the finish I stopped. And I started walking. The journalists came up to me and started walking beside me,' he says. He told them that, having raced around France, over the Alps and the Pyrenees, for three weeks, he wanted to enjoy the last 100 metres. 'I walked to the line and kissed the finish line. And then I said, "Thank God I'm allowed to do this", and the picture went all around the world.'

This, I think, was the last straw for Félix Lévitan. An ageing Jacques Goddet was still in charge of the sporting side of the Tour but Lévitan was his co-director and, while it was Goddet who famously wore khaki fatigues and a pith helmet around the race, it was increasingly Lévitan who was ruling with an iron fist. A small dark man, he was known for his icy smile, his thin, sharp features, and for imposing his will on the race with little regard for his own popularity and other people's feelings.

'I don't know anyone who called him Félix,' Jean-François Pescheux told me the day I met him at the ASO offices. 'He was a hard-nosed businessman, very exacting . . .' Pescheux had ridden the Tour in the Schönbacher-Tesnière years before taking up his post at the Société du Tour under Lévitan and Goddet. Perhaps because he had known the man well, and from several angles, he seemed to be choosing his words carefully. 'Everyone respected him when he talked, everyone followed his wishes. He was to be feared – feared by all the *directeurs sportifs*, by the riders, who maybe knew him less well, feared by all of cycling. Before you did anything, you asked Monsieur Lévitan's permission.'

Phil Liggett, meanwhile, sat on the foreign organisers' committee of the Tour in that era, when he was technical director of Britain's Milk Race. The committee was presided over by Lévitan, who Liggett found polite but formidable. To illustrate the man's character, he tells me a story from 1977, a year when Van Impe raced up the Alpe, leaving everyone behind him in trouble. 'All the sprinters pottered up Alpe d'Huez, there was a bunch of them, 23 or 25 riders,' Phil says. 'And Lévitan went berserk. He hit the bloody roof and said, "You're not going to treat my race like a touring run in the mountains and then take all the prizes on the flat. You can all go home."

'There were meetings until midnight,' Phil continues, 'and I climbed on to the roof of a place to look through a window, and I could see them banging on the table, the team managers and Lévitan saying, "You don't potter up here with your saddlebags on and then expect to race tomorrow, this is the Tour de France, the hardest race in the world." And he got rid of them all.'

There was even an instance of him changing the results of an intermediate sprint to de-classify Barry Hoban, a British rider. Of course it was out of his remit to do so, but when Hoban argued, he hit a wall of indifference. 'The commissaires even had no control over him and it was only in the latter years of his period that the commissaires reminded him they were actually the people who ran the race on the road,' Phil says. 'It was his race and that's the way it was!'

Gerhard had picked a formidable opponent. He had not, of course, invented the race for the *lanterne rouge* and, even though he was fighting to be last while others were fighting not to be, it's difficult to believe he was doing anything truly subversive and destabilising. But by playing the clown he had hit a nerve with Lévitan. 'I'll fight to the death for the moral good,' Lévitan said years later, at one of his last public appearances before he died at the age of 95. 'Because I aspire to live my last years in peace.' It's easy to believe that Gerhard's behaviour offended his moral sensibilities, and that the Tour director didn't want an upstart disturbing the tranquillity of his rule. So Lévitan set out to crush the worm. 'Félix Lévitan was upset about the way I came last, that I didn't take his race seriously,' Gerhard says simply. 'A little later Lévitan said that next year the rules would change, so that no one can come last for fun.'

It was decreed that in the 1980 Tour, from the third stage onwards, the final rider in the GC each day would be eliminated.

This did not go down well with the riders at all. Roger Legeay was vice-chairman of the riders' association at the time and he complained to Jacques Goddet on the train transfer to the start in Frankfurt that it was unfair. Given the first 10 stages were flat, with plenty of split days and team time trials, the rule would, he said, knock out all the climbers before they had a chance to use their skills, not to mention penalise those caught in the traditional first-week crashes. Goddet considered the point and put out a communiqué that the elimination would not start until after the first mountain stage. After that, confusion reigned: an official notice on the morning of the only Pyrenean stage, when Schönbacher lay 107th out of 113 riders, promised the elimination would start that night. But for some reason no elimination took place and the guillotine did not fall until the next day, when it was announced that Kelme's Juan Pujol was out. On stage 15, a Frenchman Jacques Osmont started last. 'He got in the breakaway,' remembers Sherwen, 'which might have got him away from being last overall. Except the breakaway got caught in the end.' But seeing how courageously he had ridden, Lévitan handed down a reprieve that evening and Osmont started the next day. 'He was eliminated after the next day's stage,' Paul Sherwen says. Sherwen thought the ruling was stupid: 'It was like bringing a guy to the firing squad and telling him you weren't going to shoot him until the next day.'

It only added to the bad atmosphere at a tough Tour. Roger Legeay was publicly complaining about the length of the transfers and the riders were exhausted, having climbed Alpe d'Huez twice in 24 hours. Jacques Anquetil, who in retirement was writing a daily Q+A column in *L'Équipe*, came out against the rule, though he did point out that all the teams had signed up in the full knowledge that it would be happening.

And although Lévitan was eliminating the last man, time cut be damned, he had not yet succeeded in knocking out the Boxer. He had not counted on Schönbacher's cunning and Gerhard was relishing the challenge. 'I got really motivated and really prepared,' he says. 'My aim was to win last place again, but then win the last stage in Paris. It was to challenge him and his new regulations. So I tried to come second-last in most stages.' Gerhard had also been promised a bonus by his team owner (he had moved to Marc-Carlos-VRD with DS Patrick Lefevere) should he manage another last place; once again the publicity machine played along, giving the Austrian the coverage his employers desired.[42] The journalists even colluded with him, providing him with timekeeping since none of the team cars could stick with him at the back. It was a service they were happy to provide. 'They had a great time with me, telling me I was 25 minutes behind and I shouldn't be slower than another five minutes,' he says. 'It was my own race.'

After stage 17, Erich Jagsch was eliminated from 91st position; Schönbacher, in 89th, was then only one place above

---

42 Not *L'Équipe*. Lévitan's in-house paper clearly had decided they'd had enough of that joke and didn't give him any exposure.

elimination. Bernard Quilfen was stage 18's victim, leaving Gerhard bottom, eight minutes adrift of safety. In other words, in real trouble. Gerhard had performed a remarkable Houdini act a few days before, making up a big handful of minutes, but a second great escape seemed unlikely. Miraculously, however, Quilfen was *repeché* that night – and Gerhard Schönbacher was saved.[43] Against expectations Quilfen started the next day, still propping up the GC, and failed to scramble out. He was duly eliminated.

But, last or not, Schönbacher was now safe. The 19th stage was the last elimination allowed for in the regulations.

Lévitan had been gunning for Schönbacher for a full year and in his pursuit had caused an uproar and ended five men's Tours unreasonably early. Then he had had a golden opportunity to dispatch his nemesis and he had not taken it. It is the prerogative of dictatorship to change its mind: to be irrational and erratic and to answer to no one. But those of a charitable frame of mind might also argue it is proof that the better side of human nature sometimes prevails: that the misfortune of Quilfen's situation was weighed in the scales of providence and found to outweigh Schönbacher's sins. The outcome either way was Gerhard had again outwitted his enemy.

On the Champs-Élysées he got in the meaningful break, but was caught on the final corner of the Place de la Concorde and missed his chance to win. He came in that day just outside the top 10.

It was a remarkable performance. However, even Gerhard could dodge the punches for only so long. That evening, at a fancy restaurant, he got into a row with his boss, who did not

---

43 Roger Legeay, when interviewed by Sadhbh O'Shea, said that Quilfen had crashed, which had narrowly tipped him into last – and he was for that reason given a stay of execution.

want to pay him his bonus. It ended with Schönbacher leaving the team.

When I ask him how the team felt about his second *lanterne*, Gerhard at first seems reluctant to talk about it. 'The team was happy, as far as I remember. They had publicity and it didn't cost them anything,' he says. I press and ask if he argued with the management; he hesitates and then says: 'Yes. That's true. Now you've reminded me of that. They didn't . . . I can't remember the name of the team manager of the time . . . I got in an argument with him, not about publicity, but because he didn't pay me my fee. That's true.

'I gave all my stuff back, and I rode till the end of the year at my own expense. And it was because of that argument. There was no relationship any more after that. If the team disappoints you because they don't pay the promised fee, there's no reason to continue.'

The conversation ends and I am confused, a little sorry it finished on that note and also feeling like I'd missed something vital. He's not the sort of guy to be embarrassed about a little confrontation but, I think, perhaps there's more to the memory, an unpleasantness that he had wanted not to reveal. As I sit there lost in thought, an email pops into my inbox:

Hi Max,

After our conversation this morning I tried to recall what happened after the second TdF . . . it is a long time ago and nobody has asked me that question for many years.

As far as I remember we had dinner after the last stage in Paris with the whole team.

When the boss of the team said something disparaging about me in front of everybody

including my female company (it must have
had something to do with the last place —
even though he probably might have said it
for fun I can't remember) I was too proud
to take that — got up and said something
'nice' to him as well...and then left with
my company ...

...I met him several times years later
for other occasions with Patrick Lefevere and
we had dinner together...but that subject
never came up.

Maybe we were both emotional at that moment
and said something wrong at the wrong time
at the wrong place...it had probably only
relevance at that very moment.

Cheers
Gerhard

I am relieved and write straight away, confessing I'd been
worried I'd brought up something painful. I also ask whether it
was tough to continue on his own – whether he did it for money
or self-respect. The reply pings quickly back from Austria.

Hi Max,

It wasn't because I didn't want to speak
about it — it is not such a big deal but 32
years ago is a very long time and it took
me a while — I had to go very deep into
my memories.

Now I will keep it for the next 32

years...I also tried to remember the name
of my female company but I had to give up.

No, it wasn't tough because to ride all
the criteriums after the Tour de France you
don't need a team because you get the contract
directly from the organisers.

With the start money from the criteriums
I could pay my bills until the end of the
year.

And I signed a contract already at the end
of July with the Puch-Wolber team in France
for the next year so I didn't lose too much
sleep because of existential fear.

All the best
Gerhard

He doesn't act like a man who suffers much from existential
fear. In 1981 he raced the Tour for Puch-Wolber, and he was
urged to go for the historic hat-trick of lanterns. 'I said, come
on, it's getting a bit silly now. I've done it two times, I told my
story and why I did it already, I'm not going to keep playing
the idiot. Not the idiot, but the clown.'

Not content with the boxing and ice hockey, Schönbacher
was, in 1983, the only man in Europe to be professional in
three sports. There was cycling, obviously. He cycled because he
loved the endurance challenge and the thrill of competition, of
going wheel to wheel with other men. He would get complaints
from his manager because he didn't like training, so he'd race
three times a week to avoid having to do any. Number two
was speed skiing – a discipline I, not being Austrian, had
barely realised existed, but of which he speaks in a nonchalant

manner. And there was touring car racing too ('It was a good way to make my living actually'). He even ended up on top of a car at the Adelaide Grand Prix being driven – unattached – at 240 kilometres an hour. It was, for a time, a world record.

The one big question: why? 'It's the skill, the thrill, and those moments when you stand at the start and you are about to do something that's normally not possible,' he says. 'I mean, it's crazy. But if people want to see it and pay for it, and I had fun, then everyone gets something out of it.' Because he was a thrill seeker, in other words, and an adrenalin junkie before those things were fashionable. Because he was, and is, a showman, and showmen understand that the show, despite everything, must go on.

In 1985 he was hit by a car on his bike, breaking his back and leaving him languishing for months in a hospital bed. He raced a little after but that was really the end.

After Gerhard's last-minute dive into last place, the Tour show trundled on, with little visible damage from the feud. It's true that 1980 hadn't been a vintage edition. But Bernard Hinault had withdrawn before the Pyrenees with a knee problem, leaving the winner, Joop Zoetemelk, a relatively easy run at yellow, and the *parcours* had been exhausting – so it's impossible to say whether Lévitan's meddling at the bottom was at fault. Suffice it to say that the Devil rule did not survive another year and neither Lévitan nor Goddet tried to eliminate riders again.

It's also true that the Devil rule compressed the 1980 race, speeding up the tail end. Gerhard was only two hours, 10 minutes and 52 seconds behind the winner – a 2 per cent difference, whereas most post-war *lanternes rouges* are around 4 per cent, or four or five hours behind the winner. But in 1981, the spread from first to last widened again to four hours,

29 minutes and 54 seconds as the slower riders, no longer menaced by daily elimination, relaxed.

'The riders always adapt to the rules, they do. It's no big deal.' That's Pescheux again. He's talking about his changes to the time cut in 2013, but he may as well have been talking about Schönbacher and the early '80s. Schönbacher was not playing the game that Lévitan wanted him to play, but he kept within the rules and worked the Tour's other angles pretty hard. He'd had a good time and it had suited his team just fine . . . until it was time to pay.

Pescheux does think, however, that Gerhard's behaviour had a lasting effect on the Tour, in that it diminished the institution of the *lanterne*. 'After all those games with Tesnière and Schönbacher, [the *lanterne*] got a bit lost during the '80s,' he says. 'There was less media coverage of the last man in the Tour . . . I can't think after '81 or '82, nothing like the same phenomenon.' These days, he believes, the *lanterne rouge* is insignificant and that riders try to avoid it. 'Now a guy who falls, who finds himself last in the Tour, he doesn't care about his placing: he only wants to finish,' he says. Later on, he elaborates on what he admires about the *lanterne rouge* – or rather, states it even more plainly in case I hadn't understood. 'I like it when the last man rides with an attacking spirit, tries to take time bonuses so that he is no longer last.'

Try your best, honour the Tour . . . and the Tour, in return, will be fair to you. That's why even though there will never be an official *lanterne rouge*, there is something in its ethos of which officialdom approves. It's that determination to finish and propensity to suffer for it that saw, for example, Edwig Van Hooydonck, a fine Classics rider, turn himself inside out the day a young Lance Armstrong won his first Tour stage in Verdun, riding 130 kilometres on his own to scrape in 40

seconds before the cut-off. And then repeat the effort day after
day until the end, purely to be 1993's last man. It's something
the sprinters have got down to a fine art.

Perhaps the unseemly scrap did diminish the *lanterne*'s
allure. But rising salaries and fewer criteriums did too. It may
be old hat to Pescheux, and the traditional Tour audiences
may have overdosed on the *lanterne* in 1979 and 1980, but
there are fresh generations of fans, particularly outside Europe,
who still find something fascinating in it. There is a Lanterne
Rouge cycling club; a Lanterne Rouge travel company in the
Pyrenees, and an outspoken American Lanterne Rouge blog,
whose *raison d'être*, it states, is: 'Celebrating the last-place
rider in the general classification . . . because you couldn't
hang on his wheel for 30 seconds.' There is even, thanks to
Bicycling magazine in the States, a Lanterne Rouge cocktail.
Take one measure of vodka, a half each of Cointreau and
Chambord, a measure of cranberry juice and a squeeze of
lime, and then shake, strain and serve, garnished with a
blackberry or raspberry if desired. *Voilà*.

In a strange twist of fate, Schönbacher is now a race organiser
himself. The poacher has turned gamekeeper and runs the
Croc Trophy, billed as the oldest and toughest mountain bike
stage race around. In previous years he's had former stars of
the road including Eric Vanderaerden, Alberto Elli and Phil
Anderson making guest appearances, but now it has established
its reputation he's skewing it back towards a purer test of
off-road skills. If you think the Tour is a logistical nightmare,
try transporting tents, generators, food and water tanks for
130 riders and a total retinue of 260 through the Australian
outback. And I wonder out loud as we chat if he has more
sympathy with Lévitan now: how would he feel if his riders
started racing for the back, hiding behind termite hills in order

to lose time and be last? 'I don't think anyone gets last because they can't do better. This year the guy who came last is actually a good friend of mine.' A pragmatic response, then – he also mentions that there's not the same money in mountain biking, or the crowds and the publicity that European Grand Tour racing brings. He also has a different management style. 'I don't need to have people there. I want to keep it quite small,' he says. 'Everyone can ring me, all the riders can, and ask me questions personally, or I'll ring them back. I think it gives it a family feeling.'

Of his former life he keeps nothing but memories. That show is over. Over the years he has given away all his bikes, jerseys and trophies. 'I don't collect these kinds of things. I remember them and if I remember it's good, and if I forget it it's good too,' he says. 'A trophy means nothing to me. All the positive things I remember now, and everything I do now, I have to thank my sport for that.'

Gerhard still fields calls from journalists and fans about his *lanterne rouge* years and even now is not averse to a bit of showboating. About six months before the 25th anniversary of his first last place, one of the longest-serving Dutch Tour journalists, Robert Janssens, contacted him, saying that he, Janssens, had wheeled Gerhard's bike for him that day on the Champs-Élysées as Gerhard walked across the line. A Dutch TV station was proposing to send them both to Paris to stage a re-run of that finish. So that was how, after the *gendarmes* had organised a short road closure,[44] they found themselves again walking side by side, both older now and slower, the final 100 metres of the Tour course. Janssens supplied Gerhard his lines,

---

44 Presumably this would not have been possible without the help of the ASO. Lévitan spins in his grave.

which had been broadcast across the world 25 years before, and pushed his bike (or as close a replica of Gerhard's bike as they could muster, since he'd sold it or given it away) while Gerhard, ever the showman, kissed the line.

The last-placed man in a race a quarter of a century ago, deemed important enough to stop the traffic on the world's most famous finishing straight. Making a spectacle, causing a commotion and no doubt ruffling a few feathers, just as he used to. The sponsors would have been proud.

1978
110 starters
Winner: Bernard Hinault, 36.08 km/h
Lanterne rouge: Philippe Tesnière, 34.84 km/h @ 3h52'26"
78 finishers

1979
150 starters
Winner: Bernard Hinault, 36.51 km/h
Lanterne rouge: Gerhard Schönbacher, 35.05 km/h @ 4h19'21"
90 finishers

1980
130 starters
Winner: Joop Zoetemelk, 35.14 km/h
Lanterne rouge: Gerhard Schönbacher, 34.46 km/h @ 2h10'52"
85 finishers

Chapter 9

THE MAVERICK

Beauty comes first, victory is secondary.

Sócrates, 1982

I'd rather finish shattered and last having attacked a hundred times than finish 25th without having tried.

Jacky Durand, 2000

Jacky Durand is the kind of guy old Frenchmen want to touch. I do not say this lightly. He has a presence, a kind of star quality that seems more appropriate to the heroic exploits of cycling's Golden Age than to a windswept car park in Cholet, western France, in 2013. Squint hard enough and you could imagine him wearing a set of dust-covered goggles pulled up on to a flat cap, a spare tubular tyre wrapped snakelike around his shoulders and a knitted polo-neck cycling jersey. Yet 2013 it is, and Jacky is at the start of the Cholet Pays de Loire, a 206-kilometre circular race and an established fixture on France's domestic calendar. The organisers would style it 'La Primavera des Mauges', since it takes place in the Mauges region on the same day as the opening spring Classic, Milan–San Remo, yet there's not much of the style of the *classissima* on show. It's mid-March and the clouds are scudding across the sky with inscrutable vernal intent, a Russian roulette of precipitation. Race HQ in the town's *Salle des Fêtes* looks forlorn, its sponsors' banners twisted over themselves in the wind. In the car park some of the boys' faces (because many of the riders are barely older than that) betray dread, while the older, wiser heads (there are plenty of them too) simply set their chin just so and wait. Later, as they mass for the start, the temperature drops five degrees and cold raindrops strafe the dense peloton, huddled like penguins against an Antarctic breeze, leaving some tangled in translucent rain capes, scrambling to catch up even as the signal is given and the off is offed.

But for now Jacky is bathed in golden sunlight of the particular intensity that only occurs through gaps in large threatening clouds. He is here with Eurosport France, for whom he is now a 'consultant'. At the Tour de France, that involves commentating all day every day through exciting stages and dull, but at Cholet, where there is no live coverage, it means interviewing riders before the event and capturing the local colour for the highlights package that will be shown that evening. He stands tall, intensely scanning the scene for things to do, interviews to make. The cameraman swoops right to shoot some footage of three kids sitting on a wall, waving flags and then Durand is off, threading his way quickly through the crowd to his next target. In the hour before the race he is jumping in and out of team buses, whether they be the shiny edifices of Movistar or Europcar or the relatively tiny motorhome of VC La Pomme Marseille, one of France's more prestigious domestic teams, trailing cameraman and camera behind him. He does so with authority and aplomb; he is a man who has spent his life in the belly of such private sanctuaries and knows his presence is still welcome there. One moment outside, the next, there Jacky is, glimpsed through a windscreen, with his microphone in some skinny lad's face and a glint in his eye that invites confidence. He is in his element.

Born in Laval in the Mayenne department of Normandy only an hour or two north of Cholet, as a kid Jacky stood with his grandparents on the side of the road to watch the Tour come past, and he has raced these roads since he was a *minime*. He moved up to the *cadet* age group and raced some more, though with little outright success, then to the juniors and beyond, pedalling his way along the tried and trusted route from local club to bigger club, *stagiaire* to professional, from changing in mum's hatchback to the team's estate car, minibus, motorhome, superbus, like those parked around here by the *grands fromages* of world cycling. The different buses at Cholet illustrate perfectly the gap in glamour and prestige between even the largest second-tier race and the Tour. It's not that the race isn't hard – it is. The rain that falls today at the start does not dog the riders for long, but there are vicious winds that will tear the peloton apart during the decisive attacks and the rolling *parcours* on narrow, open country roads will catch out anyone who hasn't worked through the winter. The Chinese national champion is here, racing for Champion System, a China-based Pro Continental team. This year's best out of 1.3 billion people (albeit 1.3 billion not-so-interested-in-pro-cycling people), he must wonder how he ended up in Cholet trying to keep warm on a turbo trainer under an awning while a few people mill around, more interested in working out how to cross the road than watching the race preparation. Yet look at the *palmarès* of the race and you'll see some familiar names on the podium across the years – Marc Madiot, Johan Bruyneel and Laurent Desbiens, mixing with Frank Vandenbroucke, Thor

Hushovd and Thomas Voeckler. There is also a sprinkling of *lanternes rouges*: Jimmy Casper and Wim Vansevenant sharing the podium in 2001, Casper popping up again later and Jimmy Engoulvent (*lanterne rouge* 2012) in there too. Engoulvent's on the start line again this year, as is the Minsk Missile, Yauheni Hutarovich (*lanterne rouge* 2011). A podium at the Tour de France has status and meaning outside cycling: non-cyclists understand something of the Tour and the dedication and talent it takes to compete, and a Tour stage winner or a *lanterne rouge* may surface in the wider public's consciousness for a minute, fully formed. But events like Cholet pass under the radar, and they are the unseen reality: years of honing fitness and race-craft in blustery discomfort, jostling for position with the same community of people, perhaps since childhood, meeting and re-meeting at hundreds of small towns and minor stage races around Europe.

Everyone here is, was or will be a brilliant bike racer on his day, but maybe his only shot at recognition on the biggest stage, the Tour, is as a bit-part player, or as the joker in the pack, the king's jester. And maybe that's OK. Maybe it's better to be a small fish in a big pond, the red lantern swinging merrily on the back of the gravy train.

Aside from being *lanterne rouge*, in 1999, Jacky Durand won many other awards, including individual Tour stages, and he has worn both the yellow and polka-dot jerseys for a stage or two. Plus Paris–Tours, two national championships, the Tro–Bro–Léon and stages in Paris–Nice and the Dauphiné. Ergo he is, in Cholet, something of a celebrity. He is big, burnished, weatherproof. As he moves through the crowd it parts, and the old men with their bum-bags and their windcheaters, their tracksuits and their umbrellas, turn, mouths slightly agape, murmuring 'Jacky' as he passes, belatedly sticking a hand out in his wake. Because Jacky Durand is the kind of guy old Frenchmen want to touch.

Earlier that morning when I arrive to interview him he is in his hotel, destroying the breakfast buffet with his Eurosport colleagues. He'd given me directions the night before by phone, from a car on his way from another nearby race, the Classique Loire Atlantique, but couldn't remember quite what the hotel was called.[45] 'The one on the *grande place* where the start is . . .' he says over the road noise, grasping for precision. And, though the name escapes him, he finally skewers it. 'The one where Cofidis is. They're always in the same hotel.' Because that's how it is: the years roll on and the circus moves around the country, around the world, yet race organisers are creatures of habit and some things always stay the same. I sit and wait in the lobby and after he finishes he comes past, huge and still in good shape. 'I'm going to smoke a cigarette,' he says, eyes full of *joie de vivre*, and disappears.

Jacky's biggest win was at the Ronde van Vlaanderen, the Tour of Flanders, one of cycling's Monuments. It came in 1992 when Jacky was 25 and riding for Castorama, and gave him his reputation as a long-break specialist. He was a third-year professional under Cyrille Guimard, the tactical mastermind behind stars including Bernard Hinault, Lucien Van Impe, Laurent Fignon and Greg LeMond, when he got in a break after only 40 kilometres at the Ronde. More precisely, he was riding while Cyrille Guimard was overseeing the team's efforts at another, more winnable, race that was also more important to the sponsors, a French DIY chain. Jacky's leader that day

45 Remember, the man has probably seen in excess of 1,000 nondescript hotels during his careers; I don't blame him.

had withdrawn because of injury, giving all the Castorama riders a free pass in the race. Jacky attacked with a Swiss rider, Thomas Wegmüller, and then on the Bosberg attacked again and launched off on his own. The peloton, which had been too busy marking Sean Kelly, didn't know who this kid was, and Durand was allowed to get away. He won by over 17 minutes, only the third Frenchman ever to take the race and the first since the 1950s. The long break was Jacky's style and he wasn't going to change it just because he was young and unknown and in the big league.

'Voilà, I've always worked like that,' he says. 'I rode my first races at 14, they were 25 kilometres long and I attacked from the start. It was always like that. As a junior the races began to be 80 or 100 kilometres and I did the same thing. And when I passed into the pro ranks people said, "Careful Jacky, it's not the same, it's another level, the races are harder, with more laps." And then after a bit . . .' He pauses for a moment to reflect on the justice of this, that he, a self-proclaimed middle-of-the-pack rider, somehow was allowed to tear off at will, did not have to buckle down in the system in which those with lesser talents were harnessed in support of those with greater. 'Bof,' he finally shrugs. 'I won the Tour of Flanders like that. Then no DS, no manager, dared to say: "Don't do that" since I'd won the Tour of Flanders. So I always had carte blanche and continued to do it my way.'

After Flanders, it was not just carte blanche, it was full-blown adulation from the French public. Soon he was nicknamed 'Dudu', which means something like 'Teddy Bear', and Vélo magazine was publishing a Jackymètre, recording how many kilometres he had spent off the front of the peloton that month. The Belgians, too, embraced him. In 1996 he was stopped for speeding by the Belgian police, and then let off with the words: 'Ah, Jacky Durand, you won the Ronde in '92.'

Such is the power of that race in Belgium.

Despite Flanders and his other wins, Durand is modest about his talents and his achievements. When your working life consists of being ranked daily or weekly against your colleagues, when in each race you put everything on the line and you can be ruthlessly exposed if your preparation, fitness or abilities are not up to scratch, you are constantly bumping up against failure. As an ex-pro once pointed out to me, the main reason many riders open their mouth in public is to explain why they didn't win. And while some may choose to hide from the truth, or delude themselves why things aren't working out, many *lanternes rouges* possess a brutal, matter-of-fact honesty about their talents, as if the absolute loss has brought clarity, even a kind of reconciliation, to them.

And yet there is always the possibility of upsetting the applecart.

'I had a motto: "In cycling, it's not necessarily the strongest who wins" – luckily for me, since otherwise I wouldn't have won much!' Jacky laughs. This is clearly familiar ground. Something that people ask a lot, yes, but also something about which he has thought long and hard: how on earth he, the class clown, triumphed over so many other more able riders. It's the 'you-make-your-own luck' school of racing. 'I won some races where I really shouldn't have won,' he says. 'At the Tour of Flanders, I wasn't one of the strongest. I won a stage of the Midi Libre at the top of Mont Saint-Clair, which is completely unimaginable. *Mais voilà*. It's because I dared and nobody else did.'

We're slurping on coffee he's salvaged for us from the wreckage of breakfast, which has now also been ravaged by Cofidis riders. He stops talking to chat to one of them wandering past, then turns back, and I'm wondering if he always meant it: if every single dig was an authentic break for victory. Riders regularly

attack when they know they have no chance of succeeding, make
an *échappée bidon*, a suicide break, simply for the sponsors or
to stretch their legs before settling contentedly back into the
peloton's embrace . . . but not Jacky. He warms to his theme:
'It's true you see riders sometimes, particularly on the Tour de
France, who know absolutely that they're not going to win, but
I always had a little idea at the back of my mind . . .' He stops,
backs up and continues. 'Some of the time I knew I had no
chance at all, but there is always *les aléas* that makes . . . *voilà*
. . . when I won the stage of the Midi Libre on Mont Saint-
Clair, I was on a solo breakaway, I had no chance of winning,
but there was this little *aléa* that happened – a level crossing
that closed in front of the peloton. It was thanks to that I won.
I tell you, in cycling nothing is set in stone, there's always an
élément perturbateur and I take advantage of it.'

Les aléas: it's a little phrase Jacky likes – the unforeseeable,
unpredictable, unquantifiable unknowns that make racing more
than a matter of physical prowess and training. Whether that's
the peloton refusing to chase Pierre Matignon down on the
Puy de Dôme until it is too late or something more *deus ex
machina*, more of an unbelievable B-movie plot twist. The
last-minute inheritance from a dotty old aunt that saves the
business; the solar eclipse that helps the hero escape the natives;
the freight train at the level crossing that halts the peloton,
the thwarted climbers buzzing like little wasps, and lets the
lumbering *baroudeur* win on the summit finish. These things
can happen, honest.

Les aléas did not, however, treat him at all well in 1999. It
was a Tour he went into riding for a new team, with good form
and relatively high – though realistic – hopes. 'I was coming
out of eight or nine years with French teams, arriving at Lotto
for two years, and I honestly think I was hired for that – to

shine in the Tour de France. They knew me. I'd won a stage of Paris–Nice, everything was going well, and I arrived at the Tour in good condition with . . . not a desire to shine in the general classification, since I'd never done that, but to challenge for stages. Everything went well at the start, but it became more difficult after three days because there was the famous Saint-Nazaire stage, with the Passage du Gois, and I was one of the many, many riders who hit the floor. The misery started there.'

The Passage du Gois is a four-kilometre-long causeway linking the Île de Noirmoutier to the Loire mainland at Belvoir in western France, and its appearance in the 1999 Tour has passed into legend. Twice a day the narrow road is submerged completely by the tide, and it is safe to pass only during a four-hour window around the low-tide mark. The previous time it featured in the Tour, in 1993, a group of 40 riders, including Jacky, escaped into the mists swirling over the seabed, although they were later caught. In 1999 the race accelerated in the run-up to the causeway as the teams, all wishing not to get caught behind any crashes, jostled for position at the front of the pack. Lance Armstrong was among those who was determined to go through early, and his vigilance was rewarded when a huge pile-up on the slippery road, its surface criss-crossed by drainage channels, delayed many of his main rivals. While they spent precious minutes disentangling their bikes, the front group accelerated and GC contenders Ivan Gotti and Alex Zülle eventually trailed in more than six minutes back. Armstrong and US Postal did not relax until stage nine, which finished in Sestriere in the Alps – this was his first Tour after recovering from cancer, and his likely performance in the high mountains against the specialist climbers was unknown – but the GC race was essentially over when the first rider slipped and fell on the seaweed-strewn Passage.

Armstrong had been wise and got lucky, but Jacky's luck very nearly deserted him completely. At the start of the Passage he was in the day's only breakaway, dangling 15 seconds in front of the peloton, but that did not keep him from harm. He came down in the big crash, extricated himself and checked he wasn't too badly hurt. 'I wasn't good, wasn't good at all,' he says (later he'd find out he'd dislocated his right shoulder). 'I got going again with a completely busted bike. And I had to put the hammer down to try to get back to a group, since there were riders all over the road. Suddenly my car arrived and I said to them, "I have to change bike, I have to change bike." They said, "OK, we'll overtake and stop, to give you one." Except I only had one working brake, and as I started braking, it failed. Nothing left at all. And I had team cars overtaking at 150 kilometres an hour on my left catching up with the different groups, and my team car in front of me and CLAQUE!' He claps his hands together loudly and the Cofidis riders lining up waiting to leave the hotel look over. 'So I hit the car, slammed into the boot and VVVVVRAM!!' He becomes even more animated. 'I fall on to the road, the team cars are coming, they brake and a Mapei car starts to drive over my leg.'

Right on your leg?! I splutter. But I look at the photos later and he's right. He's face down across the road and Mapei's Fiat Marea is right on his leg.

'Afterwards, it was a calvary to get to Saint-Nazaire.'

No shit, I think.

Fearing elimination, he limped in – almost literally – around 19 minutes after the stage winner Tom Steels. To his surprise he made the time cut. Even more to his surprise, he was also given the day's combativity award. Decided by a panel of judges, the Prix de la Combativité is awarded daily during the Tour to that stage's most attacking rider. For which honour the rider receives a cash prize, the right to wear a red number on the next day's stage and, in 1999, a Camembert – it was sponsored by a cheese manufacturer called Coeur de Lion. That's 'lionheart' to you and me – which seems entirely apt for Jacky that day, and not only in the way they intended. 'Every year I've raced the Tour, I've always attacked,' Jacky told *L'Équipe* that year, on one of the days he won a Camembert. 'This year because of my fall at the start of the race I've attacked, but only backwards.'

To compound his misery the following day's stage was due to finish in his home town, on his home roads, the ones he'd trained on after helping his parents with the farm work after school, then as a *jeune espoir* and a young pro. 'When I saw the route of the Tour, I marked that stage. I knew it by heart, obviously. It passed right by the village where I was born, it arrived at Laval . . . it was home,' he says. Now, everything was ruined. 'The night before I knew I had no chance of showing myself and the only goal was to get to the finish line. I remember the masseurs looking after me and I felt in their conversation that it was my last day, that my Tour de France road was stopping there. I was in a terrible state, bandages everywhere, and then after two or three kilometres of racing I was dropped.'

Jacky was left to languish among the team cars for 20 kilometres or more before making it into the shelter of the peloton. And there at the back of the bunch he stayed, unable to exert any force on the handlebars, commiserating with Michele Coppolillo, an Italian from the Mercatone team who'd taken a chunk out of his leg with his brake lever, trailing in on the increasingly familiar roads. For a while he counted the bandanas worn by his fans, who were out in force sporting his signature look. 'All my supporters were waiting for me,' he said. 'I'd told them I wasn't going to do a thing but in vain, they still had a slim hope of seeing me attack. I got to where I had decided in advance to attack, 30 or 40 kilometres from the finish, and it was there I was dropped and I finished my home stage on my own.'

Family, friends and supporters were there, and his mum cried tears of joy as he crossed the line in Laval.

Quite what more it would take to keep Jacky Durand down than a car on his leg is difficult to say, but that was his darkest moment of that Tour. Ever the optimist, he was already looking ahead. 'I had to get through the day. I knew that I'd have 48 tough hours after the fall, and I'd got through one,' he says. 'I told myself that if I could get through these two days, I'd see about attacking again afterwards.'

Did you not consider giving up at any point, I ask, and Jacky scoffs. 'Ah non, non, non, not after those 48 hours. I'm of the persuasion that you have to treat pain with pain. I mean, if you hurt everywhere, you'll forget it if you hurt yourself some more attacking. I knew it would come back after.'

Jacky makes it to Blois and then to Amiens, and then he is as good as his word: he starts attacking. He is not at this point in the *lanterne rouge* position and there is still a lot to play for. On the stage to Thionville he feels he has good legs and attacks off the front with 144 kilometres to go. 'I think I would have won the stage if there wasn't a rider from Aubervillier ahead . . . he went first and I went behind. I wanted him to wait for me, but he never did. I think it was Lylian Lebreton,' Jacky says of his adversary and potential friend who'd gone on a solo break with nearly 200 kilometres of racing remaining. Lylian's DS was telling him not to wait for Jacky because he feared that Jacky would get the better of Lebreton if it came down to a sprint. 'But when I got to him, he was dead! It was a crap strategy, because everyone knows the peloton rides to the time gaps. The peloton was watching the gap to Lebreton, who was cooked – they saw he had quite a big lead, so they began to ride hard. Now, if he'd waited for me, the gap would have been smaller and I think we could have won, since we weren't caught far from the finish,' he says.

At the finish he was surrounded by newspapers eager to hear about the resurrection of Jacky Durand: 'You might call it suicidal to ride into a headwind behind a man with a seven-minute lead, but I put myself to work as if I was in a solo break out front,' he said, bent over his bike and exhausted, after being caught with four kilometres to go. Jacky was back.

Les écarts: the time gaps. Along with *les aléas* it's something that preoccupies Jacky a lot. Whereas most of the *lanternes rouges* I speak to spend their *lanterne rouge* Tour preoccupied by the cut off, Jacky was more interested in measuring and controlling the seconds he'd gained on the peloton. Is that what runs through your mind when you're out on your own? 'I'd say that you focus on the time gaps, on not forgetting anything, eating, looking at the board,' he says, referring to the *ardoise*, the blackboard carried on a motorbike that in the days before race radios was a breakaway's only indication of what the time gap was. 'But there were times when I was riding happily, and I'd look at the landscapes, the spectators, who were always surprised to see me talking. But you have to manage your effort differently in a break. It's not attack, attack, go all out and see where it leads. You must get a lead on the peloton but not too much, so they're not tempted to come after you. It's a game of positioning – that's where my efforts went. I'd keep an eye on the board, play with the gaps a bit. It was always *les écarts*, *les écarts*, *les écarts*. If the peloton accelerated, maybe I'd accelerate too, to make them doubt. It was a game of hide-and-seek.'

He was off playing hide-and-seek with the peloton again on stage 14, just before the Pyrenees, though he'd lost a lot more time to yellow jersey Lance Armstrong on the way there. There'd been the small matter of the Alps to negotiate first, and he'd finished 45 minutes behind the American and endured a hailstorm on the Col du Galibier on the stage to Sestriere. The next day he tried attacking within sight of Alpe d'Huez – it was Bastille Day after all – but came in second last. Add in another four minutes lost on 15 July, helping his ill teammate Thierry Marichal make the cut, and Jacky was in penultimate place on the GC, over two hours down and just above the ailing sprinter Jay Sweet. His breakaway partner on stage 14, which ran from Castres, in the rolling hills of Cathar country, to Saint-Gaudens, at the foot of the Pyrenees, was Dmitry Konyshev, an experienced old stomper of pedals and former Soviet national champion. The pair had escaped with only 10 kilometres gone – and 189 left to go through the fields of sunflowers to Saint-Gaudens.

Did Konyshev seem like a good bet as a breakaway partner? 'I didn't have a favourite rider,' he says. 'Let's say I'd calculate a little who I went with. Sometimes I'd say "Let's have a go" in the peloton. I'd look for someone in good shape, who was riding well, who was someone I could beat in the end!' His eyes sparkle, he slurps some coffee, which he has had refilled by a waitress, and smiles. Unfortunately Jacky's powers of discernment failed him in this instance, since Konyshev dropped him before the finale and Jacky could only finish fifth. 'I used too much energy in the first breakaway,' he explained ruefully at the finish. But he soon perked up and, whether it was due to the heat or the effort, began uncharacteristically to talk about himself in the third person. 'Jacky Durand doesn't let a failure slow him down. He's going to have a couple of difficult days in the Pyrenees

on Tuesday and Wednesday, but he'll make the time cut and
if his legs are good he'll be there at the end of the Tour!'

Perhaps he'd been cheered by the news that he'd just topped
the combativity classification, having collected several more
Coeurs de Lion Camemberts since the Passage du Gois. 'I'm
from Normandy, I love cheese,' he explained in a newspaper
article under the headline *Jacky Durand aime le Fromage*.
He was probably less aware that he was now *lanterne rouge*,
after Jay Sweet missed the time cut on stage 15. The irony
of leading both was not, however, lost on him. 'Yes it was a
paradox,' he laughs again, as he remembers joking about the
lanterne. 'I was "fighting" for it, in inverted commas, at least in
the last week, and I was messing around with Pascal Deramé,
Lance Armstrong's teammate,' Jacky says. 'We were on almost
exactly the same time, just before the Futuroscope time trial
[the penultimate stage] and we were on a flat stage. I'd tried
attacking at the start, for that win-that-never-was, but didn't
succeed, so with seven or eight kilometres to go, I let myself
be dropped from the peloton. I knew that Pascal couldn't do
the same because he had to stay at the front to protect Lance
. . . I practically stopped. I thought, *bof*, better to be last than
second last.'

Think about that stage to Futuroscope: 187.5 flat kilometres
through a rather dull part of central France to an amusement
park that, as my 12-year-old self can attest, is frankly not very
amusing. The GC's been sewn up for weeks, it's the fag end
of a pretty dull Tour, yet Jacky keeps on trying, pinging off the
front with alacrity at the start of the stage, then sitting up to
become the last man on the course. From one extreme to the
other: there was no middle ground in his philosophy. He must
have had off days here and there, whole races of just pushing
the pedals and thinking about the hotel dinner waiting at the

end, but by nature he was 100 per cent committed, each attack completely intentional yet also a kind of *acte gratuit* undertaken for the joy of animating the race, for the sheer hell of it. To *L'Équipe* on the rest day after his Saint-Gaudens attack he said: 'I'm not a revolutionary of any sort, but on the bike I've always refused to come out of a mould. It astonishes me that most riders are followers, even sheep. A lot of them, the only people who know they're in the Tour are their *directeurs sportifs*. I couldn't do the job like that. They finish the Tour without having attacked once, maybe the whole of the season, even the whole of their career. I'd rather finish shattered and last having attacked 100 times than finish 25th without having tried.'

It's something he still sticks by. I mention to him his other placings, his top 10s and near misses, and he immediately comes back, almost defiantly: 'I never raced to place in the top 10, I raced always for the win or nothing, but so I could say to myself in the evening: "I've no regrets, I tried." I often see riders who after a stage say: "If I'd known . . . I maybe should have gone in that break . . ." Not me. You could say that 98 per cent of my attempts failed, *mais voilà*. I tried everything I had for the win.'

There's a pride in riding like that, in doing everything with purpose – and you certainly don't end your career as something of a national treasure if you play it safe, hedge your bets. Is he proud of his reputation as a rider? 'Of course – it's my trademark. There are the connoisseurs who know my *palmarès*, but for a lot of French people, Jacky Durand, who is he, he's the guy who got in long breakaways and got caught a kilometre from the line. *C'est le baroudeur*. It's stuck with me since I was a kid.'

I ask him if he's proud of being *lanterne rouge*, and the answer is a bit more nuanced: 'Yes, I'm proud.' A pause. 'Well, I didn't go looking for it, because at the Tour you think more about winning stages than getting the *lanterne rouge*. But it usually happens like that – it's the rider who one evening realises he's last and thinks, oh that could be nice. But that only happens in the last couple of days.' His thoughts return to the stage to Futuroscope, where he tried to get away before sitting up and losing the time: 'I really only thought about it on the day before the time trial, but I'd done everything I could to get in a break. If I could have got in a break I could have gained 10 or 12 minutes and won the stage, which would have been much more valuable and powerful.'

He looks slightly crestfallen at this, the one that got away, and it's clear he really *feels* the race – the ups and downs, good luck and bad, the possibilities and the missed opportunities. Durand retired after the 2004 season after getting no offers of a contract for 2005, but soon found a job with Eurosport. I put it to him that being a keen observer of the race helped him – both at the time and in his subsequent career. He agrees: 'I always read the race well, whether that was for me or even, sometimes, for a teammate, when I saw a break forming that I thought was the one, but I didn't have the legs . . . that's how I got my role as a consultant. I've seen everything. If you're "strong", you don't really need tactics. But you need them sometimes. I've often seen really strong riders who haven't the *palmarès* they should – they should have won a lot more but they raced tactically badly because they thought they were better than the rest.'

Pure strength – whether individual or as a team – is sometimes the only tactic you need. Armstrong and US Postal that year showed that. But when you don't have it, you use your head, and in Jacky's case that took him to the front, and the back, and a lot further than that.

*

Later on, as I watch Durand working the car park, I realise that I had come to Cholet to talk to a man about last place but instead had been treated to a masterclass in the art of the break by one of its greatest ever exponents. That's why his legions of fans are still so passionate, and pension-age Frenchmen are left trailing in his wake. They're part of a great French tradition of hero worship: years ago those old men probably reached their infant hands towards Louison Bobet or Jacques Anquetil. And if Jacky, along with Laurent Jalabert and Richard Virenque – either minor heroes, or flawed, or both – were the best that French cycling could do in the '90s and early 2000s, then that's perhaps a reflection of the fallen state of the sport in France in those years.

In 1999 there was no French stage winner for the first time since 1926. There was much public soul-searching and France's press conducted an inquest, attributing the failure variously to the *peloton à deux vitesses* ('the two-speed peloton' – because even then in the so-called Tour of Renewal there were doubts about how clean the peloton was) to the lower numbers of French riders in the race that year (they were outnumbered by Italians in their national Tour) and to simple general, inexorable decline and fall.

Lance Armstrong in 1999 – and subsequent years until his unmasking – proved that there can be a kind of banality to winning. Jacky made racing exciting. He still does. Days before Cholet, I watched Paris–Nice on French television, with Durand commentating on a lumpy day in the Massif Central. Thomas Voeckler, perhaps Jacky's closest modern-day counterpart, is attacking and Jacky is animated: he thinks that, whatever the final outcome, this was the right place to attack; thinks it might stick; thinks that Voeckler could win it. Voeckler is, of course, reeled in pretty sharply. Hope springs eternal. Like Icarus, Jacky usually flew too close to the sun, but, surely, every time we read the Icarus legend we do so in the hope that, this time, the boy will not fall.

And then there is that image from 1999 of the *lanterne rouge* – that award about which the Tour has been so ambivalent – taking to the podium on the Champs-Élysées in Jacky's burly, still bandaged form. Because Jacky has won the year's overall combativity award. If you didn't know the circumstances or the man, this might seem a supremely counterintuitive state of affairs – the Camembert and the *lanterne*. And Jacky was alive to the symbolism of it. He doesn't even remember how much money the combativity award was worth. All that mattered to him was standing there proudly on the Champs-Élysées as 'La Marseillaise' rang out.

'For me, the best bit was climbing on to the Tour de France podium, there in the middle, in front of the Arc de Triomphe on the Champs-Élysées,' Jacky said to me in Cholet. 'It was a joy and a relief because I remember after three days, at Saint-Nazaire, I said that the Champs-Élysées was still my goal. I wanted to win stages; I wanted to see Paris. But I knew, and the team did too, that I had very little chance of seeing the cobbles of the Champs-Élysées. So I told myself on that podium that considering how I'd got there, it was a victory.'

1999
180 starters
'Winner': Lance Armstrong, 42.28 km/h
Lanterne rouge: Jacky Durand, 40.80 km/h @ 3h19'09"
141 finishers

Chapter 10

THE FALL GUY

There is a long-held belief that sport embodies the values of fair play and honesty that we want our children exposed to. Perhaps we need to reassess that belief; maybe we should consider whether sport may, in fact, be a corrupting influence, especially the closer an athlete gets to elite level.

John Fahey, president of WADA, during the fallout of the Armstrong scandal, 2013

So the Platonic year
Whirls out new right and wrong,
Whirls in the old instead;
All men are dancers and their tread
Goes to the barbarous clangour of a gong.

'The Tower', W.B. Yeats

Cholet, where I met Jacky, has its place in Tour history, and a dark one at that. It was there on the evening of 15 July 1998 that gendarmes were waiting on the finish line to arrest Bruno Roussel and Eric Rijckaert, respectively manager and doctor of the Festina team. The previous week, a Festina *soigneur* had been stopped on the Belgian border with a team car full of illegal drugs. The team tried to distance itself from him, but eventually the Festina scandal engulfed the whole 1998 Tour. It was one of the most shocking events to happen in any sport in the modern era, but unfortunately not the last time it happened in cycling. With the pressure mounting on Lance Armstrong following his second retirement, and then his accusation by WADA in 2012, his unmasking and eventual appeal for absolution from Oprah's couch, doping had become impossible to ignore.

It's tempting to think that during all those bad years doping was just going on at the front of the peloton and that it is all about winning. Bjarne Riis, Jan Ullrich, Armstrong and Floyd Landis are collectively a decade of Tour de France yellow jerseys subsequently proven to have cheated during their careers, and these are the cases that receive the most attention. 'Winners use drugs' is the '90s' perversion of the old FBI anti-drugs slogan – and the unspoken corollary is that losers do not. But that's not true. There were also those doping simply to survive, hanging on to the tassels of the magic carpet by their fingertips, whooshed along in the crazy, brutal world of professional cycling with a long way to fall if they lost their purchase. Men just wanting a contract for the following season, to put food on the table for the kids and pay the mortgage. Learn your craft, *faire le métier*. Dig even a little into the histories of the *lanternes rouges* in these pages and it's easy to find many publicly known doping incidents. When Tony Hoar raced in the '50s there were no anti-doping rules, riders would drop back to team cars to administer the goods and he saw one man almost die. (There is also a frankly unrepeatable story about an iconic French rider self-administering strychnine suppositories mid-race . . .) In 1969, meanwhile, Pierre Matignon was penalised for a doping offence and was pitied rather than pilloried in the press. Many of these incidents I have not mentioned, because they were not relevant to the story of the back of the race. Perhaps, like a lot of people, I'd been side-stepping the issue of doping, pretending it wasn't part of my story, whereas in truth it had been something I'd been brushing up against everywhere. Now it was time to confront it head on.

It is now crystal clear – if somehow it wasn't before – that in the 1990s many riders at all levels used sophisticated performance-enhancing drugs and blood transfusions, and that includes some of the *lanternes rouges*. Jacky Durand, that improbable podium star in Paris, admitted, under pressure from a French Senate investigation, that he'd taken EPO; he'd also tested positive for nandrolone at the Côte Picarde race in 1996 and was questioned several times in the Dr Mabuse investigations, one of the era's big drugs scandals, while Rodolfo Massi (*lanterne rouge* 1990) was nicknamed *Il Farmacista* in the peloton and was arrested in 1998 (actually the first cyclist to be arrested) for 'inciting and facilitating the use of doping substances' and 'importing, selling and transferring poisonous substances' when cortico-steroids were found in his hotel room. He was holder of the Tour's polka-dot jersey at the time. And then there's Philippe Gaumont, *lanterne rouge* in 1997. We'll never know how many riders were doping in the 1997 Tour, coming as it did on the eve of the big Festina shakeout, but pick a number out of the air and it might well have three figures. And yet only one can win. If you're a rider, doping and still coming last, how do you reconcile that – and what if those performance-enhancing drugs actually made you go slower? I was going to talk to Gaumont to find out.

'I doped to exist . . . but I lost a lot,' Gaumont wrote in his autobiography, *Prisonnier du Dopage* (*Prisoner of Doping*). He

was one of the *gros moteurs*, the big engines, of the peloton in
the '90s, having come to prominence as a 19-year-old surprise
inclusion in the French 100-kilometre time trial quartet at the
1992 Barcelona Olympics, where he had helped power them to
bronze behind the untouchable German and Italian teams. In
1994 he signed for Castorama and entered a professional cycling
culture in which many teams encouraged and organised doping.
'*Chez les pros, on ne peut pas gagner une course à l'eau claire*'
('Pro racing is not won on water alone') was a common dictum,
and for many drug taking was as routine as shaving their legs.
Gaumont remembers as a neo pro watching the team's older
riders meet with the team doctor to demand he supply them
EPO; the blood booster hadn't yet entered the French peloton
but they knew the steroids they used habitually wouldn't cut it
against the Italians in that year's Tour. By then even the 'clean'
young Gaumont was injecting himself and swallowing up to 20
pills – legal supplements and vitamins – daily. That evening, 27
April 1994, he doped for the first time with Kenacort, a steroid.
There began a career during which, he said when looking back,
'I swallowed everything that might possibly make me go faster.
That was my reality. At no time during those 10 years did I
imagine you could be a bike racer in any other way.'

As a youngster he was already under pressure to get results
in the one-day Classics, and soon he would be spending a large
part of his modest salary of 25,000 francs a month (around
£2,500) on his 'preparations'.

Gaumont moved to another French team, Gan, for 1996 and
the following year joined Cofidis, a new team headed by super-
directeur sportif Cyrille Guimard, who had given him his start
at Castorama. By then Gaumont had already received his first
positive test for anabolic steroids, at the Côte Picarde in 1996
(the same race as Jacky Durand). 'Everyone was driving at 200

kilometres an hour, but I got flashed by the speed camera,' he said in an interview about a later suspension, and he was right: everyone was doing it. Yet he was unlucky or careless enough to get caught, and he had also earned himself a reputation as a loudmouth, not good in the closed circle of professional doping.

Somewhere in all of this Philippe had also discovered a latent tendency for overdoing things – 'always living to excess' as he put it later – and became immersed in a damaging culture among certain French riders at the time of abusing drugs of all kinds. 'Very quickly,' he writes, 'I noticed the gulf in our mentalities. The Italians, the Swiss, the Spanish and the Americans only used banned products to improve their performance. We French doped, but we also regularly got wasted on amphetamines and *pot Belge.*'

In the 1990s, when many countries had rave, France, it seems, had cycling, and French cycling teams were frequently riven by cliques that formed around partying and a very old-school attitude to training and racing. It was at a teammate's wedding that he first took *pot Belge*, an injectable concoction of amphetamines, caffeine and, frequently, cocaine, heroin or anything else people cared to add. A group of cyclists retreated to a hotel room, prepared a syringe for Gaumont and then each one in turn pushed the plunger down, a Mafia-esque ritual baptising him into the circle of trust and ensuring they were all implicated in the action. The weekend after was the same. This time Gaumont stayed up all night and then the following afternoon raced and won a 'gentlemen's' cyclocross race (involving teams comprising one professional and one amateur rider).

After that, it was open season – steroids, hormones, EPO, amphetamines – provided that the drugs were balanced by good results. He would test positive for nandrolone, a steroid, in 1998, and be implicated in the Dr Mabuse affair before his career finally came to an end in the drugs scandal that engulfed Cofidis in 2004. The impression his words give is one of chaos and a spiral into addiction, a man always crashing in the same car.

While racing, Gaumont was a divisive figure, seen by some as an addict and a cheat; by others, as a friend and loyal workmate; some claimed he was supplying drugs to his team (he denied this); others that he was a victim – an impressionable young man led into harm's way, introduced into an immoral system that did not care about his physical, emotional or professional well-being. Yet he was also a charismatic, handsome ladies' man who liked the rock-star spotlight as well as a reckless party animal who before a time trial in a stage race might stay up all night drinking with his partner-in-crime Frank Vandenbroucke and, still drunk, ride off the road several times the next day. A gifted cyclist too: time trials, smaller stage races and a minor Classics star. Twice a top-25 finisher in Paris–Roubaix, he had a real shot at winning it in 2001 before he broke his leg in a crash on the Arenberg trench. And, according to his former sponsor, the boss of Cofidis: 'Even if he seems big and proud, he's fragile. Every setback screws him up.' Shy and open and too frank, in his words; easily influenced, without limits, a bully and a manipulator in others.

I was simultaneously intrigued and intimidated. You can imagine how I was dreading getting in touch.

'J'entends une voix anglaise là.' I hear an English voice . . . and I hear a languorous, somewhat world-weary voice on the other end of the phone line. Playful, almost teasing. The serpent and the apple. He was pleasant, interested in the *lanterne rouge* project and not at all 'lukewarm' as I'd been warned by a local journalist who had put me in touch. We arranged a meeting.

In 2011 he'd moved from his native Picardy an hour or so north-east – nearer Roubaix, nearer Belgium – to Lens, to open a brasserie-bar. That's why I am sitting in a bar in Lens, home town of that famous first Tour cheater, Maurice Garin, watching the rain fall through the glare of the streetlights at dusk on the neat, red-brick streets, feeling as if I've stumbled into a scene from a Marcel Carné film. Philippe is a few minutes late, so I call his phone. Fumbling, static, a disoriented voice and the sounds of driving. He at first wants to rearrange for the following day then changes his mind, says he'll be there in an hour. I order a Coke and select a seat as MTV blares from several screens around the room. Above my head, a photo of Philippe – tall, well built, his arms aloft, the Cofidis sun logo shining from his chest as he crosses the finish line to win Gent–Wevelgem, the massed peloton crowding the background of the shot. It's the only bit of cycling memorabilia in the place.

That win came in April 1997, and was the biggest of Gaumont's career to that point. Among Frenchmen, only Jacques Anquetil and Bernard Hinault had won the prestigious Classic before, and it confirmed that Philippe was back on the right track after sitting on the sidelines having been banned for most of 1996. The French press had high hopes for him in 1997 (an *éclat* of wishful thinking had seen the phrase 'the new Hinault' bandied about) and it seemed he might be shaping up for a good tilt at the Tour.

In fact, in his time off he'd become heavily reliant on *pot Belge*, both recreationally and as a training aid. In the spring of 1997, in advance of the Tour, Cofidis held a training camp in the Pyrenees. They were reconnoitring one of the main mountain stages, a 252.5-kilometre epic that finished on the Arcalis climb in Andorra, 18 kilometres long and rising above 2,000 metres. The team's plan was to ride half the stage's major climbs – the Pas de la Case, the Col d'Ordino and the Arcalis – then turn around and ride back to base at Font Romeu. Gaumont's plan, hatched with a teammate, was to take amphetamines while doing so. Each put a capsule in his jersey pocket and secreted a syringe of *pot Belge* in his jacket, which they stored in the team car, and went on their way. Both waited to take the pill on the second climb, delaying to avoid the 'descent into hell' (as coming down before the end of a training session was known); but by the mid-way point the pills were doing nothing, so they retrieved their jackets for the return leg, stopped as if to pee and injected themselves by the side of the road. 'We descended all out, as in a dream,' Gaumont said – as you might have expected from two *allumé* (literally 'lit up' or 'switched on') riders. What you wouldn't expect is that on the climbs back to Font Romeu they repeatedly rode their teammates, including the specialist climbers, off their wheels. Gaumont: 1.86 metres, 90 kilograms; TT and budding Classics specialist; angel of the mountains.

The Coke is almost finished, only a weak, ice-diluted splash remains. The hour of our rearranged appointment has been and gone, so I ring Philippe again and leave a message. A few minutes later a woman comes over. It's his wife, co-owner of the brasserie. She says there's been a family emergency, he has unexpectedly had to fetch the kids and he won't make it back that evening. He's still happy to grant an interview, perhaps tomorrow; I thank her and explain my schedule, sit back down and silently chide myself for imagining something salacious going on. This is, after all, a penitent ex-doper, a family man who has paid for his mistakes and turned himself around, who now has a thriving business and a new life. For years he has been outspoken against doping. Perhaps not as prominently as his former teammate David Millar, but quietly and locally campaigning for a change in the system ruling pro cycling, which, while also recognising his own weaknesses, he has come to view as corrupting and flawed. In 2012 he said to *La Voix du Nord*, his local paper: 'There will always be a big cloud over the peloton as long as this world is managed by former dopers. We need a clean break. Those leading the anti-doping fight have to be completely outside the cycling world, and outside sports' governing bodies in general.' According to a study by the website Cyclisme-Dopage.com, in association with the crusading journalist Pierre Ballester,[46] in the 2013 WorldTour squads there were 105 ex-riders in meaningful management positions, and 33 of those – that's 31 per cent – had in the past been caught doping. Only AG2R and Team Sky were completely free of this shadow. 'We need a clean break.'

Philippe Gaumont's clean break comes on 20 January 2004 after a former Cofidis rider, Marek Rutkiewicz, is arrested in possession of banned substances. Soon another former rider and a current *soigneur* are also implicated, and on his return from a Spanish training camp Gaumont, by that point one of the senior, most influential riders on the team, is pulled aside at customs by police and arrested. This time, rather than deny, lie and stonewall as riders fingered during that era often did, Gaumont, gnawed by guilt, deranged by drugs and exhausted by lying for so long, decides to tell the ugly truth – and there is a lot of it. In the process he implicates many other riders and the Cofidis affair snowballs in importance. He also explains many of the tricks of how to get away with using performance-enhancing

---

46 Among many anti-doping pieces, Ballester co-wrote with David Walsh the 2004 exposé *LA Confidentiel: les Secrets de Lance Armstrong*.

drugs. For example: simulate saddle problems by rubbing salt on to your scrotum until it's bleeding raw, to procure a 'therapeutic use exemption' for cortisone from a sympathetic doctor. Because once the steroids are in your blood it's impossible to tell how they got there, so you can inject with impunity. Little of what he says is pretty and eventually Cofidis is adjudged to have known about – and therefore tacitly encouraged – the doping on the team. The prosecution in the case against Gaumont and other riders talks about the team's *culture de la séringue*, 'syringe culture'. The sentences eventually handed down to the riders are comparatively lenient, perhaps taking into account the systemic nature of the problem, but all receive sporting bans and Gaumont never cycles competitively again.

So Philippe is not coming. I gather my things together, wondering how to measure this missed opportunity on the yardstick of success or failure. Because even if I have missed Gaumont this time I feel that, as the last light disappears from Lens and the Grill Pizza and McEwan's Pub signs neon ever brighter, sitting in Gaumont's restaurant under a picture of him winning Gent–Wevelgem in 1997, somehow I'm winning too – somehow I'm getting to the bottom of things. That said, my glass is empty and my data-roaming bill is doubtless astronomical. It's dark and I'm starving. I go to the takeaway counter that forms part of the brasserie and get some chips. They're good. Proper Belgian-style *frites*. Mayonnaise.

After his turbo-charged Pyrenees training camp Gaumont continued to go well, and continued to use both performance-enhancing and performance-decreasing drugs. This is in part thanks to one of his Cofidis teammates, who he says took him in hand before Gent–Wevelgem, helping him with his drug regime and adding human growth hormone (HGH) to the chemical mix.

In 1997 EPO is still undetectable but the UCI has introduced a rule that bans from competition cyclists whose haematocrit (red blood cell level) exceeds 50 per cent of their blood volume. Since EPO increases haematocrit, in turn boosting performance and recovery by enabling more oxygen to be carried around the body, it is (naively at best) hoped that this will stamp out EPO abuse. In practice capping haematocrit levels only regulates and does not stop cyclists using EPO: micro-dosing can easily take a careful user up to but not over the line, allowing him to continue racing doped. Nevertheless, the new rule has significant ramifications. First, because natural haematocrit levels vary some riders will now benefit from EPO's effects more than others. Consider someone naturally at 48 per cent and someone naturally at 43 per cent. To reach a 'safe' doped level of 49 per cent the former can only boost his natural haematocrit by one percentage point, but the latter can shoot for six percentage points' change. So while the first has improved his oxygen-carrying capacity by only a tiny amount, the second has added up to 14 per cent more oxygen to his blood: the potential to improve performance is still there but, thanks to the UCI rule, henceforth more unequally distributed. Consequently, explains Gaumont, some cyclists were branching out, looking for new competitive advantages over their peers. Second, the change in EPO use affects every other part of a cyclist's drug regime. Gaumont says his 'helpful' teammate, pre-1997, would easily and deliberately have surpassed 50 per cent haematocrit thanks to EPO (and Bjarne Riis's nickname was 'Monsieur 60 Per Cent'); but without all that extra oxygen zinging round the system, it's easier to overdose on human growth hormone and, in the parlance, become *bloqué*: blocked. Gaumont's teammate isn't helping him out of the kindness of his heart: Philippe is the guinea pig he is using to work out the appropriate HGH dose in a post-50 per cent age.

Five days before the Tour Gaumont is taking two units a day, the same amount as before Gent–Wevelgem. However, this time the hormone does not 'pass', probably because of the heat, and Gaumont, faced with the biggest race of his career, finds himself well and truly *bloqué*. The race starts and there is nothing to do except get on with it and ride. In the Tour's third stage, Cofidis's number-one man, the seasoned champion Tony Rominger, abandons after breaking his collarbone – which should have been a shining opportunity for a young contender to step up and fill his Sidis. (It's one unlucky break too many for Rominger who, aged 37, consequently retires.) But neither Rominger's misfortune nor anything else that happens early in that Tour has much bearing on Gaumont's story. Water retention makes him swell up and gain three kilos, and his legs simply have no power. His mentor suggests doubling the dose; the next day, Gaumont is dropped from the peloton. After a few days he stops the injections and painfully pushes a huge gear around France, languishing at the back of the race. Only a good 10 days' riding, many, many kilometres and a lot of sweat will sort out the surplus hormone, and all these he has in prospect – except Gaumont would much rather be at the front than grovelling at the back, jousting with the big guns on the flat stages and seeing how his climbing abilities match those of Jan Ullrich, the East German powerhouse. In stage 10 to Arcalis, where during the earlier lit-up Pyrenean recce he had repeatedly distanced Cofidis's climbers, Gaumont trails in 172nd of 178 riders, 43 minutes down on Ullrich, who takes the yellow jersey and will not relinquish it for the rest of the Tour.

At some point in the race, sensing the game is lost and presumably hoping for publicity – any publicity – for his fledgling team, Cyrille Guimard instructs Gaumont, who is not quite last in the race, to aim for the bottom. Together, Gaumont claims, they devised a strategy for him to take the *lanterne rouge* – 'the media's "courageous loser who fights to the end in spite of everything"' he calls it – and, on stage 17 into Colmar, Gaumont doubles over on his bike faking an illness. He becomes detached from the peloton and rolls in 10 minutes back; after one more stage he is in last place. His job is done and Cofidis get the TV time and column inches they need.

The Tour's penultimate stage is a time trial, 62 kilometres starting and finishing in Disneyland Paris, and as the last-placed rider in the general classification Gaumont is first down the ramp. Guimard is in the team car, following him not because he expects a good performance but because Gaumont the TT specialist might be able to pass on information about the course to help the rest of the team – which corners are tricky, which you can power through without braking and so forth. Quickly, Guimard's attitude changes: his rider is flying. 'You're doing an average of 56 kilometres per hour with points at 65!' he squawks through the loudspeaker, which minutes earlier he had been using sardonically to trumpet the *lanterne rouge*'s passage. Gaumont feels great and is not suffering at all, so pushes himself deeper, faster, harder, cutting through the corners to the increasing excitement broadcasting from the team car. At the end he is congratulated by the team, but as first off and as the slowest man overall there is no fanfare. Gaumont showers and takes a tour of the amusement park, spends some time with Mickey Mouse and comes back a while later to find his name is still at the top of the leaderboard. Nobody in the lower and middle orders has been able to match the *lanterne rouge*'s average of almost 49 kilometres an hour over the distance. Eventually only two men will have the strength to beat it: Jan Ullrich and Abraham Olano, the Basque time-trial specialist, who wins. Gaumont's teammates have said he was subsequently very proud of this TT performance, but that happiness was tinged with regret for a kind of lost innocence. In one of the most telling lines in his self-lacerating, frank memoir of his descent into ignominy, he says: 'I know that first place would not have made me any more happy.'

It's a concise and poignant expression of a sentiment echoed in other ex-dopers' descriptions of their years on performance-enhancing drugs (think David Millar and Tyler Hamilton): the weariness of the cheater. The weight of the guilt, the deception and the dirty secrets wore him down; but more than that it robbed winning of any value, made winning and losing the same. Gaumont, hollowed out by a hell-bent pharmacological pursuit of victory, lost all desire for competition and all savour for his sport: 'I no longer felt that tide of emotion that rises in your chest when you cross the line victorious, the happiness of stretching your limits, of having surpassed yourself.' The only satisfaction he took from his Gent–Wevelgem win, he says, was distributing the prize money to his teammates, and his most treasured victory was the first – totally clean – performance, his bronze at the '92 Olympics. There in Disneyland just a day before Paris, as perhaps the fastest *lanterne rouge* in history, he is at a point of total exhaustion and disillusion. The particular alchemy of personality, outside pressures and team expectations that drove him there can only be guessed at, but it is probably fair to say that each played its part, and the pressure in the cooker only mounted until the lid blew off in 2004.

I leave Philippe's restaurant that night and drive back to my cheap hotel, past the rows of derelict houses, the chip factories and the slag heaps as geometric as pyramids that dot the countryside in north-eastern France. The next day I go to Belgium, but attempt to meet Philippe once more on my way back to the ferry home. I ring, we talk, he says pop by.

I swing off the motorway to head to the brasserie. Again, he is not there; I ring and get an angry response. A few minutes later, an emollient, apologetic call back – he is in Lille and won't be around, but next time I am in France we will surely meet. The tone and even the voice only five minutes apart are so different I cannot be sure I have been talking to the same person. As the weeks slide by into months, I call again a few times, but always get voicemail. I am aware that despite his professed willingness to talk, my questions, even my presence, are probably difficult for him and remind him of a bad time in his life. Little wonder he is ambivalent about our interview. After a while, I become embarrassed at leaving messages and stop.

I learn of his death while watching a fog-shrouded Giro d'Italia stage on 19 May 2013. In late April, the night before he was due to give evidence at the French Senate hearing into doping – the same one that Jacky attended – he had had a heart attack. I later hear that some French news outlets prematurely announced his passing, while he actually was in a coma in hospital, in a vegetative state with no prospect of improvement. After three weeks he dies. The summons had been troubling him, his wife told a local paper. 'I had the impression that everything he went through in 2004 was coming back to the surface,' she said. 'Nevertheless, we'd started to forget it all. Philippe threw himself into the business, but he was very preoccupied by this hearing. Nothing pointed to this attack, even if he'd had to rest a little on Tuesday afternoon. His illness happened that evening.'

'I had the impression that everything he went through in 2004 was coming back to the surface.' I've turned that line over in my mind a lot. There seems no doubt it was the drugs that killed him – twice over: the legacy of physical damage and then the trauma and stress of digging up the past. And there was also a moral jeopardy in what I was doing. Perhaps there is for everyone with an interest in cycling, cycling such as it was and hopefully will not be again – be that a Senate hearing, an inquisitive writer or simply a fan who wanted to enjoy the riders steaming uphill into the switchbacks on Alpe d'Huez, jamming on the brakes to hurtle around the corner, without asking too many questions. The Tour de France is a celestial body, a chariot careering through the sky, and we all want to live in its light. Yet undeniably there is an attraction to its dark side, its hidden face. I did want to hear stories of excess; I had wanted to know the inside gossip on the hotshot kid from Texas, who joined the team briefly then disappeared after being diagnosed with cancer. But mainly I wanted to understand the pressures and temptations of a world in which a rider can end up in such a state of emptiness and despair. Perhaps I have come to realise the truth: that I cannot understand those pressures. One of the best descriptions I have read – one that feels right, at least – of the gulf between a top-level pro's life and anyone else's was penned for *Embracation* magazine by Craig Gaulzetti, and American framebuilder and cyclist who in the '90s raced in Belgium and bumped shoulders with Gaumont more than once:

> . . . They are not like us. Their lifestyle and training regimes have nothing to do with the healthy activity of recreational cycling and domestic bike racing. It is a hard, miserable, flash in the pan galloping drive towards realising an impossible potential. The resources required have no relevance for the average person and the moral ethics created around a universe of solipsistic sacrifice, limited rewards and superhuman physical and mental efforts may as well belong to another species.

Above all I wanted, I think, to tell the story of a man who took drugs because he wanted to win so much ('I wanted to be above everyone else, always,' he wrote. 'To be superior, always, in everything') and as a result came last instead. I'm not sure this fact – doping can make you go slower – is very well understood in the wider world, and it might help people understand the complex risks and potential losses involved.

After Gaumont's year, 1997, came the Festina affair, which cast the very future of the Tour into doubt. But the 1999 'Tour of Renewal', as it was called, was a false dawn. Teams stopped being the central organisers of doping programmes, cleaving to that old CIA tenet of plausible deniability. Yes, it's OK to assassinate that leader or arm those terrorists so long as we can feasibly disavow our actions when it gets found out. Otherwise it was business as usual, with terrible ramifications for riders. The old rules pertained, men still danced to the clangour of the gong.

'You can't wave a magic wand to make these habits vanish, just because [Festina] happened, and say that in 1999 everything is pure white. It took time, and we're still suffering the consequences in 2013,' Jacky said to me. In his public statement confessing to using EPO he took full responsibility for his actions and called on the press and world at large not to blame today's cyclists for the sins of the past: 'It was a wholesale massacre at the end of the '90s. The peloton was engaged in a headlong rush forward, we didn't know how to stop.'

Jimmy Casper (*lanterne rouge* 2001 and 2004) was one of those suffering the consequences. 'I still have a sense of pride,' he told me, 'of being able to say that I finished those Tours that Armstrong won, and that I finished them *à l'eau.*' He means he was riding on water alone: clean. 'I was *lanterne rouge* twice but I was riding *à l'eau*. And everyone knows that the Armstrong years weren't easy, so, *voilà*, it was a kind of courage. I am proud to have been able to finish with those riders.'

The frequent race for the *lanterne* we've seen over the years undermines the hierarchy of winner and loser, top and bottom – or that's been the organisers' worry at least. But doping changed the whole business of winning and losing, erasing the hierarchy and rendering both almost meaningless. It provokes more than a health-related, financial or even ethical crisis, but a philosophical one: the fight against doping is, in one important sense, a fight to restore meaning to the sport. It wasn't perhaps until the Cofidis scandal, and Philippe confessing all, that things truly began to change.

I struggle to marshal my thoughts about Philippe. He came of age in a system that had lost its moral compass, a maelstrom which, if it did not create him, certainly nourished him and allowed his dangerous, unhealthy behaviour – multiple close calls, multiple wins, multiple infractions and fresh starts – to continue unchecked. He changed from a shy, talented *ingénu* to worldly, cynical professional and displayed a startling, contradictory awareness both of the danger he was in and his own propensities that were pushing him there. A man who harks back to his teenage amateur years as the best he ever lived in sport, and who in *Prisonnier du Dopage* describes injecting himself thus: 'It is drawn up inside your arm, not far from your heart, which is there, beating. You think about your heart, about its reaction as the product flows through your veins. You ask yourself if it will beat faster, if the product will exhaust it. You say to yourself: "What is all this doing to me?"'

And yet, in one of his final interviews: 'I'm still a fuckwit. I will never be on the straight and narrow. When I go on a binge, I go all out. If I want to fuck a girl, I fuck a girl. The excesses are not finished. I'm having a big party this weekend for my fortieth birthday.'

Gaumont was one of a lost generation, too many of whom – Marco Pantani, José Jimenez, his old friend Frank Vandenbroucke – have died. It is easy to condemn him and others like him, and he was vilified both by the outside world – as an unprincipled cheat – and as a blabbermouth by those in the racing world still clinging to the old unhealthy ways. *Diabolisé*, the French say: demonised. There is a legend about Robert Johnson, the Mississippi bluesman, recounting his trip to a deserted country crossroads at midnight where he sold his soul to the Devil in return for his mesmerising ability. He comes to mind because he sings, in one of my favourite songs, of the red light swinging on the back of a train, how he loses his mind as the train with its red lantern carries his love away. You can sell your soul to the Devil, but the Devil is perfidious. He promises to make you go faster, to make you famous. But Gaumont became slower. He became infamous, ignominious and then forgotten, and yet the Devil did not stint in extracting his price.

1997
198 starters
Winner: Jan Ullrich, 39.24 km/h
Lanterne rouge: Philippe Gaumont, 37.64 km/h @ 4h26'09"
139 finishers

Chapter 11

THE SPRINTER

I think you are making your own little totalitarian society,
Rey told her once, where you are the dictator, absolutely,
and also the oppressed people . . .

The Body Artist, Don DeLillo

For want of a contract Jimmy Casper retired in 2012. Although he hadn't won a race that year, given the opportunity he would have carried on, believing that at 34 his sprinter's legs still had something to give. He did not abandon professional cycling; cycling abandoned him. 'When I apply myself to something, I go all the way,' he says to me on the phone from Picardy, his native region of France, where he was born in the same town as Philippe Gaumont. Compact and built like a bulldog, Casper was for a few years the great hope of French sprinting. Even though I know he's grown out of it, in my mind he still has the bleached blond hair he sported in his early years of racing, when it was the fashion in the peloton.

We're talking about abandoning the Tour de France (which happened to him once or twice) and finishing it (he did that three times, twice coming last), and what causes you to do one and not the other. The Tour is cycling's biggest stage, the pinnacle of a professional career, and as a Frenchman Casper knew his family, friends and clubmates would be there on the side of the road. 'I was proud to finish the Tour, even last. In finishing I could show my strength of character,' he explains. 'I would say to myself, "I will not abandon, I will not abandon." When I wasn't outside the cut-off, it was out of the question that I would abandon. I think the peloton recognised the strength of character I showed.'

His determination illustrates something strange about cycling. Nobody would expect Wladimir Klitschko to play the Sugar Plum Fairy in *The Nutcracker*: he would be very out of place. Likewise, Mo Farah will never be forced to line up against Usain Bolt for the 100 metres. But road sprinters must, in the course of a Grand Tour, perform a task that really does not suit them. Before they can contest many of the sprints, they must get themselves up and over the mountains. There, the very muscles that make them so fast on the flat hold them back, literally weighing them down, while the featherlight climbers soar off into the sky. I'm not sure there's any other sport where in pursuit of glory athletes are routinely called upon to do something they're not very good at.[47]

This unsuitability for the mountains leads to a not insubstantial amount of suffering, mostly borne stoically and without complaint, and to many sprinters dipping, at least for a stage or two, into the *lanterne rouge* position. Sprinters measure their advantage over their rivals in thousandths of a second, or bike lengths at best; climbers, in kilometres and double-digit time gaps. And whereas pure climbers seem to contain and internalise their suffering in the hills, use it as

---

47 This is only relative, of course. Even the beefiest sprinter is extremely accomplished at climbing by amateur standards.

fuel to lift themselves, the sprinters' discomfort is often open and public. To my knowledge a pure climber has never been in last place in Paris. Yet Mark Cavendish has been *lanterne rouge* – before he had Bernhard Eisel or another teammate to look after him – for a single stage in his first Tour. It happened to Thor Hushovd too – *lanterne rouge* for several stages in 2002 after a stomach bug laid him low.

It also happened to Mathieu Hermans, a pretty handy sprinter for Caja Rural and Festina, who finished last twice in the late '80s, and it happened to Jimmy Casper, Jay Sweet and Kenny van Hummel – four men whose stories of suffering, perseverance and, occasionally, abandoning illustrate what sprinters endure to put themselves in a winning situation.

'When you abandon, the festival continues without you,' Bernard Hinault once said, summing up the violent feelings giving up provokes. 'You are physically weak and you feel rejected. This feeling of exclusion hurts far more than physical pain.' In his words it seems a kind of bereavement, an abandonment not only of the race but also of the self that races – the will to win and not to give up. In 1992 Lance Armstrong came last in the Clásica San Sebastián, his first professional race in Europe, which prompted David Walsh – who also collected those particular *bons mots* from Hinault – to write: 'The public humiliation of finishing last was, for him, easier than the private pain of surrender.'

Surrender must have been the last thing on Kenny van Hummel's mind as he rolled off the start ramp in Monte Carlo in 2009. His team, Skil-Shimano, had received a wild-card entry to the Tour de France and the 26-year-old debutant came to it with a solid fistful of early season wins, including a stage at the Four Days of Dunkirk, plus the runner-up's spot in the Scheldeprijs and the Netherlands Elite Road Champs. In the opening individual time trial, a 15.5-kilometre dash around Monaco's famous grand prix circuit, he is first off the ramp.[48] With the next day's sprint in mind he takes it easy and finishes second last, ahead of the Minsk Missile, Yauheni Hutarovich, a sprinter with La Française des Jeux. (It might be that Van Hummel is not built for time-trialling around principalities, but he is only five seconds slower than Mark Cavendish, which suggests they are all saving their legs.) Looking back on it, Kenny rued the difficulty of going toe-to-toe with Cavendish, then the undisputed fastest man in the world: whereas Cavendish's sprint train was a finely honed speed machine, Kenny had none. 'Only Tyler Farrar could get on terms with [Cavendish], because he had a train organised,' he said in an interview. 'And Hushovd too, of course.' Nevertheless, his sprint performances were pretty credible – his best position during the Tour was seventh. However, that was after he had hit major difficulties in the Pyrenees.

Jay Sweet's life, by contrast, took a turn for the worse way before the mountains. You may remember Sweet – the tough Aussie sprinter raced with Jacky Durand in 1999. Like Jacky, he was caught in the horrendous Passage du Gois crash that year, but he'd also gone down before it, after a spectator stepped out into the road. Jay was rear-ended in the resulting mêlée and hurt his ankle so badly he feared it was broken. A visit to the Tour doctor's car reassured him it was only a bad sprain and he chased for 30 kilometres to rejoin the peloton – only to get caught in a crash once again and hit the slippery, slimy concrete of the causeway. Eventually he limped in more than 19 minutes back on Tom Steels and the lucky bunch who'd been in front of the carnage. Jay recovered enough to take 10th in a bunch sprint on stage five, but his ankle was deteriorating

---

48 This meant that, for a few early minutes, Van Hummel was leading the 2009 Tour.

and by the last flat stage he was leaning heavily on his friends
Robbie McEwen, Stuart O'Grady, Henk Vogels and Magnus
Backstedt for moral support. With the rainy Alps in prospect,
things did not look good.

The ninth stage of that 1999 Tour, the first day in the Alps,
was the end of the road for Jimmy Casper – but that was exactly
to plan. He was the La Française des Jeux *wunderkind* who
had earlier that year nicked four stage wins from the great Eric
Zabel in the Deutschland Tour. Zabel was mid-way through his
six French green jersey wins and Deutschland was his home
Tour, so Casper had arrived at the Tour de France brimming
with confidence.

'The 1999 Tour of Germany, that was youth and insouciance
all right,' he tells me, laughing as he remembers that he really
hadn't wanted to go. It hadn't been on his programme and the
first stage fell on his 21st birthday. Naturally, he had arranged
a little soirée with his friends . . . 'I said to my partner, I don't
want to go to Germany, it's annoying, so on the first day either
I'll win the stage or I'll fall. If I win and leave the next day,
people won't say anything, since I won first. And if I fall I'll
have a good excuse to abandon. On the first day, I sprinted
quite dangerously, I took a lot of risks – because I was young
and unknown and it's difficult to make space in that situation
– and the result was I won.'

On the mountainous second stage, where Casper had planned
on ducking out, his teammate Franck Perque was under strict
instructions to bring him in inside the time cut. He didn't want to
get Perque in trouble, so he stayed the course, and then the wins
just kept on coming. The paradox was that the freer he felt from
the pressure to perform, the better he did. The Tour de France
later in the summer, by contrast, was much, much tougher. He
knew he was at a level to beat the best, but the wins were much

more difficult to find. In Germany, Casper had been an unknown quantity and Zabel the marked man. Now, at *his* home Tour, *he* was marked. With Mario Cipollini, Zabel, O'Grady, Steels and McEwen for company, all on the top of their game, he simply couldn't break free. Still, he'd gone home satisfied with a handful of top-10s. An operation kept Jimmy out of the 2000 race and when he returned in 2001 the pressure was really on.

'I went to the Tour each time set on winning, and the team told me each time, *voilà*, you've got to win a stage. The media was saying that it was now my second Tour, that I was 23, a bit more mature, and it was time to win. Everyone was saying you have to win, you have to win, and there you start to have a totally different kind of pressure from the first time,' he says. There were also the legendarily tough mountains, which he hadn't experienced in his first Tour outing.

After Casper's planned withdrawal in 1999 the injured Jay Sweet soldiered on. The famous stage to Sestriere was where, during a cataclysmic meteorological tantrum, Armstrong definitively stole the race, and it was here that Jay's race definitively fell apart. In the diary he was keeping for *CyclingNews* he wrote: 'My arms didn't want to hold up my body, I had no power whatsoever. I absolutely crawled to the top of the Galibier, which seemed to take for ever. When I got to the top I stopped to put on my rain jacket because it was freezing and my director said that I was as white as a ghost and my eyes were half open. He didn't really want me to descend the Galibier but I said I wanted to go on.' He finished three minutes outside the time cut but he was let back in, perhaps because officials admired the way he sprinted the final kilometre of the climb. By the next stage, the second in the Alps, Jay was the *lanterne rouge*.

Jimmy sprinted up a mountain once, too, in similar circumstances, using everything he'd learnt about winning races on the flat not to be eliminated on the Plateau de Beille. It was on stage 13 of the 2004 Tour, his second *lanterne rouge* year. 'I finished in a sprint. I sprinted as if I was winning the stage. I was going all out just to make the time cut.' There were no hands-in-the-air heroics, though. 'I had made such a brutal effort at altitude it provoked an asthma attack, and just past the line I fell to the floor,' he says.[49]

As for Kenny van Hummel, in 2009 he hits the mountains in last place and shows heroism in the face of adversity and suffering that endears him to cycling fans around the world. His game plan in the Pyrenees: 'Try not to get caught between the cars,' he tells a reporter for *Rouleur* magazine. And then, to shave off every possible second: 'I will drop like a stone on the descent.' His team colludes with him to get him through, the DS keeping him abreast of the cut-offs, and teammates pacing him between the hills. 'If I didn't take risks yesterday, I wouldn't have been starting today,' he says. He is not expected to last through the first week; then, with the Pyrenees dispatched, he is expected to quit at the end of the second. But he doesn't and an increasingly large band of fans from Holland, the States, Australia and the UK follow his progress, cheering him on from the sofa and sharing Kenny news on the Internet. His travails and his never-say-die attitude catch the public imagination, and Kenny van Hummel becomes an unlikely star. In the first real Alpine stage, from Pontarlier to Verbier in Switzerland, he arrives home dead last, more than 45 minutes after the winner. 'Today I literally ate my handlebar,' he tells Dutch TV. 'I didn't

---

49 Jimmy says to me he was 30 seconds inside the cut-off, but the journalist Sam Abt reported in 2004 that Jimmy had come in *hors délais*. The commissaires had let him back in because 'the huge crowd on the road in the final kilometers had interfered with the progress of the rider', while simultaneously fining him 200 Swiss francs for accepting pushes from spectators up the final climb. This detail – the clemency tempered with discipline – gives Abt's version a ring of truth.

care if I was gonna make it in time or not. I'm tough, I'll quit
when I fall off my bike. A lot of sprinters went home already,
but Kenny van Hummel is still here. And I'm proud of that.'

With both Jay and Kenny there is the sense that in their
second visit to the mountains a guillotine is hanging over their
heads. For Kenny, it falls on the Alpine stage 17, the day after
the race's technical director Jean-François Pescheux slightly
unkindly calls him the Tour's 'worst climber ever'. He tumbles
and badly hurts his knee and is forced, finally, to withdraw.
Jay, on the other hand, eats ice cream with his girlfriend on
the pre-Pyrenean rest day, and then sets out for Piau-Engaly.
He gets dropped on the first col, works to catch Bo Hamburger
on the second, passes him, then works with the French rider
Damien Nazon on the third to regain the safety of the *grupetto*.
'Big mistake!' he writes in his diary. 'I blew and absolutely
crept up the fourth col. On the last col Nazon left me. I was
so stuffed. I was going flat out because the time cut was really
short today. The last five kilometres seemed to take for ever,
I was sprinting the whole way. I crossed the line 43 minutes
behind the winner . . . the time cut was 38 minutes. I was too
tired to be disappointed, the media rushed me at the finish and
started asking questions but I could hardly talk!'

Jay and Kenny both rode the Tour only once, Jimmy Casper
multiple times – two *lanternes rouges* and his share of abandons
and eliminations. Although perhaps we shouldn't call them
that. 'One doesn't abandon the Tour, one withdraws from it.
An important nuance,' Jean-François Pescheux told me. 'You
withdraw because you have to – you're ill or whatever – but
you do not abandon.' It's not just semantics: it shows the crucial
difference in mindset between someone who gives up and
someone who battles to the end. Jimmy battled to the end at

Alpe d'Huez in 2008 after riding 160 kilometres on his own, only to miss the time cut by two minutes. He rode eight days in 2002 in a neck brace thanks to a crash. And he battled between Bourg d'Oisans and Gap in 2003. Each time he was forced to withdraw. Always in the Alps, they were his nemeses. Jimmy never abandoned while there was the slightest scrap of hope of finishing. He was always unable to continue, or too far outside the time limit, with too large and lumpy a portion of the day's stage to go to make it back. 'I'm stubborn, but I'm not stupid!' he says.

The first year Casper won the *lanterne rouge*, 2001, he played the game a little, knowing that he'd get the media attention. Once he was near the bottom of the standings, he joked with his fellow *lanterne rouge* contenders, pretending they were fighting for the win. 'You'd say: "Look, I'm ahead of you on the GC", when actually you're behind. Or "I have a minute-thirty on you", when in fact you're a minute-thirty back,' he says. Since he was French, he received a lot of attention and didn't shy away from admitting his difficulties in the mountains. 'The public were quite admiring because they really understood that I'm built differently,' Jimmy says to me. 'I'm not all that tall but I'm still relatively heavy. They can see that I'm not built to climb cols. And then when I tell them that at the end of the day, in terms of the time I spend on the Tour, I do a whole stage more than Armstrong – at each Tour it's about five hours longer than him, so one stage more – they say to me, you're a pretty big deal since you ride more!'

The second *lanterne* was not something he went for: as the saying goes, it came for him. In other races in 2004 he was having one of his most prolific years, but an early crash at the Tour meant he wasn't even placing in the sprints in the first week. The 2004 *Grand Départ* was in Charleroi in Belgium and the route took an extended meander across northern France, with not even a hint of mountains until stage 10. It was a field day for sprinters and *baroudeurs* including Robbie McEwen, Tom Boonen, Thor Hushovd, Filippo Pozzato and Stuart O'Grady, but not Jimmy. In stage five, which was won by his teammate O'Grady in a small-bunch sprint, Jimmy lost 13 minutes. Later, in the Alps, Jimmy fell into the *lanterne rouge* position. There was another Frenchman, Sébastien Joly, who was sitting barely a minute above him, but in the Jura, two stages before Paris, Joly got into a break and put more than 11 minutes between them.

The glittering prize for all sprinters is the Champs-Élysées, and it was the thought of performing well there, of taking this ultimate win, that kept Jimmy pedalling through the Alps, obstinately refusing to get off his bike. In what was probably a first for technology in the Tour, he took a small digital camera with him on the last stage and among the high-jinks that take place in the ceremonial roll to the capital, sprinted off the front for a minute and took a photo of himself in front of Armstrong, for posterity.[50] Though he made it to the Champs-Élysées, he could only place sixth.

Casper did eventually get his Tour stage win and even now the relief and the pride are evident. Because a *lanterne rouge* is one thing, but a sprinter who does not win seems a sorry creature. Climbers' exploits often can seem self-justifying and beautiful in themselves, futile or successful, but a sprinter coming in second has no worth. In 2006 the first stage looped around the Alsace, starting and finishing in Strasbourg. 'It was an absolutely great finish, very straight with a very good surface,' he says. Many sprinters say that right at the moment they pass

---

50 Lance looms large over the Tours he won in so many ways, though for the *lanternes* in that time he was a shadowy, unseen figure who inhabited the other end of the race. 'The Postal team, I didn't see them in any of the stages, only in the starts,' says Igor Flores, *lanterne rouge* 2002. 'It's true. They were always leading the group.'

under the *flamme rouge*, the one-kilometre-to-go banner, silence descends and each second elongates into 10 as they make the final reckoning of their situation and focus on the goal ahead. This was one of those times for Jimmy. QuickStep that day were working for Boonen, but his lead-out man ran out of gas with 350 metres to go. 'Too far from the line,' says Jimmy. 'There was a little pocket of dead time and I must have been in 12th or 13th when the eight or nine in front of me slowed. I came up behind them with *élan*, I didn't hesitate,' his words spilling out faster and faster in the rush for the line. 'I went very early, at 300 metres, and straight away with that acceleration I made a little gap. I managed to keep enough of a lead to finish half a wheel ahead of McEwen. It was an exceptional moment because it was already my sixth Tour. I'd said to myself that Tour, you've already done five Tours and not won yet: don't pressure yourself, stay calm . . . and finally I succeeded.'

Mathieu Hermans won several stages of the Vuelta a España, but, except for a single win, Tour de France stages eluded him. However, with that win Hermans put himself in an elite club of one. He is, as far as I can tell, the only *lanterne rouge* to win a stage in the same year as the *lanterne*. Hermans is a jovial, quick-talking Dutchman who now commentates for Dutch and Belgian TV and who still dislikes the taste of losing. In one instance, he calls being beaten on the line 'a Belgian joke'. I would like to believe it's a general Dutch expression for a nasty surprise or a sudden disappointment, as in: 'When my wife told me it was steak for dinner but then changed her mind and made salad, that was a real Belgian joke.' But I think rather that it's because the incident he is referring to involves Rudy Dhaenens, a Belgian. (Later, with his Tour stage win, he would turn the tables and the joke would be on Dhaenens.)

Hermans spent most of his best years with Basque teams and retains a lot of affection for that region of northern Spain. However, it meant that team priorities sat squarely with the Vuelta a España (in those days in April and May), so he would always arrive at the Tour de France knackered. 'If you have to be good in the end of April and also in July that's difficult. For me Spain was very important, that's where I won my stages,' he says. Like Kenny van Hummel, Mathieu was at a disadvantage in the Tour since he did not have the resources other sprinters had. 'What I missed most was a team that could control the final kilometres. For example if we count all the riders [Jean-Paul] Van Poppel had, and they rode all the last 30 kilometres on the front, you can be in the sprint in a good position without too much struggling.' Hermans claims to have been a more complete rider than Jean-Paul van Poppel (who was perhaps more famous than him – and Hermans' results over more varied terrain and in the Classics, a fifth at Flanders for instance, bear this out), but he did not have the team structure or, in the end, the out-and-out killer speed. 'Van Poppel had riders like [Gerrit] Solleveld, [Nico] Verhoeven, [Gert] Jakobs and [Jelle] Nijdam, good, hard riders who controlled the last 30 kilometres,' Hermans explains. '[Such a team] leads you like a king to the last kilometre. Van Poppel was very fast, he had a very good acceleration and when he had a good position it was difficult to beat him.'

Van Poppel was green jersey in 1987, when Hermans took the lantern for the first time. Hermans' second *lanterne* year was 1989, when Sean Kelly won green (the two are still friends); in '89, Caja Rural had bolstered the squad to help Hermans in the sprints. Says Hermans: 'I had Ludo Peeters who was a teammate of Van Poppel the year before, he knew a lot about the Classics and about sprints. That year he was with me and we took the initiative to control the breakaway five or six kilometres before the finish.' And this is where Rudy Dhaenens comes in: 'Then Rudy attacked,' Hermans continues, 'and he crashed at about 800 or 900 metres before the sprint, in a corner. Already we had him in our sights, he was very close. He crashed and I had a very good sprint. It was a very hard final stretch and I was in the front, with lots of space to start my sprint. I won with two or three metres, easy.'

It is very difficult to get Hermans to talk about his brace of *lanternes* at all. Not because he is ashamed, I think, but because he paid it absolutely no mind. Jimmy Casper, on the other hand, is used to fielding questions about his two lanterns, but when I ask if he is proud of them, he responds as if it were some sort of Belgian joke. Not really, he says, though once he had two to his name he would have liked to get three. Really, all he wanted to do was finish.

Abandoning is the dark flipside of the pursuit of the *lanterne rouge*. Inimical to it, its bogeyman. On that point, and on the desire to finish, all the sprinters are in agreement. And given the abandon rate in this chapter of sprinters – by far the highest in the book, I think – you can see why. Did Hermans ever think about quitting? His response is practical: 'You could leave the race but if everyone thinks like that, you'd only have 20 finishers! For me it was not an option to leave the race. People told me I had some good results in Spain but maybe I couldn't win at the Tour. My Tour victory was not my best or my nicest, but it was showing I could.'

Jimmy, meanwhile, who is more emotional and has more experience of 'withdrawing', is more intimate and revealing. 'When you abandon, it's a very difficult moment,' he reiterates. 'The only race I ever cried over when I abandoned was the Tour de France.'

I asked many of the *lanternes rouges* I interviewed, and especially the sprinters, if they thought we, the spectating public, understood or even could understand what they go through in the mountains. Perhaps I was hoping to be granted an insight into the professional cyclist's relationship with pain – 'my favourite enemy' as legendary hardman of the peloton Jens Voigt calls it, since inflicting pain on himself is to him a sign that he's doing his job right – but nobody I asked thought we were missing anything. As far as someone else's pain is comprehensible, it can be read in their faces in the images transmitted from the motorcycle cameras on the slopes, or while we watch on the side of a mountain as the tarmac turns sticky in the heat. Or, following the 'It never gets easier, you just go faster' school of thinking, from our own lesser efforts in bicycle rides and races. For his film *Fitzcarraldo*, about one man's obsessive quest to bring Verdi to the Amazon, the German director Werner Herzog dragged a paddle steamer over a mountain in the depths of the jungle. The studio execs suggested doing it with models, but that idea was met with blank incomprehension: 'I told them the unquestioned assumption had to be a real steamship being hauled over a mountain, though not for the sake of realism but for the stylisation characteristic of classic opera,' Herzog said. Even if you're never going to try to do something as difficult as that – and the boat being dragged over the mountain looks like a flipping nightmare – you can feel the gravity and the absurdity of the undertaking, as it pertains to something in your own life and experience. Just as when someone says: 'I raced the world's best bike racers for 200 kilometres over the Galibier in a storm', there's a weight to the statement that cannot be denied. And I'm not sure there is an insight to be gained. What is remarkable is the persistence.

Much later, looking back, Herzog mused: 'Every man should pull a boat over a mountain once in his life.' At the back of my mind Saint-Flour was calling.

1987

207 starters

Winner: Stephen Roche, 36.65 km/h

Lanterne rouge: Mathieu Hermans, 35.30 km/h @ 4h23'30"

135 finishers

1989

198 starters

Winner: Greg LeMond, 37.49 km/h

Lanterne rouge: Mathieu Hermans, 36.21 km/h @ 3h4'1"

138 finishers

2001

189 starters

'Winner': Lance Armstrong, 40.07 km/h

Lanterne rouge: Jimmy Casper, 38.35 km/h @ 3h52'17"

144 finishers

2004

188 starters

'Winner': Lance Armstrong, 40.56 km/h

Lanterne rouge: Jimmy Casper, 38.74 km/h @ 3h55'49"

147 finishers

Chapter 12
THE BROTHERS

The race is not to the swift, nor the battle to the strong.
Ecclesiastes 9:11

The towering figure of Miguel Indurain looms large over the cycling landscape in Navarra in northern Spain. In fact, where I'm standing he's looming large over *me*, hunched above his handlebars in his yellow jersey and white cycling cap, sunglasses on, mouth half huffing, half grimacing in pain. The mural, about three metres tall, dominates the entrance hall of the Miguel Indurain sports centre in Tafalla. As well as an indoor velodrome, the sports centre has handball, volleyball and tennis courts and a large heated pool where an aquarobics class for pensioners is taking place.

It's the cycling that's really inspiring, though. He's a hero to local bike riders. A product of and a motivating force behind a strong cycling culture in the wider Basque country, which until 2013 sustained Euskaltel-Euskadi – for almost 20 years a *de facto* Basque national squad that took talent only from the region. The sports centre is one way in which he gives something back, though not the only one. 'He's a perfect rider,'

says Igor Flores. 'You can talk with him, and in a very normal
way. He's a very nice man.'

During Indurain's best years, Igor was racing and moving
up the age groups on his way to turning professional. Because
he showed promise his home town arranged for him to meet
his idol, and Igor has an autographed photo of them both: the
huge pillar of muscle, heart and lung, and the skinny, floppy-
haired youth, much more of a classic cyclist's build and of
average height. Igor at 39 still has the same haircut and, if he's
heavier than the kid he was, he's probably pretty close to his
professional weight. He bounces out of the car to shake my
hand. It is autumn in northern Spain and the short journey from
my hotel in Tafalla to Altsasu where Igor lives was beautiful.
The landscape is gently creased and rumpled like expensive
fabric, the muted greens, bare brown fields and the ochre and
russet and red turning leaves, like camouflage, are soft in the
low sun. Smoke from a farmer's fire lies heavy over the hills.
Yet with the sun the heat has gone from the day, an early chill
has come and with it the melancholy that arrives at dusk when
it falls upon you and you realise you are a long, long way from
home. Next to Alsasua (to give the town its Spanish rather than
Basque name – though I'm not sure many locals do) is Urdiain
where Igor and his younger brother Iker grew up. Urdiain, a tiny
community in the lee of the mountains of the Urbasa y Andia
national park, has a 200-strong sporting club with more than
a few framed photos of members-turned-professional-cyclists
on its walls. Iker, too, was a pro. Not so unusual perhaps and
especially not in the Basque country, but no other brothers have
both been *lanterne rouge*. Igor hit bottom in 2002, Iker in 2005.
The younger brother, mortified by his downward trajectory and
probably with 2002 in mind, told Spanish journalists: 'I must
do something to escape from last place.'

'I was the last because I wanted to be,' Igor says. 'Iker was the last because he couldn't be better.'

Altsasu is not a pretty town. It has the air of a Franco-era ski resort, yet there is no skiing or the tourists that come with it. The walls are adorned with daubs of separatist slogans and political posters in ribbons and rags. A stark pelota *frontón* – the game suits the sparse look to life here[51] – and a small square, its trees trimmed severely back. What it does have is Razesa Bicicletas, the shop that built the frames Indurain rode to his first Tour win, and this is where we meet. Igor's English is good and his smile wide. It is a comfort. His house on the edge of town is also welcoming. I follow him in the car as he drives there, and watch as he beeps at joggers running through the dusk, waves a hand in greeting to them. We sit in his living room and he shows me old photos: with Iker in their Euskaltel kit on their way to a race together; with Big Mig; at the Tour of Mexico as a junior. That one, in fact, comes in two instalments. The first, a young Igor, same haircut, wearing a yellow jersey; the second, the same kid, but in half a yellow jersey, an arm sling and a neck brace. He had crashed on a descent. 'I had the opportunity to win the Tour of Mexico but I lost it in one minute,' he says. It was a rare chance. Igor won only once as a junior, and infrequently as an amateur and young pro. He is, I think, being modest when he says this, since he undoubtedly had an eye for an opportunity and rode in many of the more prestigious local and international races, where winning is consequently more difficult.

---

51 Pelota, one of the traditional games of this part of the world, consists in its most basic form of two men on a court – the *frontón* – hitting a small leather ball against a wall with their hands, though it is much more elegant and challenging than that suggests. Jørgen Leth, director of classic cycling documentaries, including *A Sunday In Hell* about Paris–Roubaix, was fascinated by pelota and made a beautiful film about it.

'But in his case he was, in every single year, the best, the best, the best. It was different. For him it was very easy for him to pass through the categories and to win.' Igor is pointing at his brother. For Iker has now arrived in a flurry of wives and children, all home after work and after school. They live in the same town, the brothers, their wives are friends and their kids play together every day. I am introduced to everyone enthusiastically by Igor, who jumps up off the sofa to help the new arrivals with their coats and bags, and then we're left to our conversation. In Altsasu, the brothers are surrounded by the roads they trained on every day as kids, together, where their dad gave them both the encouragement that would lead them to pursue cycling seriously. Their mum was less keen: even as pros she could not bear to watch them on television, fearful for the sort of crashes that had put her eldest son in a Mexican hospital.

Iker ended his career after the 2007 season with the Fuerteventura-Canarias team and then moved to Barcelona for a while, but returned and now is the regional sales rep for the clothing manufacturer Bioracer.[52] Igor works as a carpenter for his wife's family business, which has interests in everything from building apartments to large-scale container shipping in Spanish docks. 'When Iker was young he was very good, playing football, playing pelota. I was always in the middle. Not too good, not too bad,' Igor continues, and as he explains how easily his brother passed from one level to the next, Iker sits there on the sofa next to him, looks down towards the floor, arms crossed, legs apart, and smiles, as if remembering another life. Igor is sitting forward, quick-witted, leaning towards me, always more animated; Iker, though younger, has prematurely greying hair

---

52 Bioracer also employs Mathieu Hermans, which means it has two *lanternes rouges* on its payroll – in all probability a record.

and is slower to react, more considered perhaps. He is relaxed and doesn't dispute what Igor is saying. In professional sport, where people's talents are ranked so routinely, there is often a disjunction between a sportsperson's own perceived worth and the objective measure of their abilities. Not here. Perhaps being given the *lanterne rouge*, the booby prize, removes all possibility of denial or self-delusion; or perhaps cycling is simply quicker and crueller than other sports at stripping away illusions. Nevertheless, all the *lanternes rouges* have seemed both aware of and content with their place in the pile.

And Iker knows that he was actually something. A talent who almost fulfilled his early promise. He coulda been a contender.[53] In 2003 he came 18th in the Vuelta a España and took some podium positions in smaller races. The 2005 Tour was his third and he went into it as one of the team's key *domestiques*, but his performance was a huge disappointment, both to himself and to others. Unlike Igor, who is taking lessons, Iker's spoken English isn't up to much, though he understands everything that's going on. Consequently, when Iker tells his story our conversation is a glorious three-way affair, which I realise once I have the transcript translated is part faithful translation, part amplificatory echo chamber, part game of Chinese whispers as Igor's enthusiasm takes flight. They clearly know each other's personal experiences and careers inside out; both start each other's stories and complete the other brother's thoughts, but because Igor speaks my language this is very much his show.

How did you feel that Tour, I ask.

'Tell him I felt very tired, drained,' Iker says.

'He felt very tired, drained,' Igor says.

---

53 After he retired, he appeared on a Spanish reality TV show. We have Christopher Biggins and Kerry Katona, they have ex-pro cyclists. That's the culture gap right there.

Iker looks at his brother then continues: 'In that moment I didn't realise what was happening. I thought my body was not . . . was not responding. I felt strange and four months later they told me I had been in contact with the hepatitis virus. That's when I looked it up on the Internet and I saw that the symptoms they described were exactly what I had been feeling. I didn't have any appetite, I was swollen, I mean I couldn't really physically compete.'

'He says he prepared the Tour de France very well,' Igor says, only diverting mildly from the script. 'But when the Tour de France started he felt that he couldn't stay with the top guys – and not only with the top: he couldn't stay with any competitors. He wanted to finish the Tour de France, because it's the Tour de France. If it were another race he'd give up. But it was the Tour de France and he wanted to finish. He felt different things during the Tour and after the Tour he struck the block and he made an analysis, I don't know how to say . . .' A blood test, I offer. 'Yes! He made a blood test and he realised that he was sick during the Tour, and he had contact with hepatitis.'

In 2005 there was a tough, 67.5-kilometre-long team time trial where Iker was dropped and his problem became very apparent.

'I mean, I stayed in there all I could. I couldn't even cope with taking a turn,' Iker says. 'And I think I did stay: I kept holding on for my own self-esteem till I got to around seven or eight kilometres to the finish line.'

'He's saying that in the time trial he couldn't take a turn on the front, and he stayed all the way behind the group,' relays Igor. 'He did all that he could to follow the group, because he knew that if you drop back . . .'

'I was a world away,' Iker says.

After finishing significantly back on the eight other members of his team, he went to see one of his managers and told him he wanted to quit. He was refused permission to do so. Neither Igor nor Iker has good memories of that particular staff member. In Iker's opinion the man did nothing more than drive the car.

Igor adds that at races where this manager was in charge there was little working structure and few planned race goals. The year that Igor rode his only Tour, 2002, was Euskaltel's worst ever showing, for which he in part blames the same man. That year the team had an embarrassment of talent: a young Haimar Zubeldia (now the highest-placed rider in the 2003 Tour not to have had a doping positive); Lance Armstrong's sometime nemesis, the climber Iban Mayo; a young Samuel Sánchez, later an Olympic champion; and old hands Unai Etxebarria and Roberto Laiseka.

The team's goal at the outset was a top-five placing, a tough ambition even at the best of times. But, Igor says, 'I remember when I was in the bus the first day, he told us that we had five leaders in the Tour de France. "Five leaders?" I said to him. "It's impossible to go to the Tour de France with five leaders, because we are only four [others]. It's impossible. You have to choose one, one leader, and the others . . . we have to work for him."' It's hard to serve five leaders with four *domestiques*. Igor continues: 'My work was to help them, and to stay with them. I had to be with Haimar, with Mayo, but it was impossible to be with all of them. You have to choose one and stay with him. We were working a lot for the five guys, and they felt very bad.'

After dividing his attentions and energies for two weeks (the team lost a man along the way, so then it was three men helping five) Igor found himself completely exhausted and in second-to-last place. 'There was one guy below me and when there were three days left we were in the peloton arriving at the stage finish. And in the last 10 kilometres he decided to stop. I saw him and I thought, I'm the last, and I want to be the last, so I decided to stop too. I stopped in the road for three or four minutes.'

Meanwhile, in 2005, Iker was doing everything he could to gain time, including drafting his team car, for which he was sanctioned both financially and with a time penalty: 20 more seconds to add to his already weighty total. His deficit to second-to-last place, Wim Vansevenant, who had yet to start accumulating his hat-trick of *lanternes*, was irrecoverable. On one mountain stage Iker was feeling so bad that in the first 10 kilometres he was dropped from the peloton, with two big cols and a long, long way to go: '240 kilometres,' Iker says. 'Odyssey.' Even with two other riders by his side it was going to be a tough day. To keep himself going Iker pretended he was in a winning break and was shooting not simply for survival but for glory. Igor starts the tale: 'He was thinking how to win the stage because he needed to motivate himself. In this situation if you go down you are lost. And he was thinking all the time that he was in this *escapada*, and how to beat these two guys, for motivation.'

Iker takes up the pacemaking, 'I had the last col to finish. So I thought I'd try to leave those two behind. They moved sideways and looked at me as if to say: "What is this guy doing now?" and then they dropped me. And after that, on top of that, at the col when I came in last, all the people were in the road, they were all leaving and I still had to finish. They had to make way for me. That was probably the most humiliating day in my whole cycling career.

'I remember crying,' he finishes.

'He said that he was crying at this moment because he felt tired, the last of the peloton, he thought he was going to be dropped from the Tour, and he began to cry on the bike,' Igor finishes.

Out of self-respect and sheer bloody-mindedness Iker kept

going. 'A Spanish journalist came to me and told me I was last. I said: "No, make no mistake, 200 came here, I am 120th. In another race I might be last, but not here."'

At their final time trial, which for both of them fell on the race's penultimate day, the brothers decided on opposing tactics. Igor, realising that Lance Armstrong, who had dominated the Tour, would not let up in this last race against the clock, decided to speed up. He knew that even on a normal day he might lose seven minutes to the American and he did not want to be eliminated. Iker, meanwhile, decided to embrace his last place. 'I said: "This is it. I am going for the last position."'

To which Igor adds, embellishing only slightly: 'He had tried not to be the last, but on the time trial of the last day he saw it was impossible to change position in the classification. He wanted to be the last on the last day because he felt he was the worst rider. He says he can feel proud.'

Both, however, had aroused the ire of the team management. 'On the last day they came to me asking for explanations,' Iker says. 'I'd spoken to him eight days into the Tour. I said to him: "Fuck, I don't feel well." I told him I recognised when my body . . . I knew that something weird was happening to me. And they didn't pay any attention. I mean, they completely ignored me during the whole Tour but when they knew I was going to come in last, they came to me asking for explanations.'

'On the last day we had a very bad moment with the boss,' Igor says. 'He told us that we had very bad tools, that we were lazy people and . . .' he makes a baffing noise and shoots his hands up in the air. 'I exploded and I had a very bad argument. It was the last race in which I took part.'

Igor had never really liked life as a professional, never really adjusted to it. He has difficulty explaining why and this time Iker fills in: 'When you're amateur it's a hobby, which you do because you love it, not because you're thinking about the future . . . when you're a professional it's a lot of money, a lot of interests, a lot of pressure on you, and in the end it's not the same.'

Did you want to race the next year, I ask Igor.

'No, I didn't want to,' he says. 'I had the opportunity to continue in another team but I decided to give up because I was psychologically very down.'

Disillusioned?

'Yes, the Tour de France killed me. Not only the race. The atmosphere in the team, the pressure of the manager, the pressure of the director, the pressure of the physician.'

The Tour de France killed me. Racing while ill with hepatitis. Both flogging themselves for managers they didn't believe in, just to make last place and for no thanks at all. How did it feel to finish, I ask, expecting perhaps relief, perhaps something darker.

'For me, I had a very good feeling on this day because it was the last day of my career,' Igor says. 'I can say that in my case I feel proud of my position in the Tour. I felt the support of the people from here,' – he means his town and region – 'I knew that some friends of mine would be in France in Paris, waiting for me. I wanted to finish the Tour for many reasons, but one especially was this: that I wanted to stay with them in Paris.'

Iker is even more effusive. 'It was the happiest day in my life,' the younger man says, eyes down, in his quiet, considered way. 'Out of all the competitions I have ever done, I think it was the one where I felt the happiest, because after suffering so much I felt very proud. I think it's the day I felt the proudest, because I knew I wasn't well . . . on that day I felt proud to have finished the Tour. Every year, once you finish it, you think you don't want to do it ever again – but then the following year comes and when they tell you you'll be in the Tour's team, you want to go.'

Neither of them would have got to the Champs-Élysées, the brothers say, without the fraternity of teammates who helped them through. And, in Iker's case, the *grupetto*. *Grupetto* regulars are sensitive to who should be there, who should not, and they tried to cheer Iker up every day he sank back, since it was obvious that something was wrong. He also forged a close bond with his room-mate, Iñaki Isasi, who was also having a bad race. 'In the race we had to do what we had to do, but each evening in the room we would tell each other that outside of the race we had to enjoy ourselves. He would say: "And now, let's live our lives. Let's enjoy things, let's speak to our wives, to our children, let's laugh together,"' Iker says. 'The idea was, we are having such a bad time in the race, let's make everything else nice.'

Igor, meanwhile, was pushed up the hills by Roberto Laiseka, who took turns with the spectators to keep him going.

Neither brother wanted to quit, out of *amor propio*, and also because they knew that an empty space at the breakfast table damages team morale, makes everyone's lives that little bit harder, even if there is no practical purpose to be derived from continuing. So they kept going, in part for their teammates, and for fans, friends and family too. Many of Iker's family and friends – including Igor – made the journey over the border for one of 2005's Pyrenean stages to cheer him on at the finish line. But the stage was a low point for Iker and only with Isasi's help did Iker make it to the end at all. 'It was the worst day of my life, physically,' he says.

The trip over the Pyrenees is one thousands of Basques regularly make, to support their riders and claim sovereignty over this corner of the Tour de France. Watch the race on TV and the mountain roads, especially on whichever stage travels closest to Spain, seem carpeted in Euskaltel orange. Travel to the mountains, however, and the noise, the atmosphere . . . the sheer amount of orange are on another level as Basque fans bring a party to the cols, with beer, barbecues and vociferous support for the Euskaltel riders. It is as if, for those few days, the Basque nation that straddles the mountains between Spain and France – at any other time a folk ideal – is made geographically real. For the riders it passes in a blur of suffering and encouragement. The only way he could tell which side of the border he was staying on, Iker jokes, was that in Spain it was cheaper to call his wife in the evenings.

'Right from the first day of the Tour I felt that it would be very difficult for me, because my legs didn't feel well. But I wanted to reach the Pyrenees because all the people were talking about the Pyrenees,' Igor says. 'And when I arrived to the Pyrenees, for me it was incredible. My skin, it was . . .' he makes a vocal sound imitating an electric shock. 'I had a very hard moment between Menté and Aspet, because I was alone and I felt that it was my last day in the Tour de France. But after this moment I was with the group climbing Plateau de Beille and I couldn't follow them. It was incredible. I was with Roberto Laiseka and he was pushing me a lot. I remember I arrived at the seventh kilometre [of the climb] and there was some guys from Montpellier and they were pushing me for a kilometre, and it wasn't legal. But it was *emoción*.' He thinks some more. 'The best moment I had riding the bike was in the Pyrenees.'

We talk about finishing the Tour some more and Igor shows me the painting a German TV channel presented to him that day on the Champs-Élysées, along with some cheese (long since eaten) and a magnum of champagne (which he still has). Finally, I ask them what they will take from their *lanterne rouge* Tour. Both had embraced coming last: one because he liked the idea of being the *lanterne*, the other, rather nobly, because he truly felt he was the worst rider in the race and it was the position he deserved. Each had experienced that peculiar mix of pleasure and pain that seems unique to endurance sports and particularly special to bike riding, and run the gamut of emotions from hope to shame to pride. Perhaps because I've been hearing from two of them at once, because they've been so kind and welcoming or because it's in the relatively recent past, their stories somehow feel more emotional and overwhelming to me than some others. So, guys, what's left?

'That whole experience taught me many things,' Iker says.

'He says he learnt a lot of things, about himself and about cycling too. But especially about himself,' improvises Igor.

Iker pauses a moment. It's as if he has all along been formulating short, neat answers so that his brother can expand upon them – teeing them up for Igor to knock out of the park.

'In that Tour, the bad moments I went through have made me value a lot more all the good moments I had with you guys,' he says, gesturing not at me (obviously) but at his brother and former teammate Igor.

And Igor puts the cherry on the icing on the cake, 'He says that the bad moments he had riding made him remember the good things he felt during the Tour. Those moments made him stronger, not only for riding the bike, but for his life. He says I know I can, I have to, work to do things better, to be better, to be happy.'

After that, what more can you want? Ham, it seems. Local cured *jamón* sliced wafer thin on the kitchen counter, and a little wine to round off the evening. They joke about the competition between them, the natural feeling between brothers that is still very much there. Igor still rides a lot, but of Iker he says: 'He doesn't ride too much. Now, I'm better than him. He's very fat compared with a year before.' They laugh. Igor competes in duathlons – those runners he was beeping at earlier were his friends and training partners – and last year both the Flores brothers took part in a famous local running race, the Behobia–San Sebastián. Igor beat Iker by eight minutes, a feat of which he is very proud.

'Yes, yes, the problem now is that I am better. I train more than him. But he's fat.'

'I am very good. He is very *delgado*,' Iker says, mainly in English. Thin. '*En profesional no estabas . . .*'

'He says, when I was professional I wasn't so. He's fat,' Igor says.

'I am now very good,' says Iker, in English again.

It is time to go. Iker is on his way home too and guides me back through the town to the main road. He honks his horn and flashes his lights to send me on my way. And as I drive back through the dark I think of the families I have left behind, the warmth, the fraternity, the community – and simply how nice and how normal their lives were.

Mathieu Hermans, the Dutch sprinter, spent a long time in the Basque country. 'The first time I went there, it looked a bit old, like 50 years ago compared to Holland,' he told me. But eventually he fell in love with it. 'Most of all the people, you discover it afterwards. They are very nice, warm people. Once you are a friend they are friends for life.'

There is a whole pile of academic research looking into the psychology of winning and losing, examining such ideas as intrinsic and extrinsic motivation, reward, competition and achievement, but there's not very much on the personal, emotional or developmental sides to it. One *New York Times* opinion piece, however, puts its point of view neatly in its headline: 'Losing is Good for You'. The gist of the article is that if you praise kids too much and make sure everyone receives a trophy, they grow up with a sense of entitlement – and without the sense that working hard, and trying, and failing, are a necessary part of life.

It quotes the author of a book called *Generation Me*, Jean Twenge: 'You're going to lose more often than you win, even if you're good at something. You've got to get used to that to keep going.' I have no idea if losing is actually good for you (apart from any other personal experiences, mine was the sort of school where at Sports Day everybody got a gold star). But that feels like sound thinking. And, without forgetting that the *lanterne rouge* is only one small moment in its recipients' lives – a low or a high or simply a blip – compare most of the last-placed men with the monomaniac, borderline psychopathic characters some of the great champions are painted to be, and it feels doubly right.

The Flores family, at the very least, seem to have something important nailed.

2002
198 starters
'Winner': Lance Armstrong, 39.92 km/h
Lanterne rouge: Igor Flores, 38.25 km/h @ 3h35'52"
153 finishers

2005
189 starters
'Winner': Lance Armstrong, 40.56 km/h
Lanterne rouge: Iker Flores, 39.66 km/h @ 4h20'24"
155 finishers

Epilogue
SAINT-FLOUR

I can't ride fast, I can't climb, I can't sprint . . .
I'm a complete roadman. A Tour-man, therefore.
Roger Chaussabel, *lanterne rouge* 1956 and
Prix de l'Humour that year.

'You feel like the Champs-Élysées is paradise,' Igor Flores told me, on the subject of finishing the Tour – in all probability unaware of how literal he was being. His words summed up the general feelings of joy, relief and amazement among the *lanternes rouges* at getting, finally, to the end. And for the Tour to finish anywhere other than the Champs-Élysées would seem wrong. It was Félix Lévitan who instituted the now-traditional ending in 1975, so you'd have to be 50 or so to remember it doing anything else.

But for me, there was nowhere else this race could end other than in the Auvergne, given my masochistic attachment to the region and the unfinished business I had with stage nine of the 2011 Tour. That bloody Étape I abandoned. I had to go back and make it from Issoire to Saint-Flour. Because if I've learnt one thing from the *lanternes rouges* it is the value of finishing the job in hand. Do it for your self-respect, for your teammates, for your DS, for your sponsors, for your wife and family. But just do it.

When I tell David, my teacher friend who lives near Issoire, the *ville-départ*, that I am returning to ride the route he looks at me like I am a little bit sick. I am not staying with him, because in the intervening period since my failure he has had a new arrival. His house is busy with the baby boy and his two other children, whom his wife is trying to corral – all signs of someone who does not feel obliged to (re-)ride 208 kilometres through one of the hilliest, and on its day, least hospitable parts of France. People move on, things happen. Apparently. I mention that in certain worst-case scenarios I may need rescuing by car and he laughs half-heartedly.

So, another day, another early start in the Massif Central. But this time the sun is peeking over the volcanoes in the distance and the peacocks at my *chambres d'hôtes* are rustling their tail-feathers and making coughing noises in preparation for another day of strutting, preening and pooing on the lawns. Down in the valley it is cool and cloudy, but there's no forecast of rain. I have knee warmers, arm warmers, gilet and a cap; tools and two tubes, one taped under my saddle, a couple of bars, credit card, €50 note and a few coins for coffee. Plus a well-used GPS unit with a knackered battery that I'm wagering will not last the day. No rain jacket, since I retain a bizarre and irrational faith in the weather reports.

Aside from whatever obscure forces compel us to do these things, a long bike ride is also a good way to ruminate on the *lanterne rouge*, a way to close the circle and to piece my thoughts into a philosophy. Being *lanterne rouge* is about so many other things than being last it is barely about being last at all. It's about money and about a job, about doing what you can do to the best of your abilities and not giving up. About responsibility and determination and dignity and sacrifice, yes, but also about pain, naivety, bad luck and drugs; fun and cheating and crashing; bravery, injustice and friendship . . . and even winning, sometimes. It's all the things the Tour is, but with less emphasis on crossing the line first.

And a lot of it, for me, is about history and the stories we tell around bike racing. The *lanterne*, for all its notoriety and on-and-off attention-seeking, does not generally figure in the official histories and, where there are no cameras, myths are made. Myths of the underdog, the glorious loser, the plucky fighter and the joker, of Zaaf and Vietto and Samuel Beckett. Stories where truth is not really the point, but whose truths are an essential part of the meaning we bring to and take away from the race. As soon as the riders pass, so do the noise, the bright colours and the smells – the sweat, the suntan cream, the clutches burning out. Everything that had been so eagerly anticipated is quickly gone, ephemeral and irrecoverable, and we're left with the numbers on the leaderboard, the pictures and reports in the papers the next day and the stories that have caught our imagination, that we tell and re-tell and which animate the bare facts of the race long after.

I set off and am derailed even before leaving Issoire city limits when the Tour route wants to take me on to the motorway – not a good plan when the roads aren't closed and the morning rush hour is just starting. I rejoin my intended path further south and get hit by déjà vu, fragments of the wet Étape hurtling back into consciousness as if from a nightmare. It feels apt that I'm retracing my tracks, since during my journeys around France and back into Tour history the same places come up – the Tourmalet and Alpe d'Huez and Galibier, but also Cholet, Béziers and Albi, Chateauroux, Tours and Saint-Flour.

Saint-Flour where Thomas Voeckler took yellow, where Richard
Virenque won and where Christophe Bassons, the outspoken
anti-doper, abandoned in 1999 after being intimidated by Lance
Armstrong; where Jay Sweet was still *lanterne rouge* and Jacky
Durand one place above him, was waiting to take the mantle
when Jay abandoned. Where Jacky said, in vain: 'I only hope
for one thing, that the next stages are less miserable. Because
for five days it's been terrible.' Each time the Tour visits a town
or a road it adds another layer of history; and another winner,
another loser, another story.

As I retrace my journey, back up the road on the banks of
the Allagnon river, it's clear to me that I was going way too
fast two years ago, and that I would have absolutely blown my
biscuits somewhere along the line. The Côte de Massiac is
shrouded in a moist, damp cloud and climbing it is barely more
fun than the first time round, while the Aubrac plateau at the
top is as featureless and bleak as I remember. It is completely
and utterly deserted. Go to a mountain, even a famous one, two
days after the Tour has passed and there is nothing left, no sign
that anything momentous has happened; and this isn't even a
famous mountain. But that's the magic of it: the Tour takes the
little places, the villages and churches of *la France Profonde*,
and gives them presence and meaning. Turns non-places – a
country lane, a mountain pass – into the centre of the world
for a few short moments. It holds them in the web of invisible
traces of the Tours gone before, as if the roads are a Mobius
strip and the ghosts of riders past are forever on their journey
around France. Bobet, Anquetil and Merckx passed a while
ago *en tête*, and here we are trailing in the swirling dust. They
are out there ahead of us still.

The Aubrac is no good for anyone except cows, I decide
after a few more kilometres, and today the cows are making me

nervous. I pass a field of them, then fields and fields more, but no humans. It's really the weather I'm nervous about, obviously, but the cows, those supposed indicators of what the weather might be up to, aren't helping. Half are standing up, half are sitting down. What does that even mean?

On the descent to Allanche, which last time had been the final straw, the skies begin to brighten. I have two *pains au chocolat*, in honour of the feed station that was, and then carry on into the sunshine. As the weather cheers up my mood brightens and I realise that's something else I've taken from the stories of the *lanternes* – the equanimity to make the best of whatever the race day throws at you. And in Pierre Matignon and Jacky, especially, that determination to gamble, that spirit of giving it your best because nothing is decided before the end. In horses, a particular genetic variant was identified not so long ago that gives one animal superior speed over courses up to seven furlongs; another that guarantees superior stamina[54] – and the racing world is becoming justifiably worried that their animals' talents may be deduced by a prowler stealing a hair. Because what would the handicappers and the bookies and the gamblers do then? Their world would be ruined. We need that ability to gamble in bike racing too: a small crack of uncertainty through which a finely placed attack can escape and succeed – whether that be caused by the weather, the landscape or by a renegade determined to upset the natural order. If *les aléas* were eliminated and genetics or watts alone were the cast-iron determinants of inevitable success, would we still watch?

I'd like to pretend I'm thinking these things on the way up to the Puy Mary, the highest climb of the day, but really

---

54 The thoroughbred stallion Northern Dancer had it: he sired more than 150 winners and charged a million dollars a 'shot'.

I'm just trying to keep my breathing in check and looking at the mountains in the sun. How the meadows cede to scrub and then to warm golden-brown rock faces, with pockets of blinding white snow and dirty icy fringes. This ascent and the knife-edge road leading off the other side of the col are some of the most fantastic stretches of tarmac I've seen anywhere, the views breathtaking.[55] There's a case for panache and beauty in most sports (in our school playground in the 1980s, kicking round a panel-less former leather football, we all wanted to be Brazil; *nobody* wanted to be West Germany) but cycling is particularly concerned with aesthetics. So much goes on at the Tour outside winning and losing, the easy sway of either/or – from the million-and-one unseen battles within the peloton, to the helicopter shots of the alpine peaks and the trashcan dream of the caravan – that it's OK to appreciate the shape and form of the race, the noble intention, the doomed break and, yes, even beautiful losers. The romance of the *lanterne* is an antidote to the driven, sometimes clinical approach to sport.

On the descent from the Puy Mary there is a series of warning signs haphazardly spraypainted on to the road, then, on a tight corkscrew left-hander, a squiggly arrow pointing to a familiar forked tree trunk and the words 'Vino Out'. So it was here, the carnage. I take it slow, snap a photo for posterity, and carry on down. On the Col de Pertus, which starts with no warning after a sharp left-hand turn, the road is so steep and the loosely gravelled surface so sticky with hot tar my triceps start to hurt from pulling on the bars. Shit, shit, shit, shit I repeat in my head to the rhythm of my breath. I spend the climb and the gravelly, claggy descent thinking about Vino and

---

55   I wouldn't have seen a thing during the Étape because of the freezing clouds. Also, I stopped to have a hamburger, chips and Coke on my victorious second sortie. That wouldn't have happened with the stopwatch going. Double bonus.

his broken femur, and about Juan Antonio Flecha and Johnny Hoogerland, wondering where on the route the television car decided to take them out; and I think about Vincent Jérôme, recovering from his injuries but stuck as *lanterne rouge* behind the crashes while his leader flew into yellow. Bad stuff happens. It happens to the best of us and the worst of us, and all those in the middle. You might be a national champion, a yellow jersey or a Classics winner and still through accident or misfortune be brought low and dumped into last. And while the urge to win can sometimes bring out the worst in people (and not just in cycling), there is plenty of evidence among the *lanternes* that losing can bring out the best. They were, the ones I met or read about, a pretty remarkable bunch of characters. Take a cross-section from the peloton according to any other criteria and I doubt you'd arrive at such an interesting selection. They were also, to a man, decent, well-adjusted people. Decent enough that not one of them thought I was a swivel-eyed loon when I told them about my project, but instead happily shared their stories of the sometimes extraordinary events and tough breaks they confronted. None had been defined by the *lanterne*: it had just been a moment in their lives that had happened, they had dealt with and moved on from. 'I don't think about it much,' Aad said to me. 'It's just one small part of my career. I don't know who the *lanterne rouge* was last year, or any year.'

I pass through the Lioran ski resort, where they're making summer repairs to the chalets under blue skies, and head down the wide, straight service road to Murat then take a right towards the Prat du Bouc, the seemingly endless final major climb. The bonus is that afterwards there's a 50-kilometre freewheel almost to the end, down tiny roads surrounded by meadows and more cows. I wouldn't have realised if I hadn't ridden it how the day's *parcours* had been meticulously planned for good racing: tough mountains in the first half to sort the wheat from the chaff; long, sometimes technical descents to help the break stay away and then, I was to find out, some short and sharp hills with 15 kilometres to go, to make the decisive selection. Somewhere very close to the end, on a hill above a lake crowned with an impossibly beautiful castle, my Garmin runs out of batteries. That'll teach me to rely on electronics, and to fiddle around with buttons when I should be concentrating on pedalling and looking at the scenery. I follow the route on my phone for the final few kilometres, and the foreboding dark stonework of Saint-Flour on its sugarlump hill finally appears on the horizon. My Champs-Élysées. Soon I'm at its foot. I throw caution to the wind and, since 3G has deserted me and I don't know the exact Tour course, take a fairly direct route to the top. This results in a horrifically vertical climb through the back streets, the only virtue of it being that it proves to me my legs are still working. When Sánchez and Voeckler climbed the hill the right way, the apparatus of the Tour – the TV trucks and team buses and finish-line gantry – were completely occupying the top square and spilling down into the rest of the town. Mathieu Hermans would have been there commentating, sitting in his habitual spot in the technical area between Sean Kelly commentating for Eurosport and Pedro Delgado for Spanish TV. He looked forward to the reunion every year, he told me; they were almost like a family. Does it also feel like a homecoming, I wonder, when you come over that hill in the race and see the end, after 200 kilometres in the mountains, to see all the Tour machinery waiting to swallow you back up again? Is it a relief?

When you're a writer following the Tour, arriving at the start or end usually is a relief. Because following the Tour is an inaccurate way of describing it: you're never following the Tour, you're chasing it. You're constantly on the verge of being dropped and you're hanging on for dear life. You're driving in a hire car between a stage start and a stage finish at 155 kilometres per hour, going fast because, damn it, that's what races do – they go fast – and a Lampre car has just overtaken at an incredible speed, which spurs you on because you need to get a fucking parking space within a stone's throw of the finish or else you'll be walking lost through rows of identical hire cars in a field in the 37°C sun (but not too close to the finish or else you'll never get out in time for a steak and a bucket of wine later at your hotel 200 kilometres away); and there's only one road up this particular valley so you have to reach that bottleneck before everyone else. Sure, you're beating the special Tour Norbert Dentressangle lorries, but that's no good because they're going to the *next day's* start, to set it up and keep this whole crazy show on the road; all the while, barrelling up the *autoroute* at 160 kilometres an hour now, you're thinking of the day's deadline that will soon be whooshing past, musing on why the French Internet is so backwards, stuck with Jimmy Casper's first *lanterne* in 2001, and the consequent impossibility of actually sending the bloody copy and pictures without inflicting fatal damage to your bank account with your mobile data bill, when all of a sudden there's a motorway sign announcing you're crossing the Greenwich Meridian; and you realise you're alone in a rented Škoda surrounded by pâtisserie crumbs and empty Cristalline bottles, accumulating speeding tickets for no real reason, and you feel a pang of homesickness for the parallel life across the same Meridian all those hundreds of kilometres (they do things in miles up there) north across the Channel; simultaneously linked to home and incredibly isolated, because it's unimaginably distant – even though it was only two weeks ago you left and if you turned around now you could be there by the small hours of the morning. But you don't turn around because even though it's uprooting and profoundly alienating – a three-week daily ordeal of bad mattresses, fast food, late nights and early starts, where your best friend is your satnav and you eat madeleines in school gymnasia while watching on the press-room LCDs the race that's passing yards from the door – you wouldn't want to be anywhere else.

And you imagine – or try to but cannot – what it must be like for the riders. Because if this is what happens to a writer going a bit Major Tom in France, shuttling from one non-place to another via the recommended off-course route, one Campanile hotel to another, one service-station *expresso* to the next, what must it be like for them? Being last is not glamorous, it's not fun and it's not easy, but it's the eye of the storm, the centre of things, or as close to it as you're going to get. This is for these three weeks your community, your family, and you don't want to be dropped.

I remember Igor Flores again: 'It's the Tour de France. It's different. Other races you can give up and nothing happens, but in the Tour de France it's incredible, because every single day is a new experience. You go to the start and you're with the people and it's incredible.' He is leaning forward, eyes bright, his sense of wonder undimmed by the threadbare facts of his participation and last place.

Of them all, the image that remains is of the Camembert and the *lanterne*.

'The symbolism was just too good,' Jacky told me. 'The bloke climbing on to the Champs-Élysées podium like the winner is actually the last guy. Is it the last man? No, it's not the last, it's the most aggressive rider! For me, the ambiguity was too good. The first and last on the same podium.'

I'd done it. I'd finished the Étape. Now I knew Saint-Flour were not just pretty words to say. The official figures state that

6,500 signed up, 4,056 made it to the start line and only 1,982 got to the finish. Make that 1,983.

Before I think about riding the 20 kilometres to the station for my train back to the start, I sit in the town square and have a Coke in the sun. It's the same hotel bar in which we had previously huddled, warming up and drinking hot chocolate. Outside, on Étape day, trucks had arrived laden with hundreds of expensive bicycles to be reunited with their owners, and when we'd revived a little we'd braved the elements to cheer on the first two finishers (who apparently had worked as a pair for many long hours to keep their lead) as they rolled up the final steep incline to the finish and disputed a slow-motion sprint. I sit there, exhausted and half dozing with the gentle early evening sun in my eyes, in that grey-stone square that I'd last seen so cold and windblown, and it occurs to me that, only one year and 333 days late, I am indisputably the last person to finish that Étape and – while lacking in many, many other qualities, not least of which being able to ride a bicycle at any sort of competitive speed – I am therefore something of a *lanterne rouge* myself.

LANTERNES ROUGES FROM
1903 TO 2013

Year	Name	Country	Year	Name	Country
1903	Arsène Millochau	(Fra)	1925	Fernand Besnier	(Fra)
1904	Antoine de Flotrière	(Fra)	1926	André Drobecq	(Fra)
1905	Clovis Lacroix	(Fra)	1927	Jacques Pfister	(Fra)
1906	Georges Bronchard	(Fra)	1928	Edouard Persin	(Fra)
1907	Albert Chartier	(Fra)	1929	André Léger	(Fra)
1908	Henri Anthoine	(Fra)	1930	Marcel Ilpide	(Fra)
1909	Georges Devilly	(Fra)	1931	Richard Lamb	(Aus)
1910	Constant Collet	(Fra)	1932	Rudolf Risch	(Ger)
1911	Lucien Roquebert	(Fra)	1933	Ernst Neuhard	(Fra)
1912	Maurice Lartigue	(Fra)	1934	Antonio Folco	(Ita)
1913	Henri Alavoine	(Fra)	1935	Willi Kutschbach	(Ger)
1914	Henri Leclerc	(Fra)	1936	Aldo Bertocco	(Fra)
1919	Jules Nempon	(Fra)	1937	Aloyse Klensch	(Lux)
1920	Charles Raboisson	(Fra)	1938	Janus Hellemons	(Ned)
1921	Henri Catelan	(Fra)	1939	Armand Le Moal	(Fra)
1922	Daniel Masson	(Bel?)	1947	Pietro Tarchini	(Sui)
1923	Daniel Masson	(Bel?)	1948	Vittorio Seghezzi	(Ita)
1924	Victor Lafosse	(Bel)	1949	Guido De Santi	(Ita)

1950	Fritz Zbinden	(Sui)
1951	Abdel-Kader Zaaf	(Alg)
1952	Henri Paret	(Fra)
1953	Claude Rouer	(Fra)
1954	Marcel Dierkens	(Lux)
1955	Tony Hoar	(UK)
1956	Roger Chaussabel	(Fra)
1957	Guy Million	(Fra)
1958	Walter Favre	(Sui)
1959	Louis Bisiliat	(Fra)
1960	José Berrendero	(Esp)
1961	André Geneste	(Fra)
1962	Augusto Marcaletti	(Ita)
1963	Willy Derboven	(Bel)
1964	Anatole Novak	(Fra)
1965	Joseph Groussard	(Fra)
1966	Paolo Manucci	(Ita)
1967	Jean-Pierre Genet	(Fra)
1968	John Clarey	(UK)
1969	André Wilhelm	(Fra)
1970	Frits Hoogerheide	(Ned)
1971	Georges Chappe	(Fra)
1972	Alain Bellouis	(Fra)
1973	Jacques-André Hochart	(Fra)
1974	Lorenzo Alaimo	(Ita)
1975	Jacques Boulas	(Fra)
1976	Aad van den Hoek	(Ned)
1977	Roger Loysch	(Bel)
1978	Philippe Tesnière	(Fra)
1979	Gerhard Schönbacher	(Aut)
1980	Gerhard Schönbacher	(Aut)
1981	Faustino Cueli	(Esp)

1982	Werner Devos	(Bel)
1983	Marcel Laurens	(Bel)
1984	Gilbert Glaus	(Sui)
1985	Manrico Ronchiato	(Ita)
1986	Ennio Salvador	(Ita)
1987	Mathieu Hermans	(Ned)
1988	Dirk Wayenberg	(Bel)
1989	Mathieu Hermans	(Ned)
1990	Rodolfo Massi	(Ita)
1991	Rob Harmeling	(Ned)
1992	Fernando Quevedo	(Esp)
1993	Edwig Van Hooydonck	(Bel)
1994	John Talen	(Ned)
1995	Bruno Cornillet	(Fra)
1996	Jean-Luc Masdupuy	(Fra)
1997	Philippe Gaumont	(Fra)
1998	Damien Nazon	(Fra)
1999	Jacky Durand	(Fra)
2000	Olivier Perraudeau	(Fra)
2001	Jimmy Casper	(Fra)
2002	Igor Flores	(Esp)
2003	Hans De Clercq	(Bel)
2004	Jimmy Casper	(Fra)
2005	Iker Flores	(Esp)
2006	Wim Vansevenant	(Bel)
2007	Wim Vansevenant	(Bel)
2008	Wim Vansevenant	(Bel)
2009	Yauheni Hutarovich	(Blr)
2010	Adriano Malori	(Ita)
2011	Fabio Sabatini	(Ita)
2012	Jimmy Engoulvent	(Fra)
2013	Svein Tuft	(Can)

GLOSSARY

Autobus: The French-language term for the group of slower riders, mainly sprinters and *domestiques*, who band together in the mountains to make sure that nobody misses the time cut. In Italian, *grupetto*.

Criterium: A short circuit road race, often of an hour plus a set number of laps, that usually takes place in a town.

Cuite: French term for bonking, cracking, hitting the wall. Literally 'cooked'.

Départ fictive / départ reel: The *départ fictive* is the ceremonial roll-out at the start of the stage. After a few kilometres at a steady pace behind the lead commissaire's car, the starting pistol is fired and the racing begins – that's the *départ réel*.

Directeur Sportif: The sporting director, who makes a team's strategic and tactical decisions, and looks after its performance. Can encompass anything from a manager and mastermind combined in one man to simply the guy who's in charge in the team car on the road that day.

Domestique: A supporting rider, working in the service of one of his teammates.

Faire le metier: An expression that denotes learning the trade of a professional bike rider. The rituals and etiquette of riding in the peloton; the lifestyle and practices of someone committed to that path. Back when being initiated into doping was part of one's passage into professional life, it had sinister overtones.

Grupetto: See ***autobus***.

Kermesse: A circuit race, but one that takes place over a longer circuit and longer distance than a ***criterium***. May be 100 kilometres or more in total.

Maglia rosa: Italian for the pink jersey worn by the leader of the Giro d'Italia.

Maillot jaune: French for the yellow jersey of the Tour de France leader. Most histories say it was first awarded in 1919 and that Eugène Christophe was the first to wear yellow.

Musette: Small cotton bag used to pass food to cyclists during races.

Palmarès: The roll call of a cyclist's race wins and achievements.

Parcours: A fancy French way of saying 'route' – though it encompasses the ups and downs as well as the lefts and rights.

Prime: A prize, usually money or goods, offered by the race organisation or private individuals in the course of the main race. In the early days there were lots of '15 francs for the first Frenchman through Amiens', for example. These days, there are intermediate sprints and mountain *primes*.

Ravitaillement: The feed zone.

Recordman: French for he who holds the record.

Repêchage: The French word for the act of allowing a contender back into a contest after they have been eliminated. In the Tour often *ad hoc*, even arbitrary. It is also planned for in track events such as the Keirin: after the knock-out rounds, beaten riders fight for a chance of reinstatement.

Rescapé: Survivor. In modern times usually said of men in a break that has broken up or been whittled down, but in the old days was often used to mean all of the remaining riders in the race, since the Tour's attrition rate was so high.

Rosbif: An Englishman. Just as the French are sometimes unkindly called 'frogs', we are 'roast beef'.

Soigneur: Team helper with multifarious roles. Everything from masseur to rider's confidant, adviser, healer and spiritual guide. Helps riders learn to *faire le métier*. May also hand out food and drink on the road and undertake general dogsbodying. In the old days often an unofficial pharmacist, the guy who sorted out a rider's *soins*.

Soins: Literally 'care' or 'treatment'. Euphemistically, pills and drugs.

ACKNOWLEDGEMENTS

In thank yous I must first offer my profound gratitude to all the riders and others connected with pro cycling whom I interviewed or who helped me out. Without their willingness to give their time and memories, this would have been nothing. Second, to Matt Phillips, my editor at Yellow Jersey, for his thoughtful work and the big improvements he made, and to Jon Elek, my agent.

After that, I must also thank: Graeme Fife, Bill McGann and Les Woodland, for generously answering my no doubt annoying numerous questions. Feargal McKay, of PodiumCafé, for the interesting articles and painstaking tables of average speed information across the years. Professor Christopher Thompson of Ball University, Indiana, who will see the strands I took on from his book, particularly in 1919. Nigel Dick, for generously allowing me to see the transcripts from his interview with Tony Hoar. Basia Lewandoska Cummings, for transcriptions, and Lia Alba and Soren Evinson, for translations. Craig Gaulzetti, Jeremy Dunn and *Embrocation* magazine. And Steve Jones, for inspiration and for letting me make his bolthole temporarily mine. Also, in no particular order: Thierry Durand, the Inner Ring, Sadhbh O'Shea, Pierrot Picq and Dominique Magnier, Bill Strickland, Femke Hoogland, Tom Southam, Richard

Moore, James Fairbank, Camille McMillan, Kristof Ramon, David Campano, Simon Mottram, Felix Lowe, Marion Gachies, Frédéric Rétsin, Fabien Conord, Christian Wolmar, Carlton Reid, Emma Davies, Charlotte Easton, Nathalie Palomino, and Thomas Cariou and Fabrice Tiano at ASO. Any errors that remain in this work are all mine and not theirs.

Last but definitely not least, to Anton and Claire, Rémi and Catherine, and John, whose company in Nice and on long rides through the Alpes Maritimes helped give this idea legs. And to Laura, who made it happen.

FURTHER READING

This eccentric endeavour illuminates some parts of the Tour where others frankly have not been interested in going, but it relied on the huge foundation of writing and research on the race in general that's already out there. Aside from the old newspapers (the *Miroir Sprint* Tour specials in particular are very good fun) I could not have written the book without these resources, so if you want to read further here's a short and by no means exhaustive list:

Antoine Blondin – *Tours de France: Chroniques de L'Équipe, 1954–82*

Pierre Chany – *La Fabuleuse Histoire du Tour de France*

Daniel Coyle – *Lance Armstrong: Tour de Force*

Graeme Fife – *Brian Robinson: Pioneer*

William Fotheringham – *Roule Britannia*

Philippe Gaumont – *Prisonnier du Dopage*

Bill and Carol McGann – *The Story of the Tour de France* (two volumes)

David Millar – *Racing through the Dark*

Bill Strickland – *Tour de Lance: the Extraordinary Story of Lance Armstrong's Fight to Reclaim the Tour de France*

Christopher S. Thompson – *The Tour de France: a Cultural History*

Jeremy Whittle – *Bad Blood*

The best reference websites out there are:
The official Tour stats: Letour.fr/HISTO/fr/TDF/
Memoire-du-cyclisme.eu
Bikeraceinfo.com
Cyclingarchives.com
LaGrandeBoucle.com
LeDicoduTour.com

LIST OF ILLUSTRATIONS

INDEX